No (
Without
a
Dad

Ryan, you are an awesome
thanks for being a Leader
of influence for the Kingdom
of God...

6/23/21

NRB

No Child Without a Dad

A Global Mandate to Bring Healing to
Hearts, Homes and the World...
Know your Glory Code - Know Your Impact

Advantage
Books

Paul R. Benjamin Sr.

Published by: ADVANTAGE BOOKS™
                Longwood, Florida, USA
                www.advbookstore.com

Library of Congress Catalog Number: 2020943300

First Printing: August 2020
20 21 22 23 24 25   10 9 8 7 6 5 4 3 2 1
Printed in the United States of America

Table of Contents

Introduction

The Mandate, for Such a Time as This

With very little hope of change, we are witnessing the increase of crime, violence, and abuse in families, and cities across America and around the world. I feel compelled to not only share some insight and wisdom about these symptoms, (*the problems we spend trillions of dollars trying to fix without any impact*) but to address the root-cause in a manner that would:

- Address the source of all the problems
- Guide any **willing** reader on the path to a solution that can result in healing and victory
- Explain the **"Why,"** behind the scenes of the pandemic in our homes, and society at large
- Equip readers to become champions who can help engage others to make a positive difference.

Throughout these pages, we will only wade five feet deep in the ocean of information. I promise to expand on various topics in future books and blogs.

I believe this information is a God-given mandate to address key issues/symptoms resulting from our broken father relationship. You might ask, what about the role of mothers? Yes, even the pain inflicted by mothers stem from the father.

Could the role a dad plays in a child's life correspond to the number of prisoners, teenage suicides, murder, crime, high school dropouts, drug users, school shootings, and racial conflicts? What about those who have not known a father? Or perhaps had less-than-desirable fathers? Is there any hope? How could we bring healing to hearts, homes and the world?

Why am I committed to every child having a dad? It's because I know the significance of fathering *(whether positive or negative)* and its far-reaching impact. Our relationship with our father and ultimately our Heavenly Father, influences our society and the world.

If I could give you one word that would answer most of your questions about yourself, your family, your relationships and how your beliefs were formed, would you not want me to share it? Of course, you would. We all would respond with a resounding, Yes!

Follow along as Deborah, (Deb) a reporter from *Global Impact Magazine.com* and I delve into the interview of a lifetime.

Warning

I do stress one warning! After reading, your level of responsibility will change. More will be expected of you after being exposed to this truth. For the ease of reading and comprehension, I chose to write this book as an interview. After many years of being interviewed on radio, TV and in newspapers, I felt you would receive more insight as we sit around the table in a quiet restaurant having dinner, dessert and a cup of coffee or tea. So, place your order, pull up your chair and let us begin this journey from discovery to destiny. Some *names were changed to protect the identity of the real individuals.*

Chapter 1

The State of our Nation

After returning home at 10:31 PM from a *Father of The Year Awards Banquet*, John, chief editor of Global Impact Magazine was troubled and concerned. He heard Paul Benjamin speak about the alarming statistics regarding children who are being raised without a good *(well balanced and authentic)* father and the moral decay of families in our nation and world.

John couldn't sleep. Images of his childhood abuse kept flashing before him. Tormented by his thoughts, he reached for his smartphone, considering calling his number one syndicated reporter, Deborah.

As he reflected on Deborah and her family, he couldn't help but note the differences between her family and his own family of origin. Deborah had encouraged her two children, 10-year-old Ashley, and 15-year old David, when they wanted to nominate their Dad, Joel, for the "***Father of the Year Award.***" Joel had received that prestigious award earlier that evening.

Meanwhile, over at the star reporter's house, Deb and Joel had returned home and spent time discussing the award ceremony and the topic of the evening. They then said goodnight to their children, prayed and kissed each other and went to sleep. Deb was fast asleep snuggled next to her husband when her cell phone rang.

The Mandate – Urgent Call at 2:00 AM

John had been ruminating about his family and was just about to speed dial Deborah's number before he noticed that it was 2:00 AM. He hesitated for a moment, but felt such and urgency that he made the call anyway.

As Deb was jolted awake, she looked at the caller ID, and realized it was her boss, John. Startled, her heart was already thumping from the late call, but the fact that it was her boss, she began to imagine the worse, "Is he ok? Am I fired?"

She answered the phone in a soft, crackling voice, "Hello?" "*Sorry Deb, It's John.*" His voice reflected that he had been crying. "I had to call! I have an urgent request for you. I would like for you to drop all your other assignments and begin a new one first thing in the morning." Deb was thinking to herself, it's already 2:00 AM. Before she could finish her thought, John said, "*It's regarding the topic we heard about at the awards ceremony last night, please research the broken state of our nation and the role fathers play in the current state of our families and nation. I am looking for answers. Why are so many children growing up without fathers in the home? Why are some fathers in the home, so abusive to their wives and children? Please set-up an interview with Mr. Benjamin regarding this topic. I want some answers. I couldn't rest after hearing the unsettling statistics. What he spoke about are the same signs I felt growing up in my own home; pain, anger, and rejection. Even today, in my current position, I struggle with feelings of inadequacy. Subliminally, I am still waiting for my dad to come and pat me on the shoulder and say, "Son, I am proud of you!"*

"*Even with all my money and success, I question why I am still yearning for more. Nothing seems to quench that for me. What I experienced as a boy in my own home, I want to help correct for others. If I can help just one boy or girl not to experience what I did, it would be worth it. I want to invest my life to making a difference*"

John emphasized this point, "Deb, I don't want fluff. I want you to get to the source of where we, as a society, went wrong. We need to make changes, no longer masking the problem, but fixing it. Cancel all the other assignments that I have given you. This is now going to be your number one priority. I would like for you to work on this assignment for the next 30 days or for whatever amount of time you need to get to the bottom of this universal problem. You have all of my resources and finances available to you to accomplish this assignment. I have a vested interest and my hope is that this information will help me once and for all resolve the issues in my soul. I need to understand why I feel and function the way I do. Thanks Deb, I am sorry for the late call. Please apologize to your husband, also."

Joel was able to roll over and go back to sleep, but Deb couldn't sleep. She rolled out of bed and went to her home office near the kitchen. After fixing a hot cup of coffee, she pulled out her MacBook Pro and began typing some questions to ask Mr. Benjamin. Taking a quick pause from typing, she decided to send an urgent email to him requesting an appointment ASAP.

The email that forever changed her life

Deb remembered that Joel had requested Mr. Benjamin's business card earlier that evening. She quietly returned to the bedroom to retrieve the business card, which she found in his blue suit.

After sending the email, Deb continued to type. As fast as she thought of a question, she added it to the list, which grew from one page to three. Yawning at the end of each page, she looked at the time on her laptop. It was 4:30 AM. Knowing that she couldn't keep her eyes open any longer, she returned to bed.

Deb tried to be quiet getting into bed, but her cold feet touched Joel and woke him up. He said "Wow, Deb! Your feet are ice cold! Where did you go?" Deb said, "I was in my office making notes. Sorry for waking you up. We will talk later. Let's try to get some sleep."

Before too long, both of them were fast asleep, only to be awakened by Joel's alarm clock at 6:30 AM. Deb rolled over and said *"Morning! Honey, could you drop the children off at school for me today?" I need to get a few more hours of sleep before I begin my long day."* Joel rolled out of bed and kissed her and said, *"Okay honey, I got you covered. Get some rest."*

Deb could not fall asleep after her husband left the room. She began reflecting on all the questions she typed. She wondered how soon she would be able to make an appointment and begin her assignment. Just as she was about to head for the shower to start her day, she heard her phone vibrate. It was an email alert. She reached over to check the message. To her surprise, it was Mr. Benjamin. Deb was lost for words. It was around 8:35 AM. Mr. Benjamin said he had just left a meeting, saw the urgent nature of her email, and had responded without delay.

His email read, "Hi Deb, I am glad to learn of your desire to do an article. I would love to meet you to discuss the root cause of the problems in our nation and around the world. I can clear my calendar today and meet with you at my office at 10:05.7 AM. My wife and I would be blessed to meet with you. I will be happy to share the truth and facts about how we, as a people, and the nation arrived where we are today. Blessings to you and your family, Paul Benjamin".

Deb was so excited to see the email, she quickly responded and said, *"Thank you, I will be there today."*

Deb called her boss to give him the good news. He said, "Deb, someone must have been praying." Deb said, "Yes, sir. I was."

Deb did not do her usual morning routine of exercising, reading a devotional message or skimming the daily newspaper while having her coffee. She took a quick shower and got dressed for a meeting that would impact the rest of her life, her family, and her boss, John.

The Drive into the Hood

Deb left home a little early because she was not sure how to get to Mr. Benjamin's office. She had not driven in that part of town before. She had entered the address into her phone and was on her way. The phone reminded her that she was 2.1 miles away. Deb quickly realized that she was in an unfamiliar part of town. She saw some school-aged young men hanging out in the front yard of a home. As she continued driving past a cluster of apartment units, she noticed some were boarded up and in disrepair. Some women were sitting on the front porch, and others were standing on the sidewalk talking with each other. As Deb was looking, her phone said, "You have arrived. Your destination is on the right."

Deb pulled into the parking lot. She took a deep breath and said to herself, "Where in the world am I?" As she was about to get out of her car, she heard a loud vibrating sound passing her, as she looked out her window, she noticed a young man driving a car with huge tires, the music he was playing was so loud that the spare change in her cup holder began to vibrate and make noise.

Meet the Benjamins

She entered this large facility where she was greeted by Helga, a warm, friendly receptionist. Helga took her back to Mr. Benjamin's office. Deb walked into his office, Mr. and Mrs. Benjamin greeted her kindly and offered her coffee or orange juice. Deb quickly replied, "Coffee please, two creams and two sugars."

The Urgency!

Deb explained about the call she received from her boss, John. She shared his urgent request and the need for the information. She thanked Mr. Benjamin for the previous evening's event and commented how she, her husband and their children were blessed that night. Mr. Benjamin stood and gestured that they should move the meeting to the conference room where he would not be interrupted by frequent phone calls. He said, "Deb, I have seen the lives of many men, women, and youth who have been relationally wounded in their past, learn how-to walk-in victory. The truth and principles that I will share with you are not a quick fix. Even though, if anyone chooses to implement them, it will begin to have an immediate impact on their lives, and will ultimately impact many generations to come. Deb, I will explain the concepts in simple language and terms so that the majority of your readers will understand."

The first question Deb asked was, "Mr. Benjamin, to avoid appearing rude, what should I call you? Should I call you Pastor, Reverend, Apostle, or I noticed on your business card your title, 'Chief Servant'?"

"Deb, there is only one person that should be Revered here and that is God Himself. You can call me Paul. I usually introduce myself as *Paul, and that's all...* Or sometimes when I speak at events I may introduce myself as *Paul from the tribe of Benjamin.* Okay, all kidding aside, Deb, let's begin. Just to warn you though, my wife, children, and friends will tell you, I tell corny jokes and can give a pun for almost every sentence you may say. I am usually the best customer of my puns and humor."

Deb: Paul, I was up for over two hours this morning, typing out a list of questions to ask you. As I mentioned, my boss, John, is anxious to know the answers to these problems. By the way, I was wondering why did you schedule our meeting for 10:05.7AM?

Paul: Deb, I just wanted to get my *point across...*

Paul's wife, Dawn, groans and interjects. *"Here begins the puns. Welcome to my world!"* Paul continues, I usually add a point in the time of our meeting to help people remember.

Deb: This now explains why you said 10:05. Point 7.

Dawn: Maybe if he can get most of his puns out on you before he comes home tonight, I won't have to hear too many, as he will already be punned out.

Deb: Dawn, you will owe me a big-time favor for this. I guess this is part of the price I will have to pay for this urgent assignment.

Paul: Deb, there is a cost to everything in life. We have to determine if we are willing to pay it.

Deb: Talking about cost, I know that your time is valuable and this assignment is urgent, let's get back to our interview. Every day when I turn on the TV or pick up the local newspaper, these symptoms you referred to last night manifest itself: a young boy or girl committing a crime, or choosing to drop out of school, dying by suicide, shooting another student on the bus, or in the school, car-jacking a woman's vehicle with her children inside, a rape occurring in the school bathroom, gang shootings or being vandalized in the community. Sometimes I feel like we are living in a war zone where the battle never ends.

The Origin of The Father Fracture Syndrome (FFS)

Deb: Joel, my husband, and I were shocked when we heard you share the statistics of children raised in fatherless homes. You said they are products of the ***Father Fracture Syndrome (FFS).*** You explained this was part of the global ramification due to the disobedience or rebellion-witchcraft of one man. I heard you say that the one man was Adam, and it was disobedience against The Heavenly Father which produced abnormality.

Symptoms of the Problem that we spend Trillions of Dollars on today!

Paul: Yes, Deb, you heard correctly. This plunged all of mankind; men, women, children, and society, into a broken diminished state of glory. This results in murder, crime, violence, mental health issues, sorrow, suffering and pain that we experience today in families and in the world. Let me expound on some of these statistics which all relate to children who were raised in homes without their dads *(or biological father in the home)*.

Some Ramifications from the FFS

This accounts for:

- ***90%*** *of runaways*
- ***85%*** *of those incarcerated,*
- ***80%*** *of rapists,*
- ***75% - 80%*** *of those living in poverty,*
- ***71%*** *of school drop-outs,*
- ***63%*** *of those who are cutting themselves and ultimately committing **suicide**, and*

- *92% of these girls and boys are **more likely to get divorced** if they ever decide to get married.*

Deb: You also mentioned here and in urban inner-cities across America, *9 out of 10* children are growing up without their fathers in the home. You shared that every six minutes here in Florida, a youth is arrested for a crime. I was very startled to hear that 100% of all the crimes, violence, abuses and problems we encounter today in our society and around the world stems from **The *Father Fracture Syndrome***. The list of these symptoms just keeps growing and it spills over into all aspects of our society. Paul, where and how do we begin to address and mitigate this huge problem?

Paul: I will answer your question, but first let me add some more information for you to consider. In divorce cases, **95%** of the time, the judge awards custody to the mother. Of those, **70%- 80%** are molested while in the custody of the mother contrasted with only 7% while in the custody of their father. **33%** of girls and **25%** of boys who have been molested or abused have lost their innocence (Virginity) to a man called father, the majority by step-fathers.

Deb: Wow, Paul! I did not know that. Why do you think that happens? Why so frequently?

Paul: Here is another fact for you to consider. Most judges are also victims of *Father Fractured Syndrome.* They are trying help other children from being abused, neglected or abandoned like they were. Not realizing the potential for abuse is much higher when a child is placed with the mother. The majority of the cases where abuse occurs in the home stems from the mother's live-in boyfriends or step-fathers. It would take hours to explain all the underlying reasons why some of these moms end up in a pattern of relationships that are abusive. The consequence of this impacts their children for generations.

Deb: This is startling information. It seems hopeless! Just thinking of all the ramifications of the FFS can cause someone to be depressed.

Paul: It is overwhelming just thinking about how huge this global problem is. Before I lay the foundational history and the solution to this dilemma, I would like to address our American view and the way we usually process and deal with issues and problems in our society. I will share it through a story of a farmer and his wife.

The Farmer's Story

A farmer and his wife lived near a large lake that ran south through their farm. Every day they would see dying fish floating on their backs. From time to time, they would wash up on their farmland.

The farmer and his wife would treat some of the fish that did not die by placing them in their freshwater pond located on the east end of their farm. Those that died, they would burn with their trash. He and his wife would give them medication to try to fix them, but they noticed that the side effects caused them to become deformed and dysfunctional. Some would attack other fish in the pond and refuse to bond with the other fish.

Months turned into years, this small problem turned into an epidemic. While talking with other farmers in their city, they too were talking about the impact this problem was having on them. They listened to the news and talk show hosts. They, too, were talking about these symptoms. One day, the farmer and his wife got sick and tired; they had enough! He and his wife decided to drive thirty miles up to the top of the lake, to the **source.**

The thirty-five-minute drive seemed like an hour, but they were anxious to know the cause. To their surprise, there was a huge rusty barrel filled with chemical waste at the head (**source**) This was slowly leaking chemical waste, poisoning the water and impacting the fish. The farmer had a decision to make.

He and his wife thought of these options:

- *Start a national fundraiser,* "*Save The Fish Campaign*" to raise billions of dollars perpetually for research and treatment of the deformed fish. We can keep the *source* of the problem to ourselves and a select group of people for our team, thereby keeping the money for ourselves.

- *Get physicians to come up with a medical diagnosis* for the condition of the fish, request pharmaceutical companies to produce a drug treating the symptoms and a team of doctors to write prescriptions for the families affected. The farmer and his wife knew they can make billions from this plan.

- *We can get our political leaders to create laws or pass a bill* stopping anyone who would seek to solve the problem at the source. After all, it would dry-up the funding stream generated from all the medications. Earmark "special" funding for the treatment of the fish and their families. We could get the pharmaceutical company to give us stock options in their company and to the political leaders so they can approve the drug.

- ***Encourage religious groups or organizations pray about the problem,*** start support groups and even write self-help books on how to deal with this problem.

- ***We can call our friends to help*** us remove this one-ton barrel from the source of the lake and stop this epidemic by addressing the root cause.

The farmer and his wife had a choice to make. While reading this book, you too, will discover the source of all the symptoms and problems in our nation and world. Like the farmer and his wife, you have a choice to make.

The outcome and the impact of the farmer's decision, and yours, could positively or negatively impact this generation and future generations to come. I believe you will make the right choice.

Today we are treating so many symptoms in our society, just like the farmer. We need more people with courage and commitment to address the root cause. Together we can turn the tide in our families, nation, and the world as we begin to apply these truths and principles.

Deb: Wow, Paul! The farmer's story was a great illustration. My emotions were running wild. I was angry, sad and ticked off at myself for falling for many of the tactics portrayed in the farmer's story. Now more than ever I am motivated to find the solution, learn the impact on our nation and make a positive difference.

The far-reaching impact of our *failure to act* responsibly could abort the destiny of this, and future generations. Especially when we have this kind of knowledge. Paul, I am anxious to know what decision the farmer made?

Paul: I would love to tell you what decision the farmer made. The truth is Deb, to some degree, there is a farmer story in all of us. One day we will be held accountable for the decisions we make with the truth. Like the farmer, we will have to decide what we will do with the knowledge and information we receive. When we know our **source**, we will know our purpose and destiny.

Paul R. Benjamin, Sr.

Chapter 2

The "What Was Phase"

Know Your Source

Paul: Deb, in life, everyone and everything has a beginning and end. There is a ("-") dash between the beginning and the end. We usually see this ("-") on tombstones. *"John or Jane Doe, born January 5, 1964 - September 11, 2001."* The ("-") between these two dates is what we call the season or cycle of life.

Everything in our universe has a ***source and a purpose*** for its creation. When Henry Ford founded Ford Motor Company, his vision of the first Ford Car already existed in his heart.

While reflecting and planning the ("-") for the life of the first car, he saw a shining black car driving families to the beach, to places of worship and to and from work. As his mind continued to process and draw from the vision and purpose in his heart he saw a huge manufacturing plant employing thousands of employees multiplying his vision around the world. Henry Ford is called the **Father** of Ford. From his heart came the vision, it was written out and implemented.

Today we all know someone who drives a Ford. I have driven many of them over the years. I used them for the intended purpose for which the father of Ford had designed them. The ("-") of my green Ford minivan and black Ford SUV well surpassed my expectations.

Identity is Sealed

Today every Ford model, whether it's the Mustang, Focus, Expedition, Explorer, Fiesta, F-150, Taurus or any of the other models, they are all part of the Ford Family of automobiles. Regardless of what may happen during the "-" of a Ford, it will forever be from the source, the father (Dad) of Ford, Mr. Ford himself. Whether the Ford is in a new showroom, a repair shop, in an accident or the junkyard; the birth certificate *(title, seal)* of each Ford vehicle has the name of the **Father** on it, Ford.

The father *(source)* determines the identity, destiny, and purpose of his offspring. We, too, have a Father (source), His seal (title, birth certificate) is within us. When. we know who He is, we can understand our identity and know our true purpose. Just like the Ford, regardless of where we are in the cycle of life, once we reconnect with our true purpose and identity in Him, we can change our destiny.

Deb: Paul, this is another great example of us knowing our identity and purpose. Without that, we are lost and directionless. I like what you said about the Ford vehicles, whether it is in the showroom, repair shop, or in the junkyard, it is still a Ford with the birth certificate (title) to prove it. This sounds like so many of us in the world today, many of us are in the repair shop and junkyard so to speak. I want to hear more…

Phase: What was, What is and What is to come

Paul: I am going to take you back to where it all began and reveal the root cause of the problem and the solution throughout the three main phases of the life cycle.

These three phases are a parallel of the three phases in all of our lives:

- *The What was Phase.* This phase goes back to our beginning and all the things that happened to us before we had the power and ability to choose or make our own decisions.

- *The What Is Phase.* This is where we are living today. Many continue to battle with the sum of their decisions, things done to them that was beyond their control.

- *The What Is to Come Phase.* This is the exciting phase. In this phase, when we are **armed with the truth, and the power of choice,** we can choose a new path that will revolutionize our lives, the destiny of our family, and society for generations to come. Our nation is at the tipping point of destruction. Together we can turn things around, if we team up to make a positive impact in the lives of individuals and families.

Some symptoms of the FFS

Paul: One Man (Adam), the father of the entire human race, yes, that includes you and me, rebelled, by disobeying The Loving Heavenly Father of the universe. This plunged the entire human family, all of mankind, into a cycle of spiritual, physical, emotional, moral, social and financial deterioration.

Deb, there is a teaching about the seven mountains in society. It relates to the various sectors we need to influence. Some of these sectors include, "Media," "Education," "Government," "Family," and so on. I teach the ***One Mountain Principle***. The ***"Family Mountain,"*** *and the head of the family mountain is the "**father**."* This **one mountain** impacts all sectors of the world. As the **father** goes, so goes the family, every other ***mountain*** and the world…

These are just some of the ***symptoms*** of the *Father Fracture Syndrome* that we need to mitigate in our nation and world today:

- **Divorce** shatters the safety, protection and the mental health of children and families, further resulting in…

- **Domestic Violence**, which crushes and hurts individuals while destroying the image of "family", leading to…

- **Multiple Marriages** and **Relationship Conflicts** perpetuates the blemished dysfunctional cycle from one failed relationship to another. The detrition of family values from broken relationships leads to…

- **Abortion** *(The Murder and Slaughter of Babies)*, Child Abuse, Parents Murdering Children, Children Murdering Parents, Drug Abuse, Alcohol Abuse, Animal Abuse, Senior Abuse, and increased Mental Health Issues (resulting in more Homelessness), and Feelings of Hopelessness. Subsequently, many men, women and youth turn to…

- **Suicide**, Cutting, School Shootings, Bullying in School, Low Self-esteem, and Depression. Some turn their pain into a Quest for prominence or become a Workaholic. For others, this may manifest as…

- **Anorexia**, Bulimia, Bipolar Disorder, and Narcissism. Others, may turn to...

- **Pornography**, Human Trafficking, Prostitution, Rape and Child Sex Slavery, resulting in millions of Children living in Poverty and Hunger. Seeking to alleviate their plight, many end up encountering...

- **Abusive Priests**, Pastors, Parishioners, Church and Faith Leaders, who along with many other people, are struggling with...

- **Homosexuality**, Lesbianism, Promiscuity, Gender Identity Issues, and Feminism. With their failed attempts, to heal their wounded, plus the desire to find "Family," and their identity, many turn to...

- **Crime, Gangs** and Violence, Murder of Police and Law Enforcement Officers. Many then populate...

- **Jails, Prisons**, Detention and Drug Treatment Centers, thus revealing the Plight of Urban Inner Cities where 9 out of 10 children are being raised without dads in their homes. Raised on *Social Control Welfare* resulted in poor work ethic and high unemployment which only adds fuel for...

- **Racism, Class Warfare**, Injustice, Black Lives Matter Movement, Terrorism, Mass Bombings, and World Religions. This spawns...

- **Anti-Semitism**, Replacement Theology, hatred of Israel, Humanism, Atheism, Cults, Religion and all other Societal Abnormalities plus much more.

Lunch and Learn

Deb: Paul, I like where you are going with this process. Just hearing this partial list of symptoms of "FFS" makes me realize how all facets of our society are impacted by this one root-cause, with the source laid at the feet of one man, Adam.

Paul, could we pause for lunch? My stomach is making all kinds of noises. Let me treat you and your wife to lunch. I will charge it to our company credit card. After all, my boss told me, *"Deb, spare no expense to get to the bottom of this national epidemic."* So, lunch is on my company.

Paul: Sure Deb, my wife, Dawn, and I would love to join you. I didn't realize it was way past lunchtime. I was in my zone! We can all go in my car. It would be easier than having you try to follow me. I do not drive fast, but my car does sometimes.

Deb: Ha-Ha! I see you are at your jokes again, Paul. So, when the police officer pulls us over for speeding would he or she issue the citation to you or your car?

Paul: I would say it is a 911 emergency. Deb and Dawn are very hungry and I am rushing them to the restaurant to stop their stomach pain. I am sure the officer would be sympathetic to my plight.

   Disclaimer: To all children and those who are children at heart, I recommend you obey the traffic laws and drive safely. Deb, this is classic teaching I talk about in our mentor training program. We, fathers, tell our children to do what we say and not what we do, but in fact, they will ultimately do what we do. I saw my father drive fast, my children saw me drive fast, now guess how they drive?

Deb: Now I see what Dawn was warning me about. I can see now this interview will take me a lot longer with the many puns and wise guy humor in between. Well, I guess this is part of the price I have to pay for getting to the bottom of this epidemic. My boss told me to clear my calendar to get this done. It was a good thing he did.

Paul: My wife just gave me that look! That means, Paul, cool down on your speed, puns, and jokes. Okay, Deb, you both win! I will calm down until the next episode.

Deb: Dawn and I are now best of buddies. We will both keep you in line. Let's make this a working lunch. I can't wait to get to the bottom of this. You can continue to share from where we left off and I will record all your answers. I have arranged for us to sit in the quiet section of the restaurant where I host many of my interviews.

Paul: Thanks Deb, I can feel the love. You and Dawn have teamed up on me. Now that I know who my real friends are, we can continue…

Paul R. Benjamin, Sr.

Chapter 3

Before the FFS,
Religion or Relationship?

Deb: Paul, are we going to be talking about Religion? I know this will be a controversial topic and path for me and some of my readers. You may turn-off some of them before we even begin. If this God and Heavenly Father you speak of is anything like my father, I don't want to accept this assignment. I will call my boss now and asked to be re-assigned. Please, will you both excuse me. I need to step outside for a few minutes to get some air. I feel as if I am about to have a panic attack!

Paul: Dawn, it's been about 15 minutes since Deb stepped outside. Could you please check on her to see how she is doing? Thanks!

Deb: Paul and Dawn, I apologize for my outburst. I had to step outside to regain my composure. My Dad was a preacher and a hypocrite. He said one thing in church and lived another life at home. He didn't physically abuse me or my two brothers, but the verbal abuse at times was unbearable. I remembered my mom crying in her room after his tyrannical episodes. He constantly spoke down to her and all of us. Sometimes, my brothers and I would join mom in her room hoping, that… "this too shall pass." This was the reason I pursued a degree in Journalism. I wanted to express myself emotionally through writing. Growing up I was not allowed to express my true feelings and emotions. I was told by my dad to "suck it up" and deal with it. I began journaling to express the suppressed pain in my heart from my childhood. Every time I was able to write I felt a sense of freedom. Writing became my therapy!

Paul: Sorry, Deb! I asked Dawn to see how you were doing. I didn't mean to upset you. Millions of people just like you have experienced the impact of the ***Father Fracture Syndrome***. As I begin to unravel the truth and healing principles, emotions and memories will be stirred up. For some, this is putting it mildly. Just the mere mention of the word father, dad or Father God, activates rage, regret, anger, or fear.

You and many others who have been wounded by their fathers will find hope and healing once you receive and act upon the information and solutions I will share.

Deb: I feel awkward listening to the preacher when I go to church with Joel and our children. In the back of my mind I am always wondering, *"How is he treating his wife and children at home?"* I seldom hear the word father mentioned. They sing and pray mostly to Jesus.

Paul: Deb, I am sorry to hear how your dad treated you and your family. This may come as a shock to you but, this is not about Religion *(mankind's way of doing good deeds through religious acts or rituals to obtain approval and acceptance from God The Father in order to earn their way into heaven)*.

God is not Religious. He is a relational Loving Father. Like Him, I am not a religious man. I am a son in relationship with Him. God, my Heavenly Father, passionately loves me and I love and work alongside Him. Deb, just like the farmer, each person, once they discover the truth for themselves, will have to make their own decision and course of action.

Deb, your dad treated you and your family terribly. There is no excuse for his actions. As you travel with me through this brief journey from *Discovery to Destiny,* you will finally know the truth of how things were meant to be. The answers and the healing for the symptoms manifested in our lives and society can now be implemented.

Where we are today as individuals, families and as a nation is based on decisions! We were impacted by the decisions made by our parents, their parents, and all the way back to our first parents, Adam and Eve. Now, we too, will impact our children and their children by the decisions and choices we make today.

We will examine how things were before the worldwide FFS pandemic. How one decision landed us here and how one decision can change our destiny and the destiny of the next generation.

The Quest for Inner Peace

Deb: Thanks Paul, just being here with you and Dawn I feel a sense of peace. I am looking forward to hearing what you have to share. I am a little fearful, and excited, all at the same time. Deep down, I know everything will be okay.

Paul: I understand where you are coming from. The relationship with our parents, and our beliefs, shape our worldview and the way we view and process things in life.

Core values can either be positively or negatively influenced. Traumatic experiences, key influential relationships in school, places of worship, media, *(fake-news)* and society at large, can either solidify or diminish your values.

Deb: At my office, there is a broad spectrum of *world views* and core values. I see it in the way people react to various tragic events. Some panic and throw-up their hands in hopelessness and others respond in prayer and hope. Paul, let's continue with how we arrived at where we are today.

Paul: Before Adam (our earthly father) rebelled against Our Heavenly Father, there was a healthy, balanced and cohesive family relationship. The family didn't know what sorrow or pain felt like. They only experienced joy, peace and complete harmony in the family.

Origin of the Glory Source and Glory Code

Adam and Eve enjoyed being in the perfect and complete presence of the **Glory Source (GS)** *(The intrinsic Effulgence, Glorious, Exuberant Bright Splender and Beauty of The Heavenly Father)*. Which is equivalent to:

- *The Physical, Emotional, Spiritual Zenith, and oxygen of the heart and soul.*

- *The Capstone and Highest seal of Love, (the Super Bowl Ring).*

- *The Award-winning Trophy, the Splendor of beautiful jewelry on the neck, ears or hands.*

- *The only thing that brings complete Spiritual and Emotional Satisfaction.*

- *Significance and the Spiritual-Emotional DNA in every human life. Derived only from the one True Source, The Heavenly Father, God of all Glory and Life)*

The Heavenly Father imparted His Glory Code (GC) to His children, Adam and Eve, so they can influence future generations and the world.

Deb: Simplify what is the Glory Code (GC) to make it easier for my readers to understand?

Paul: In simple terms. As oxygen is to our physical body, so is the Glory Code to our soul. Our *emotional, intellectual, psychological and mental health levels* are directly influenced by our GC. When we are in a balanced relationship with the Heavenly Father, this results in complete soundness *and wholeness* of our heart.

The Greatest Love Comes from the Father

The Heavenly Father placed His capstone (highest) Glory Code in fathers. Dads carry the ultimate love and Glory Code seal in the lives of his children. We will discover how this **key principle** has impacted us and the entire world today.

Deb: Thanks Paul, I am beginning to understand why my dad had such an impact in my life. I would have given anything to experience what life was like before Adam and Eve messed things up for all of us.

Paul: Adam and Eve lacked nothing in their lives. Their Glory Code was complete in their family relationship. The Heavenly Father and his family were all living in harmony in their garden home. They could play with all the animals. There were no societal problems like what we experience today.

Every day the family sat down for dinner and family time. They had the perfect Glory Source (The Heavenly Father) in their lives. There was no need to seek fulfillment in any other person or substance. They were fulfilled in their relationship with their Heavenly Dad.

Knowing the Heart and Character of The Loving, Heavenly Father

The Heart of their Father is filled with all Love. The very character, nature, and image of their Heavenly Dad is Love. He is The *Source* and the personification of Love. They had everything they needed!

The word Family comes from the word Father. He revealed the true heart and Love for His family. He celebrates our joy and happiness. When we hurt, He hurts, too. He is Perfect, Holy, Righteous, Loving, Kind, and Just (*Fair*). It takes Him a long, long, time to get angry.

The voice of their Father was soft, calm, gentle, and affirming. He Loved them for who they were, His children, not for what they do (*performance*). His voice was always peaceful.

When they heard his voice, it brought them peace, joy, and comfort. They loved spending time together as a family. The voice of the Father sealed and framed their emotional and spiritual identity. They were solidified in who they were as part of the family. It did not matter what they did, they knew that they would still be loved. His Words were Life itself. Everything He spoke came to pass. He always kept His Word; every promise He made He kept!

Even though The Heavenly Father is all-powerful, there are a few things He cannot do:

- He cannot Lie *(He is Truth Personified)*

- He cannot break his promises *(He is a Promise Keeper)*

- He cannot Fail *(Every mission is successful)*

Deb: Paul, I wished my dad's tone of voice was like The Heavenly Fathers'.

Paul: The voice of The Heavenly Father will soothe and bring healing to every heart that is willing to embrace His Love.

The Eyes of The Father were warm, gentle and approving. Adam and Eve always felt welcomed and peaceful in His presence. His very character is peace, He sees and knows everything before it happens. He made provision for them that will one day, lead and guide them back into His Loving arms.

The Face *(countenance) of their Father* was radiant, sincere and inviting. They always felt applauded. He loved them and was pleased to spend time with them. They were always received with a smile of acceptance and approval when they entered His presence.

The origin of The Father's Family Table

Deb: As a child, I longed for this type of family relationship. Our dinner time was just another occasion for my dad to criticize my mom for her cooking or ridicule my brother and I for our grades in school.

Paul: I am sad to hear of your family dinner time. That was supposed to be a time to reflect and model the image of the Heavenly Father's family time. The "***Father's Family Table***" was the place where the Dad would connect and communicate His Heart. While enjoying a hot dinner, Adam and Eve would ask questions and share the events of their day with their Dad. The Heavenly Father knew the question and the answer even before they would ask Him, but He welcomed their questions.

After dinner, they played games and laughed together with their Dad. He would let them win sometimes. He always knew the moves they would make in the game before they made them. However, He made them feel valued and never condemned. He always had a radiant smile on his face. They could ask him anything. He was always kind and patient with them. He knew the beginning, middle, and end of everything they would even think or ask Him. Their Dad always complimented them daily after they completed their work. They always felt appreciated as He listened to their dreams. They felt safe under His protection, direction, and governance. Their Dad warned them of the evil enemy. Satan's. desire is to lie, steal, kill and destroy the family relationship.

Deb: I would like to be a child again and join this family. I want to hear more…

Paul: We would all like to be part of a perfect family. We have to guard and protect our hearts from relationships filled with deception and lies.

One's Glory Code is Subject to be Tested

Paul: The Heavenly Father was pleased to bless His children. Their Glory Code was complete, but subject to be tested. They lacked nothing. Everything was great. They belonged to an awesome family.

The mind and thoughts of their Father were always good towards them. He thought only positive things about them. He told them that they would be doing great things around the world. He told them to model His character (image) of Love, Joy, Peace, Truth, Unity and the right way to live for their children and future generations.

The ears of the Father were always open to hearing their concerns or questions. He knew the answer to any question that they may think or imagine. He never called any question stupid or foolish. He is a loving father and He cared about everything concerning His children.

The hands and arms of their Father were strong, yet gentle enough to hold them. They can cuddle for comfort or just to feel His strength. Nothing, or no one, could defeat them when they were in the arms of their Dad.

His Strong, Right Hand represented His perfect, righteous character. Like a shepherd, His strong right-hand lead, protected, provided and carried them when the troubles in life were overwhelming. They got into trouble by rebelling against Him, but one day His *Right Hand* will reach out to redeem and save them. He told them they will be restored and reunited with Him again.

Dad's lap was a place where you could enjoy an embrace while reading a book or sharing a story. They felt *joy, comfort, safety, and peace* in His presence. He applauded, celebrated and blessed them. He always told them that He was pleased and proud of them. They always felt complete in His presence.

When they heard **the footsteps** *of their Dad* they would run to meet Him. He was their joy, glory, and hero, His presence brought them comfort. They were always delighted to be in His presence. They felt His *acceptance, approval, and affirmation*. They knew that He had given them his *authority* and blessing to do what they were assigned to do.

Deb: I never knew what mood my dad would be in. So, when I heard his footsteps, I ran in fear from him, not to him.

Paul: Deb, as you learn and grow in intimacy with The Heavenly Father He will renew your heart.

Their Assignment was Clear

Paul: Adam and Eve had full access and blessing to speak with their Dad at any time. Without fear, guilt or shame, they could enter their Dad's presence to speak with Him or to hang-out and have fun with Him. They believed all He told them. He protected them from all the pain, heartbreak, death, and worst of all, being separated from His loving presence. He told them that He would pay the ultimate price to restore His family.

Obedience = Protection

To keep them and future generations safe from the great pain of the *Father Fracture Syndrome* their Dad said that there is **only one thing they should not do**. Adam and Eve asked. "What is the one thing, Dad?"

Their Father responded, **"*all you have to do is obey me."*** Obedience *(The Father's Hedge of Love and Protection from the evil adversary, The Devil)* will keep you safe. Our family will never have to be broken or experience any loss or pain. I cannot bear to lose my family. It would break my heart. He mentioned obedience to Him was not to hinder their freedom, but rather, it was to give them unlimited freedom to walk in His love which has no limits.

Love Trumps Law Everytime

There are no boundries to His Love. Without Love, there will not be enough books to contain the laws that would have to be written to produce what He has given us the freedom to live by and to walk in. The Father told them to make the right choice, to walk in His character, Love. His character will not harm anyone, it will only seek to help and serve others. He mentioned that ***the proof of true love*** for Him is to obey His commands. Living according to this core principle will keep the world in perfect peace, which is the core of His character.

His children responded, *"Dad, we love the knowledge, honesty, integrity, love, and insight you bring to our family. Your joy and jokes at dinner time make our daily journey in life fun. Your encouragement and counsel have set the expectation and capstone in our lives that only in you will we find True Life. Dad, you are our Glory, we are complete in our relationship with you. We know obedience to you is our only hedge of protection from the enemy."*

Deb: Paul, to know this kind of relationship existed is unfathomable. To know such a Dad and his relationship with his family, was what I longed for as a child growing up. I want this type of relationship for every child and family in the world.

Paul: Deb, this is brief glimpse into the Heart of The Loving, Heavenly Father. He desires to reveal Himself to a lost and hurting world through dads, moms and their children. **There are 7 relational cycles of life.** Each cycle reveals where we are in relationship to The Heavenly Father and how it impacts our lives. I will come back around to those 7 cycles later.

Dads and moms need to love their children regardless of where they are in the relational cycle of life. Fathers carry the capstone Glory Code and are to reflect the true character of The Heavenly Father to their wives and children.

Chapter 4

Five Core Needs
(Desires that Drive our Actions)

Deb: I agree and I do love my children. I can't imagine why someone would reject or abuse their children.

Paul: Adam and Eve were deeply loved. Their Dad placed ***five core needs*** in them and in all of His children. His Glory Source completes and accomplishes these five needs, which are:

1. Desire to know their ***Father*** – *to know their source (identity) and answer the questions, where did I come from? To whom do I belong?*

2. Desire for ***Family*** – for loving *acceptance, approval, affirmation and a sense of belonging.*

3. Desire to know one's ***Function*** – *the quest for personal ownership or autonomy* The Father gave them authority and made them managers *(stewards)* over everything He made on earth.

4. Desire to know one's ***Future*** – *destiny, vision to move forward with a goal in sight.*

5. Desire for one's own ***Foundation*** - to build upon, reproduce, and establish their *own family, following, and footprint, based on their own core beliefs.* The need to leave a legacy to influence in perpetuity *(how would they be remembered and who will keep their memory alive for generations to come)*.

Origin & Influence of Fake-News

Deb: This really incapsulates my personal motivation and why I am so driven.

Paul: We all have the same power of potential. One day Adam and Eve paused from their daily work in their family business. While relaxing, the adversary *(the enemy of their Father, the Devil)* began speaking to Eve.

Tugging on her freedom of choice, he mentioned, "If you stepped away from your Dad's loving protection *(obedience to Him)* you and your family will not truly die *(be eternally separated, both physically, and spiritually from your Heavenly Dad)*. You will be able to know as much as your Heavenly Dad." She reflected back to the nights when she had dinner with her Dad how He knew all the questions and answers before she could even ask him. She said to herself, yes, that would be cool! I can know as much as my Dad? Wow! That will be a game changer during our family time. I can win some of our word quizzes.

Eve remembered her Dad said, "Stay in His loving protection *(obedience to Him)*." Not knowing what pain and separation felt like, she began to rethink her choice. The *enemy* told her she will be as knowledgeable as her Dad, *knowing good and evil.* Contending with her thoughts, the voice of her Dad kept replaying in her heart. *"Do good my child, obey Me and enjoy peace and prosperity. Always choose life! Disobeying Me, will lead to death, separation and the breakup of our family."* However, she yielded to the lies *(fake news)* of the enemy, the ***father of fake news***. She was tricked and manipulated to believe his lies which led her to disobey her Dad's command. *She thought to herself, this cute talking snake would not lie to me, would he?* Her husband Adam realized his wife Eve was tricked into disobeying their Dad's command. His **intentional choice** to rebel and disobey their Father compounded the problem. The ***Father Fracture Syndrome*** was launched the moment Adam united *(came into agreement)* with his wife Eve in their rebellion.

Immediately after their rebellion, their hearts and eyes were opened to the knowledge of good and evil. What they once saw as pure and precious, now seemed *profane* and *perverted.* Adam realized his decision impacted his family.

The Actions of a Dad Impacts their Families

Deb: In our family growing up, the decisions that my dad made impacted all of us. I am still living with some of the effects from my dad's actions.

Paul: The impact of Adam's action is still reverberating around the world. Both he and his wife were embarrassed and ashamed of their naked appearance. Guilt and fear overwhelmed their wounded hearts and crumpled their Glory Code. Realizing that they had broken their Dad's heart, they tried to hide from Him. They remembered, that they cannot hide anything from Him. He knows everything! Just as they were thinking these thoughts, they heard their Dad walking to meet them for dinner and family time.

Dad called to his son Adam *(the father of the entire human race)* to give an account for what he did to bring this devastation to his family. The Father appointed him to be the servant leader of his family. Adam knew his actions negatively impacted his family and the world. Adam thought to himself, *"should I take responsibility and admit my wrong or should I pass the buck and blame my wife, Eve?"* Before this tragic event, Adam never heard disappointment in his Dad's voice before. He immediately perceived a change in his Father's voice. He and Eve only knew their Dad's calm and soothing voice all their life. This time, His voice sounded sad and hurt, like a parent who lost their children in a tragic accident.

Fear and Failure to Take Responsibility

Deb: As a mom, I can identify with the sense of betrayal The Heavenly Father felt.

Paul: Parents don't realize that many of the same emotions we experience today, originated from The Father.

A deep darkness and guilt enveloped Adam's soul, a feeling he never experienced before. With a trembling voice, he quickly said to his Dad, *"I was hiding because I was naked and afraid."*

Shifting the Blame

Adam felt an immediate disconnect from the True *Glory Source,* his heavenly Father. He felt hurt and loss. The brightness of his Glory Code was darkened. Knowing that he had disappointed his Dad, he said, *"The wife you blessed me with was tricked and I disobeyed you when she asked me to join her in this rebellion. Now both of us have brought this global pandemic upon our family and the world."*

Their Glory Code was now in a diminished state. The Heavenly Father knew if Adam or Eve entered His presence His Holy and Perfect Glory would instantly destroy them. He killed an animal to provide temporary *(spiritual & physical)* covering for them so they could communicate with Him on a limited basis. This compassionate act was a foreshadow of His First appointed Season when He would provide the ultimate Lamb, His Son, (Jesus) to pave the way for His children to be reconciled with Him.

Adam knew his action unleashed and activated the ***Father Fracture Syndrome.*** *The broken Glory Code and the consequences resulting from the damaged relational state between The Heavenly Father and earthly fathers with their families, resulting in, malfunctions, abnormality, atrocities and the entire breakdown within families and the world.*

Adam and Eve didn't understand the full ramification of their decision to disobey and rebel against their Heavenly Father. Their Glory Code would not be completely satisfied until they are reconciled with their Heavenly Father through a personal relationship with His Son. One day, their maximum Glory Code will be realized when they are home, living with The Heavenly Father and eating at *"The Father's Family Table."*

Adam knew he was powerless to undo the negative impact of his actions. As the father of the entire human race, his bloodline has impacted all of our families. Yes, including me and you. Adam thought to himself, *"I know my Heavenly Father knows everything from the beginning to the end. He, and His strong right hand kept us all these years from harm. I know He has a plan to restore us, back to Himself."*

Father - Shammah
(He is There and Present in Every Situation working things out)

Deb: This explains why my dad found it hard to take responsibility for his actions. He blaimed my mom for most of the problems in our family.

Paul: The responsibility for what happens in the family lands at the feet of the dad. The buck stops at the Father. The term Father-Shammah *(Adonai-Shammah)* is just one of the many character attribuits of The Heavenly Father. It means: *The Father is there (present) before we even get there, He is always present mitigating things ultimately for our wellbeing.*

Deb: This reflects the heart of The Father. He is always there working things out to ultimately turn them around in His perfect time and season.

Paul: Regardless where we find ourselves in life, The Heavenly Father is there with His arms stretched out to heal and renew. Just as Adam was thinking about the mess he made, The Heavenly Father called him and said, *"You broke our family unity by rebelling against Me (leaving the safety of my loving protection). By default, you have* *chosen rather to follow, serve and obey the father of lies, Satan. He runs his family by lust, deception and murder. He will drive you with his strong left hand to only do evil and bring devastation to you and families around the world."*

"As your Heavenly Father, I led you gently by my Right hand only to do good. The agenda of Satan is to:

- **Steal** *(by deception and twisting the Words of the Heavenly Father through false information)*. Words can ***build Faith*** or ***instill Fear*** in the hearts of people. Words can also bring **hope** or **hopelessness.**

- **Kill** *(he will drive people away from Me, The Father of Life, resulting in the "FFS")*

- **Destroy** all I have done for you and our family. The voice you listen to and obey, you will serve.

"Adam, your wife and all women after her will give birth to children in much pain. The ground that was easy for you to grow and harvest crops will now become difficult. There will be conflict in your relationships. Some children will be born with birth defects. There will be crime and violence in the world. I love you and want to be back in a relationship with you and all my family."

Father - Jireh
(He sees and provides from the foundation of the world)

Deb: Having given birth to two children, the labor pain caused me to remember the price every mother has to pay because of Adam.

Paul: Sorry, Deb, this is one of the times I am thankful that women have this role in the family. The term *Dad-Jireh (Adonai-Jireh) relates to one of the many facets of the Heavenly Father's character. It means that "The Father sees and provides for every situation from the foundation of the world."*

Deb: Now, this all makes sense! So, The Father knew before the foundation of the world what Adam and Eve were going to do and He already had the provision in place

Paul: You got it! There are so many aspects to The Heavenly Father's character. I only have enough time to just scratch the surface on the height and depth of His character. That is why He told his children *"I Am that I Am"* *(I AM everything that my children would ever need)*.

The Father told Adam, "One day, I will destroy the adversary, Satan, once and for all! He cannot keep you and the rest of my children slaves to his rebellious agenda forever. He was a leader in my Kingdom. Pride ruled his heart and he rebelled against me. I banished him and his loyal operatives, from my presence forever. Now, they are on a mission to destroy, pervert and corrupt the family that I love. They are after my family. That is why he will always misquote (falsely misrepresent), steal, and manipulate, the Words that I speak to you. He and his followers will do this to every generation. Many would yield to his rebellious schemes until I finally put him and his operatives away forever."

The Heavenly Father's Appointed Times and Seasons

"Adam, your rebellion placed an eternal chasm between us and your entire human bloodline. I have established Seven Relational Seasons. This will be my timeline (calendar)for the entire human race.

Before the foundation of the world, I planned for My Son (who is currently sitting at my Right Hand) to become human and live on earth for a period of time. He would be born through My chosen people. In My Appointed Seasons, He will manifest (reveal) My character of Love, Mercy, Compassion, and Forgiveness. His bloodline will be holy, untainted and perfect. He will not rebel against Me or yield to the adversary in any way. His supernatural birth process will occur at the appointed time and Season. He will pay the ultimate price by offering His life on a tree. Thus, fulfilling My Perfect, Righteous requirements to reunite My family. I have considered this ultimate cost. The joy of knowing that one day I will have My Family back with Me is worth it all.

My chosen people, The Jews, will suffer greatly. Satan and his operatives will persecute them because My Son would come through their lineage. People and nations will turn against them because they were assigned to reveal My ultimate Glory Code through My Son. I will bless those People and countries that bless the Jews. Anyone that comes against them, will ultimately have to deal with Me...

The Jews will reveal and remind the world of My Seven Appointed Seasons. My Son, The Messiah (Savior of the world) will fulfil them in My Appointed Time. My Spirit will be in Him. He will do what He sees Me do.

Until the completion of My Seasons, there will be pain and sorrow on the earth. Billions of families around the world will be plagued with death, violence and broken hearts."

Deb: What are the Seven Seasons of the Father?

Paul: I will give you some more details about the Seasons and the Cycles shortly. I wanted to lay a foundation for you first.

Paul R. Benjamin, Sr.

Chapter 5

The "What is Phase"

Dads are Responsible for the Spiritual Condition of Their Family

Deb: Before my husband Joel and I met you, I didn't know the seriousness and impact of dads and the *"Father Fracture Syndrome"* in our society.

Paul: The impact from this one key factor is the most overlooked problem in the world. The Heavenly Father appointed and ordained dads to be the servant leaders and heads of their families. Their core responsibility is to communicate and model His character *(lifestyle, principles and teachings)* to their wives and children. Until The Father concludes His Appointed Seasons, their children are to lead and influence the next generation.

He mandated that every man must provide a *Lamb (Guide his family into a reconciled relationship with The Heavenly Father)*. The dad should first be the example, then lead his family. This was not a suggestion for dads, but a *command*.

The word Command makes me Cringe

Deb: Paul, when you use the word command, it stirs up oppressive and domineering images for me. Immediately I hear the voice of my dad and see his immense image towering over me as a child. I think about rebelling against whatever he commanded me to do. Why do you think I feel this way?

Paul: Deb, thanks for your transparency. This is one of the many symptoms of The *Father Fracture Syndrome*. The reason you and I want to rebel every time we hear the word *command* is because our earthly father, Adam, aligned with the father of rebellion, Satan, against The Heavenly Father. We are all born with the same natural human spirit of rebellion.

Deb: Even though I know when the Heavenly Father commands *(instructs)* us to do what is right and good for us, on the inside there is still that little tug to resist.

Paul: You and millions of others who have been physically, sexually, emotionally or verbally abused by a dad, or a person in authority, rebel against the command because God represents our ultimate and highest authority. Deb, you had mentioned how your dad was verbally abusive. This is another reason that the word "command," affects you so much.

People who are still living in rebellion and refuse to *repent (Turn towards the Loving Heart of the Heavenly Father)* and obey His divine will, would naturally live forever *(eternity)* with the Enemy *(if they continue living this way until death)*.

Just to lose one child would break The Heavenly Father's heart. This is why He commands us to obey and follow His divine, good and perfect plan for our lives. When we choose to rebel against His commands, it proves that we are continuing to walk in rebellion against Him; and we are still in allegiance with His nemesis, Satan. We obey the one we love. The proof of our love for the Heavenly Father is in our obedience to Him. This is only for our good. It draws us closer to His heart and perfect protective plan for our lives.

Spiritual Influence in His Family

Paul: Dads carry a key spiritual influence in their families. Fathers seal and impart the capstone *(definitive)* value and character of The Heavenly Father to his entire family. This is not about male chauvinism, as a matter of fact, most men would like to abandon this mandated role and responsibility. Just like women who would like to abdicate their mandated role of bearing and delivering children, many men would like to alleviate their mandated role.

Deb: I was smiling when you mentioned that some women would love to not have the pain of delivering children. I am one of them but, the overwhelming joy after giving birth to my children was worth it all! I can now understand what The Heavenly Father was talking about. The pain of His Son's death to restore His Family was dwarfed by the joy of having His children reconciled to Him.

Paul: You just echoed The Father's heart. This is one key reason why many men shrink back from their roles. Fatherhood is not taught, but **caught** through a modeled relationship with another man. Today, most men have not seen authentic manhood or fatherhood modeled in their homes. They don't have a true audio and video on the role or responsibility of a dad who reflects the character of The Heavenly Father.

Maximize Community Outreach Impact

Deb: My father-in-law was a great role model to my husband, Joel. Subsequently, I am the blessed recipient. He is now replicating the attributes he caught from his dad. I am married to an awesome man!

Paul: The church we attend invests about 90% of its efforts in community outreach programs to women and children. Very few dads attend these community events. There is a stark retention and engagement difference when children have their dad's involvement. Sorry to say, without their dad's endorsement and involvement, many children become disengaged. This is one of the key factors why teenage men and women leave the church and are easily radicalized on college campuses.

When a dad is the first in the family to be reconciled with The Heavenly Father and assumes his mandated, intrinsic, leadership role in his family he has a *93-97%* impact on his entire family. If his wife is first to be reconciled with The Heavenly Father, she only has a *17- 22%* impact and influence upon the family. When a youth *(son or daughter)* is first in the family to be reconciled with The Heavenly Father there is only a *3%* impact and influence on the entire family.

Deb: Wow, these results are staggering! I now understand why so many young men and women disengage with church life in their teenage *(young adult)* years.

Paul: This is why there is an urgent mandate for men to know their Heavenly Father and what He requires of them. This would yield the highest healing and renewal in families, cities and the world. Dads are required to model and teach the principles, seasons and character attributes of The Heavenly Father to their children; and their children are to proclaim it to their generation unto the ends of the Earth. Remember, children will value *whatever their dads value.*

Dads, your children will often follow your example. Good or bad! I pray and hope, it's good…

Love beyond Rebellion

Deb: Paul, I know just from being a mom, if my children should ever rebel and leave home, their dad and I would be devastated. Now I understand more about my dad and the impact his verbally abusive dad and the Father Fracture Syndrome had on him and our family. This explains a lot about my childhood experience and what is occurring in society today.

Paul: Deb, The Heavenly Father told His children, Adam and Eve, that their Glory Code (GC) is only fully complete in Him. He is, The One and only, True Father; the source of life and all that is good. He told them that they would pass on His Glory Code to their children, but that the capstone Glory Code *(finishing, crowning)* for their children and family, *He has placed in earthly fathers.*

The Heavenly Father told Adam to encourage his family with these words; one day we will be reunited as one big family and all the tears, pain and violence will be over. Remind them to place their hope and trust in my Son who will come in my Name. He will obey me. What you lost in this family garden, He will restore. It will cost Me everything. Yes, even My Son's life. The ultimate price will have to be paid. It is required to fulfill my mercy and justice, allowing my family to be reunited again.

Power to Transform a Crushed Glory Code

"My Glory Source will never allow anything to end in the negative. In my presence, I will transform your crushed Glory Code into my exuberant Glory. Three days later, I will resurrect Him and I will prepare the biggest celebration feast for all my children who will trust in the finished work that He will accomplish. Every word and action He will perform, is from me. I will be doing the work through Him. When you listen and obey Him, you are listening and obeying me. I love you and think the world of you. That is why I will pay this ultimate price to have you back in my loving arms again. The only way into my presence will be through Him. Until then, when you hurt, I will hurt, too. I am longing for that day when we can be a complete and reunited family again."

"Remember, I love you with an everlasting love, but you still have the *power of free will.* I have given you the freedom to choose to love Me and return to our loving family again. Remember, choose love, life, joy, and peace. Choose Me. Not choosing to return to Me through My Son, you will continue in your state of rebellion. In league with the Enemy, the adversary, the father of pride and lies who rebelled against me and was expelled from my Kingdom forever, you will be cast out with no path of return. They will be separated from My loving presence, where there is no darkness, pain, sorrow, tears, regrets, and guilt of the past. There will only be joy, peace, happiness, and an abundance of food and family time for eternity. I will always compel you to choose Me. I am looking forward to our big reunion. *I Love you, your Heavenly Dad."*

Deb: Paul, I can't stop tearing up. The description of the Love that The Father expressed for His children, I have not seen or experienced in my life. Why would anyone want to walk away or rebel against that type of love? I guess you are now going to explain the next phase of their journey?

You now have me at the edge of my seat. I want to hear the rest of the story. I know that we're probably less than one foot deep into the ocean of information, but, this is great to know the *"why"* to these things that have plagued me throughout my life.

Paul: Deb, I too had tears in my eyes as I was talking about this phase. When you experience the true love of The Heavenly Father nothing else in life can shake it. Death, hardship, sorrow, nothing can separate you from this eternal relational Love. We, as humans, use the word love, which is like a coffee cup full of water. The Love of The Heavenly Father is as deep as all the oceans of the world. He is Love personified. To walk away from that kind of love and compassion, would be the ultimate rebellion and tragic choice of our free will.

Raising a family with a Compromised Glory Code

Paul: Now that the family is no longer under the Divine Protection that they enjoyed before, they rebelled. The desire and quest for approval and acceptance by the Father were now sought after by the first father and all the family members on earth.

Adam and Eve's GC was greatly diminished as a result of their rebellion. Eve provided a certain level of the GC satisfaction for the children. Adam was given the complete responsibility to provide the final and complete capstone *(final seal, approval)*. Between both of them, their combined GC was not enough to give their children a sense of completeness that can only be found in a healthy, restored relationship with their Heavenly Dad. Life seemed empty without Him. Nothing they did ever seemed to give them the capstone approval they felt and experienced at the beginning.

Adam and Eve initially had two sons, Cain and Abel. Their sons were offering their gifts to get The Heavenly Father's acceptance and approval. Their earthly dad could only fulfill a part of their GC. Without a restored relationship with The Heavenly Father, they would never find fulfillment and completeness of their *Glory Code*. Cain's offering did not gain approval and acceptance from The Heavenly Father. He approached The Heavenly Father with pride, and on his terms, and his offering was rejected.

Rejection is the most Powerful Root

Without feeling accepted, approved and affirmed, (three keys to help seal his Glory Code), Cain became disappointed, discouraged, disillusioned, desperate, and dangerously enraged with anger. The light from his GC had reached (-7), *(critical level of suicide or murder)*. His light had become darkness. *Rejection is the most powerful root of anger and hate.* His dark spirit had become just like that of the Enemy of the Heavenly Father, the Devil, Lucifer. All because his GC had been crushed and his prideful offering had been rejected. Cain was not aware that his Glory Code comes from the father. It is like drinking all the water in the world and never being able to quench your thirst. When the GC is crushed, it will lead to many negative internal and external manifestations and symptoms.

When we refuse to accept the Truth, we attack others

Cain chose to manifest his anger, rage and hate towards his brother. His brother, Abel, chose to do things as his Father required of him, for which he received the Father's approval, acceptance, and affirmation. One day, jealousy and anger overwhelmed Cain. The hurt and desire to be accepted and approved by his Father clouded his judgment. He saw his brother working in the field and he murdered him and buried his body in the ground. This is where the term that we use so often, "Am I my brother's keeper?" comes from. The spirit of his brother, Abel, cried out from the ground to The Heavenly Father for justice. The Father, in the fullness of time, will settle all injustices committed by man on earth.

First Murder in our FFS World

This was ***the first recorded murder*** in the history of our earthly family. Since this first murder, the spirit of murder has never left our families. Today parents are murdering their children every day. We have softened the emotional impact of the word *murder* by substituting it with the word *abortion*. The moment we lose value for life from its inception, we have lost value for everything else. When Adam, the father of the entire human race, chose to rebel against his Heavenly Father, he came into agreement and covenant with the father of darkness and death, the Devil.

When the head of a family, city or nation decide to enter into a covenant to either do good or evil, he or she brings the weight and impact of their decision upon their spouse, family, city and nation.

Paul R. Benjamin, Sr.

Chapter 6

Protector or Predator

Deb: I thank God for my husband, Joel, he is a good balance for me. When I get into one of my mood swings and about to make a rash decision, he lovingly helps to deescalate my anxious soul. He is a great balance for me and our family.

Paul: Deb, you are blessed. There are many men who were influenced by dads who model attributes of the Heavenly Father and are able to be balanced husbands and dads. When Adam rebelled, (which is like the sin of witchcraft) he unleashed the powers of darkness into his family, and subsequently the world. The character of the evil one, Satan, is rooted in Pride and Lust. He desires only to steal, kill and destroy all the children of The Heavenly Father.

Adam uncovered his wife and family:

- He exposed his family to death, pain and the entire evil portfolio of the father of lies and deception.

- He was the **protector** and covering for his wife and family. Since then, many men have become **predators**, causing pain and anguish to their wives and families, and yes, even to themselves and others.

- In essence, by his decision to rebel, he said to his wife and family, *"When you do something wrong I will choose to embrace the deception of your actions rather than standing firm on the conviction of truth."* At the first sign of conflict, most men today would quickly compromise with their wives rather than to maintain resilient love and obedience to The Heavenly Father.

- He did not take responsibility for his actions, but instead passed the blame back to The Heavenly Father. Today, many men are not taking responsibility for their actions. They shift the blame to others or situations. *Responsibility* leads to a *resolution*, resulting in a *renewed relationship*.

- The seed of his example has now become the prototype for every wife, child, man and family in the world.

- **Predatorial** men who have physically and sexually abused women, girls and boys further paved the way to the diminished value of life. As a result, women and girls with crushed Glory Codes find it easy to murder *(abort)* their children, whether in or out of the womb. This spirit of murder has devalued all life in the world.

Deb: I am feeling overwhelmed right now! I was thinking of all the millions of children (babies) being murdered every year in America and around the world. Paul, why is this heinous act so rampant in our nation today?

Paul: Deb, one key impact of the Father Fracture Syndrome is the diminished (crushed) Glory Codes in dads and moms. The capstone seal of dads solidifies and gives value for life. With the massive absence of dads in the lives of sons and daughters, this further erodes the value for themselves and subsequently the life of their babies (children). This is the reason why 92% of the girls that murder their babies live in homes without their biological dads.

The symptoms resulting from FFS have reached and impacted every individual, family, and nation. There is nothing capricious *(whimsical or without purpose)* in society. There is an intended purpose behind every action or event. The core values of a person are revealed by their actions. If their actions reflect love, *which saves lives,* they are reflecting the character of The Heavenly Father. If their actions reflect lust, lies and the murder of babies *(children)*, they are reflecting the character of the Enemy.

Dawn: Deb, Paul can teach and explain a topic in great detail. He can even take you back to the source. So, Paul, please give the condensed version for the sake of time.

Paul: Deb, I just got that look from Dawn. That means, move it along. I will shorten my long answers as we progress. The deeper revelation and nuances behind every situation will take too long to explain. *You would end up with an encyclopedia.* The key take-away is to know the *"Why"* and the Source of every problem in life.

Deb: Paul, I was looking right at her when I too, saw the "look!" Ok, I am glad you are painting a picture by laying the historical background and core principles of the

"Why." Everything else you mentioned flows from that. I would only interrupt you, if and when, I have a burning question I need answered.

Paul: Thanks, ladies! I got the message loud and clear. By the time I speak the next sentence, another woman, girl and boy would physically or sexually abused.

Money, without the Right Process, will not Mitigate the FFS

Every symptom that we are spending millions and billions of dollars on each year is traced back to this core fatherhood issue, resulting from the FFS. My thoughts and prayers go out to the men, women, girls, and boys who were victims of abuse at home and in our society. The Father of Love and Peace is longing to heal every wounded heart and soul.

A father raped his daughter and she gave birth to Twin

One evening I was speaking to about fifty women in Orlando about the impact of the "FFS". While speaking about the abuse inflicted by fathers in their families; one of the young ladies burst into uncontrollable tears. I paused my message and invited her to come forward. Janice *(not her real name)* mentioned her dad raped her when she was a teenager. As a result, she became pregnant and gave birth to twin boys *(her brothers)* who were residing with her father.

After a failed attempt to murder her dad, she was sentenced to 15 years in prison for attempted murder. Five years into her sentence, the Governor granted her clemency. I briefly explained her own dad's childhood abuse; then I stood in the gap *(proxy)* for her father as a point of contact. I repented on *his* behalf for what *he* did to her. Then I asked Janice to *"forgive me for what her dad did to her."* Immediately, she collapsed upon the floor and with a loud outburst of tears. She began convulsing, for what seemed like 10 to 15 minutes. While this occurred, some of the women began to cry and three came up to console her. Her tears began to subside into a mellowed, soft tone.

I prayed for Janice and led her through the process of acknowledging the abuse. Coupled with the act of forgiveness, it released and blessed her. Upon completion, a quiet peaceful spirit came over her. Her countenance changed. It was lifting a 100-pound weight off of her. I stood in the place of her Heavenly Father and gave her a huge Father's hug. This helped to seal and solidify the internal healing The Heavenly Father was doing in her heart and soul. Her Heavenly Dad began mending her crushed Glory Code and restoring her.

There are millions of women like Janice around our nation and world. On behalf of our Heavenly Father, who feels every pain that you have gone through, with tears in my eyes and His, I would like to ask you, *"Would you please forgive me for what was done to you?"* Receive His gift of healing and renewal…

Love vs Lust, The character of 2 fathers

Deb: Paul, my heart broke for Janice. Just to think, there are millions of girls and women who have experienced the same thing and identify with the *"Me, Too"* movement. The far-reaching impact of the "FFS" never seems to end.

Paul: Deb, I too feel the hurt. As a dad, this is hard to fathom. Let me explain true love and how to tell the difference between fathers motivated by love and fathers that walk in lust. By observing people and their character, you will know which father they serve. Let me expound on the core character of The Heavenly Father which is Love.

Love:

- Pays the huge cost. Yes, even to the point of death. It sacrifices for the one loved. Is always satisfied in doing good. It never fails.

- Keeps no record of wrong and is quick to forgive others.

- Hopes and speaks the best of others.

- Is an act of your will.

- Is not a feeling, but the result is joy, peace, fulfillment, and contentment.

- Holds the family together.

- The Heavenly Father is "LOVE" and His children are commanded *(an act of obedience)* to walk in this Love. They will be known by their actions.

In contrast to love, the core character of the Enemy, Satan, is Lust.

Lust:

- Is selfish, demands its own way. Takes from others, even killing and murdering. Is never satisfied, even to the point of death. It will fail.

- Seeks revenge and is unforgiving.

- Uses others to benefit its own self-serving agenda.

- Will justify itself, only to destroy others at all costs

- Is an *emotion* acted out by choice, only to benefit itself, disregarding the needs of others.

- Rips individuals and families apart. Is rooted in pride. Lucifer, the Devil, is the father of lust and pride. His children walk in lust and pride. They are known by their actions *(fruits)* and what they speak.

Deb: In this comparison of love and lust, you described some people I know. My eyes are now open to the truth. So many people in our nation profess to be one thing, but their actions reflect the character of their father, Satan.

Paul: Deb, this is called "the battle for the heart." From the beginning, the battle has always been for the heart. That is why, to whom you yield your heart to obey, is the one you will serve, and whose character you will emulate. Examine the behaviors of people and you will know which father they serve. What's in the heart, comes out through the mouth and actions of everyone…

Deb: After I invited my boss John to attend your Father of The Year Awards event with Joel and our children, he reconciled his life with The Heavenly Father. Now, he is funding me to do this interview with you. I am now seeing how God works through us to love others back to Himself.

Paul: I am blessed to see how The Heavenly Father loves people so much, regardless who of they are and what they have done. He is willing and yearning to love them back to Himself and into His family again.

As I mentioned, it's all about influencing the heart. Here are some of the character attributes of the **Enemy**:

The heart of the Enemy is full of deception. He is called the father of lies. He is a murderer, and all who obey and yield to his ways, come under his influence and model his evil character. He is a master at manipulating the Words and stratagies of The Heavenly Father. Thus, derailing the already fragile hope in people that fall prey to his schemes. This causes doubt, fear, and unbelief. People will question their trust and identity with the Heavenly Father. He is the father of fake news. He is evil personified! He encourages and strengthens the pride in people so they can hold on to anger and unforgiveness towards those who have hurt or offended them.

The voice of the Enemy creates fear. It stirs up negative emotions and anxiety. At times, it creates trust and sympathy, in an effort to manipulate latent resentment and disguised hostility towards others. His motive is deception. His drive is to have you act quickly without thinking or processing the ramifications or outcomes of your actions.

The eyes of the Enemy are deceitful. They lure you in with warmth. They draw you into his presence, but the result is disappointment and disillusionment. You can never win his approval or acceptance. You will always be required to do more for him, never reaching fulfillment or a sense of completeness. His eyes are filled with anger and vengeance. He is always asking more from you without the satisfaction of being part of a loving family.

He will even promote you to great material success. Some may even reach the level of CEO for a major company, with millions or billions in the bank. Some may be elevated to become a Mayor, Governor, King, or President. At the end of it all, their lives will be empty and void. The emptiness inside can only be filled by the love that comes only from the Heavenly Father.

He will use your charisma and charm to open doors for you. However, you will fail as you lack the character to sustain you. He brags about the many professional players and movie stars who sign huge contracts, only to end their careers in moral failure.

The ears of the Enemy will hear and even grant you the evil desires of your heart. He will use the forces of darkness to accomplish his agenda, but ultimately it will fail. All the accomplishments, which promised to bring joy, peace and fulfillment, result in the feeling of emptiness.

His left hand only draws you into danger, disrupting your family life, with the ultimate goal; "leading you to a lifetime of pain and suffering with him for eternity." He will not let you know that you will be permanently separated from the love of The Heavenly Father and His family. This emptiness and discouragement lead many to commit suicide.

Deb: We are seeing an explosion of girls and boys committing suicide in school and on Facebook. The increasing number of girls cutting themselves is just another cry for help! This is part of the agenda of the Enemy to destroy lives and families around the world.

Paul: My prayer is that people will open their eyes to the agenda and strategies of the Enemy and awaken to the plan of The Heavenly Father for their lives.

Paul R. Benjamin, Sr.

Chapter 7

Seven Seasons *in The Father's Relational Time Clock*

Season One, Passover

Deb: With this insight, it helps me to understand the character that has manifested in some of my media associates. Paul, you reminded me of the story in John chapter eight. Jesus, while speaking to the religious leaders of His day, said to them; *"You are of (the same character like) your father, the Devil, and his lust (desires) you will do."* He also mentioned that, *"the Devil was a murderer from the beginning and the father of lies (fake news)."*

This statement has never been clearer to me than it is today! With over **90%** of the news *(propaganda)* today being fake news *(lies)*, you don't know who to trust. America, the nation that was founded on the principles of the Bible is now number (#1) in murdering children *(babies)* and (#1) in fatherless homes. How do the Seven Seasons of The Heavenly Father play out in the world today?

Paul: You are so right. The character of the father of death and lies is seen everywhere. Yes, even in churches!

The **First of the Seven Seasons** is ***Passover.*** Before the foundation of the world, The Father knew the price that He would have to pay to save *(redeem)* His children; so, they can have access to return into His loving arms again.

This Season and all Seven Seasons were set from the foundation of the world. Each season has a specific day, time, and place when The Father will ultimately accomplish His desired purpose.

Deb: In my church we only celebrated Easter, but, many of my Jewish friends celebrated Passover. They always told me about the broken Matzah that was hidden and then returned.

Paul: Remember, The Heavenly Father told His children if He loses them, He would die so His family can one day be back in His Loving arms again. The Father sent His Perfect Son to die on the cross so we could be reconciled to Him again. The pain of this decision was swallowed up by the joy of knowing His family will one day be reunited with Him. Every time the middle Matzah is ceremonially broken during Passover, it is a reminder of His Son, Yeshua, the perfect Lamb, and the price He paid to pave the way to have His family back with Him. *(He was broken, crucified, hidden, buried and then in the third Season, was resurrected from the dead.)* Dads are required to personally accept this gift and lead their families to do the same. If we reject Him, we are rejecting the greatest gift of love in the world.

Deb: So, Paul, the actual fulfillment of this season has already passed?

Paul: Yes, Deb, this was one of the first four Seasons that were already fulfilled and accomplished. They occurred on the exact appointed day, time, and place *(Israel)* set by The Heavenly Father two thousand years ago. Dads should celebrate these Seasons with their families. In celebrating them, it shows appreciation and brings honor to The Heavenly Father for the price He paid to reconcile His Family. There are only three Seasons left to fulfil in *The Heavenly Father's Seven Seasons*. He is now getting his children ready for the Fifth Season; this Season will be a huge game changer. *Stay tuned…*

Season Two, Unleavened Bread

Deb: In church, we never spoke much about this Season. Give a quick overview…

Paul: The Second Season is ***Unleavened Bread***. The Father knew that his children would be tested. When tested, one should not reason or negotiate, but run from and not yield to the temptation. Dad knew that from each heart flows all the issues of life; it only takes one bit of

Leaven, *(act of disobedience)* to spread throughout the entire person and family, just like the impact from Adam's decision.

It took only one disobedient act from Adam in the first garden to affect the entire human race. The Heavenly Father knew He would have to send His obedient Son, Yeshua, to accomplish His plan. After leaving His position in heaven next to His Dad, He became human. Through a supernatural process, bypassing the sin-tainted, leaven-infected, bloodline of Adam, He was born by God's intervention through a virgin named Mary. He did this so that one day, in the second garden, He would pave the way for His children to be reconciled into His loving Family.

This Season reveals that His Son, the perfect Lamb, Deity, will have no *Leaven* in Himself. There was nothing corrupt, or imperfect in Him. His life and character would not be tainted by any form of disobedience or sin. Just like how leaven *(yeast)* produces fermentation to cause bread to rise, His Son modeled, that He was perfect in all His ways, with no leaven in His life. When Pilate, the Governor, issued the order to crucify Yeshua on the cross he said, *"I find no fault (no leaven) in Him (Yeshua/Jesus)."* In other words, He was *The Perfect Lamb of God* without blemish!

Dads in their own strength and works cannot remove the leaven from their lives. By the strength of The Heavenly Father's Right Hand, they would be able to remove the leaven from their lives *(corrupt things hindering them from experiencing the fullness of life.)*

Season Three, First Fruits

Deb: I now see the value and importance why dads need to model and keep the standard of Jesus for their families. He has to empower them to live up to His character of love and righteousness.

Paul: The Third Season is *First Fruits*. On the third day, Jesus, who is symbolized during Passover as the broken Matza that returned, resurrected from the grave. He was the *"First Fruit"*, the first to resurrect from the dead. With His new glorified body, He visited hundreds of His followers. This was to show His children that they too will one day, be resurrected from the grave to spend eternity with Him, and His Heavenly Family. This has given hope to His children. Now, they too will have the same glorified body in a future Season.

Season Four, Shavuot

Deb: This is awesome to know! One day when I die, I too would have a glorified body like Jesus. This removes my fear of death. I will be with The Heavenly Father and His Family forever. *In which Season will we have our glorified body?*

Paul: Our glorified bodies would be in Season Five. We will discuss that later. Every Season of The Heavenly Father, reveals His heart towards us.

The Forth Season is **Shavuot** *(The Feast of Weeks, Pentecost.)* This Season is where the Father promised that He will not leave His children alone. He promised to send *His Holy Spirit* to comfort, equip, empower and walk along-side them. He promised not leave them alone in their struggles. His power and strength will help them walk in victory through the impact of the *Father Fracture Syndrome* (FFS). This Season also reflects harvesttime and abundance for His children prior to Season Five. He lavishes His children with gifts. Like a bridegroom showering his bride with gifts prior to their wedding.

Season Five, Rosh Hashanah

Deb: Paul, I can so relate to this! Throughout my struggles to this point in my life, I felt His comfort and peace. I am looking forward to know more about Season five, let's go…

Paul: Regardless where life takes us, The Heavenly Father is waiting to comfort us and bring us into His loving arms.

The Fifth Season is **Rosh Hashanah** *(The Feast of Trumpets.)* This Season points to the appointed day when the Trumpet will sound and The Heavenly Father will gather, from the four corners of the earth, all of His children who placed their trust in His Son Jesus. Together, they will live with Him forever, never to experience the pain and sufferings of the *Father Fracture Syndrome (FFS)*. Before the final culmination of this season, there will be:

- A short season to awaken those who are asleep on the side lines.
- Increased persecution of churches and Jewish Synagogues.
- Christians and Jews will be thrown in jail and their faith tested.
- The leftist Anti-Christ spirit will be unleashed in government and media.

- There will be great fear and economic challenges. Eyes will be on Israel.

- The implementation of a digital tracking system will be forced upon many.

- People on the left *(many who attend church)* will turn on those on the Right.

- Tyrannical leftist communist leaders will seize more and more control.

- The true character of people will be revealed and violence will increase.

- Persecution solidifies passion and purpose, thus, strengthening the church.

- The remnant Church will be unified and taken before Gods' wrath is poured out.

Many celebrate this as the head of the New Year. It ultimately points to the new era where all symptoms, tears, and heartache from the death of family members will no longer be felt in His presence.

Season Six, Yom Kippur

Deb: It's amazing! We are preparing for Season Five, *"Feast of Trumpets,"* and our President's name is "Trump". I believe there is a correlation with him in office for such a time as this.

Paul: You are right, there is great anticipation for this Season. This is why we need to get the good news about The Heavenly Father to people around the world before it is too late.

The Sixth Season is ***Yom Kippur,*** *(The Day of Atonement.)* This season points to a time of reflection and repentance before appearing before The Heavenly Father. One day, Yeshua will reveal Himself to the remnant of His chosen people, the Jews

Because of unbelief in *Season One,* their hearts were blinded to the true revelation of who He is and how He revealed himself in prior Seasons. Yeshua said, their eyes will be opened when they say, *"Blessed is He who comes in the Name of the Lord."* During this crucial season, while under a severe military attack from hostile enemy nations, they will cry out for help! Yeshua, Himself, will come and devastate their enemies, saving them from destruction. Then their eyes will be opened and they will look upon Yeshua, the One who was pierced. They will welcome Him with deep tears of joy and celebration.

Deb: With all the conflict escalation in our government and around the world, I believe we are very close to Season Five. Is this why we are seeing so much Anti-Semitism in America and around the world? So many Jews are going home to Israel. Could this be in preparation for Season Six?

Paul: You are on the right track Deb! The Jews are making Aliyah, *(going-up.)* This will lure their enemies who were seeking an opportune time to launch a comprehensive attack to destroy them once and for all. *There will be a big surprise awaiting them!*

Season Seven, Sukkot

Deb: This is feeling so surreal. To think of finality, knowing the way things are on earth will soon be shifted into a new system of government. Tell me more about this *Final Season.*

Paul: The last and final Season is **Sukkot.** *(The Feast of Tabernacles, The Ingathering.)* This *Final Season* points to the ingathering of all the children who chose to love and embrace the will of The Heavenly Father.

His chosen children, the Jews, dwelt in booths, *temporary shelters* during their Exodus from Egypt and from generation to generation. He is their shelter and their home. In this Season, His children will be back in His presence, living under the covering of His home. In the Brilliant Light of His Glory there will be abundant provision. This will be a time of celebration! Once again, His children will eat at **The Father's Family Table.** Overwhelmed with joy, The Father knows His family are never to be separated again.

This season also marks the final judgment for the Enemy, Satan, and his operatives. The Father will once and for all crush him under His feet.

Deb: In all my years attending church, I never quite heard it put this way before. I never heard of these Seven Seasons of The Heavenly Father and how it ties into our entire world cycle.

Paul: You are right! Many churches leave out the Jewish influence of the Bible. I always remind the church, Jesus (Yeshua) is not a Christian. He is a Jew. Dads, we need to teach our children these principles, the more they know of their Heavenly Father, the more they will know who they are, why they are here, what's their purpose and destiny.

Deb, it has been a long day. Let's conclude for today and start again tomorrow morning.

Deb: I think this a great idea. I need some time to process all this information. (*While smiling at Paul, she continues*) Would tomorrow at 9:31.7 be ok with both of you?

Paul: Funny, Deb, point well taken! You are a quick study. We will pick up where we left off tomorrow. Please say hi to Joel and the children for us. Good night.

Paul R. Benjamin, Sr.

Chapter 8

The 7 Cycles of Life

Paul: Morning, Deb, I hope you got some sleep this time. My creative thoughts were flowing last night. I am ready to share the next round of information with you.

Deb: I did get more sleep than the night before. I was up until midnight processing all the information you shared. I wasn't aware of the far-reaching responsibility on the shoulders of dads to teach and reveal the character of The Heavenly Father. I am looking forward to hearing about the first cycle.

Paul: One of the many roles of a dad is to set clear expectations for their children. Without it, they become disappointed, discouraged and disillusioned. Their expectations are not realized. These Seven Cycles, when explained to our children, set the tone of what will, or could, happen when they exercise their *free will* to make choices in life. Children also need to know their actions impact others and society at large. These core principles apply to all relationships; marriage, partnerships, churches, business and yes, even while dating.

The **First Cycle** is **Relationship**, this reflects what a healthy balanced, harmonious family relationship was and is intended to be. The way things were before our *Earthly father, Adam,* rebelled against Our Heavenly Father. The family did not know what sorrow or pain felt like. They only experienced joy, peace and complete harmony in the family.

The **Second Cycle** is **Rebellion**, which is like the sin of *witchcraft*. Satan, is the father *(source)* of rebellion *(witchcraft)*. When someone rebels against the Heavenly Father, it is likened unto the sin of witchcraft. When Adam made the intentional choice to rebel, *(disobey)* he exposed his wife and family to pain and suffering by launching the *Father Fracture Syndrome (FFS.)* Rebellion breaks relationships. Adam and Eve were no longer welcomed at *The Father's Family Table.* We are all born with the same spirit of rebellion and freedom of choice. Your choice would either positively or negatively impact your Glory Code (GC).

Deb: I am seeing the spiral effect in this Cycle. Just like Adam's rebellion ruined the entire world, anyone following in his footsteps will do the same to their family.

Paul: You are right! The **Third Cycle** is **Ruined Relationship**. There are many reasons that lead to fractured relationships. Everyone who is not reconciled with The Heavenly Father is still in a state of rebellion. This is the life cycle the entire world is experiencing; the full ramifications of the Father Fracture Syndrome (FFS). The Heavenly Father's solution was already paid in Season One. His arms are open wide to receive anyone during any cycle of life. He will help guide, comfort, and fight on your behalf through all the chaos in your life and society.

Deb: My boss, John, was a changed man when he repented and reconciled with The Heavenly Father. Even the tone of his voice became gentle, he was not as harsh as he was before.

Paul: When there is a true heart change, many things begin changing in our character. This is why in the **Fourth Cycle, Repentance,** *(change of heart and mind)* reflect true remorse and a complete U-turn *(180 degrees)* back to The Father. This is the pivotal moment in our journey where relationally, things begin to shift into place and will ultimately begin to affect the entire outcome of your life. This is done as we repent *(acknowledge our wrong)* to the one that we rebelled against *(The Heavenly Father)* and begin the journey to a restored relationship with Him through the finished price His Son, Yeshua, paid in Season One.

Deb: This sounds very inviting. What a welcome reception waiting for anyone who repents and is reconciled with our Heavenly Dad.

Paul: For many who had abusive dads, the very mention of the word father is repulsive. *Truth creates Trust.* The Heavenly Father is not only the source of Truth, but He is Truth Personified. It takes an act of faith to place trust in anyone called *"Father."* The **Fifth Cycle** is

He, and the host of angels in Heaven, are waiting to accept you. His arms are open wide to welcome you. He loves you and He is waiting for you. His table is already set.

Symbolically, He has rolled out the red carpet. He has a ring to place on your hand, new shoes for your feet and royal clothes to reflect your renewed Glory Code (GC).

Reconciliation. The ultimate process to bring healing to your heart, home, and society. The renewal of all broken areas in your relationship with The Heavenly Father resulting in a greater, and newly realized, wholeness, peace, and joy in your life.

The Father separates *(forgives and releases)* all of your sins. Just as the east and west, never meet, is as far as He has detached your sins from you. Never to remember them against you again.

Note, the father of fake news, Satan, just as he deceived Eve, he will tell you (through family, friends, and yes, other Christians) "You are not worthy. You are no-good. Your hair is too long. You have tattoos, etc." He will work very hard to remind you of all your past sins and mistakes your Heavenly Father has already forgiven.

The Enemy could use people in your home, workplace, church, close friends, and yes, even your spouse. When, not if, you experience this, rejoice! *Say "Thank you, I am a work in progress. I am being formed into the image (Character) of my Heavenly Father. I love you. Thanks for being patient with me."*

Deb: I thought when I finally committed my life to the Lord that everything would be all good. Boy, was I surprised! I have since come to realize that it's a process. I am still learning and growing in my own relationship with The Heavenly Father.

Paul: This is why I try to set some balanced expectations for others. This is a lifelong relationship. It's not a sprint, but a marathon. The **Sixth Cycle** is **Restoration,** *the renewed life.* Now being restored to right relationship with The Heavenly Father through His Son, Yeshua, Jesus, all the benefits of a son or daughter are restored. You are now a joint heir with Jesus. All the Benefits of a child of *The Father of the Universe* have been conferred upon you. Wow! Can you imagine! Your Dad made the world and all that is in it! You have restored access to talk with Him, Father and child. Share you heart with Him, even though He knows all your past hurts and pain. He will help soothe your hurt. He wants you to get to know Him. He has revealed His heart and plans in His written Word *(Torah-Bible)*. The Enemy has infiltrated and manipulated some versions of the Bible to distort the Words and meaning that The Father wants to communicate to you. The Holy Spirit will lead you and guide you. Ask Him to guide you to truth. After all, He is the Father of Truth.

Deb: This is awesome! Just to know the heart of The Father towards His children who are being reconciled and restored to Him.

Paul: The part I like is the restored privilege as sons and daughters with The Father. In the **Seventh Cycle**, **Renewed Relationship** with The Heavenly Father. This reunion establishes a vibrant and wholesome family bond. The Father sequentially, layer by layer, begins healing your crushed Glory Code. Your distorted image of fatherhood will be healed with a new healthy image of the Perfect Heavenly Father of Love. You are now back in a healthy relationship with the Heavenly Father and in a place where true family unity and peace abides as a way of life forever.

While here on earth, you will still experience hurt, loss, trials, conflicts, and pain, *with one big difference*, The Heavenly Father is with you. Unlike some earthly fathers, He will never leave you or abandon you.

The desire of every heart is to be part of a family. If, or when, you die *(fall asleep)*, you *will* awake in the presence of The Heavenly Father. In the effulgence of His Glory in Heaven, you will be completely healed of any disease, sickness, pain, or tears. Past hurts will be eradicated and wiped away forever.

I can hear The Heavenly Father say; *"Welcome Home my Child. I have been waiting for this moment to have you back in my Family. I Love you with an everlasting Love. No one or anything can take you out of my Loving arms again. I have healed all your pain and hurts from your earthly father and those who caused you deep emotional wounds. Thank you for forgiving them for what they did to you in obedience to me. Your pain became my pain. In my presence, you will never experience pain again, only peace, joy and everlasting Love." Signed, Your Heavenly Dad, God Almighty"*

Chapter 9

The "Spark Event" that Fundamentally Transformed America

In Search of a Dad

Deb: Paul, please share the events (The rest of the story) that led to the shooting of Trayvon Martin. I remembered this incident as if it were yesterday. Our news room was overwhelmed with articles and calls about this tragic incident. I can still hear the cries and stories of many single mothers in the urban community who called us. Paul, we need to bring hope to our nation.

Paul: Deb, when you publish this interview we would be able to educate and engage many people who are on the sidelines. Many of them are just waiting for a clear call to action to make an impact in our nation, for such a time as this.

For many years myself, and a team of volunteers at the Central Florida Dream Center, ministered to men, women, and youth in the urban inner-city of Sanford, Florida. We were located near the public housing projects where about fifteen hundred residents called home. Partner church groups and community organizations came from around the country to volunteer. Thousands of volunteers served annually. There was one challenge, no church would anchor down with us to serve the community on a daily basis. Most were only willing to serve once a month.

Whenever I spoke at clergy events, I would make an appeal that we needed to link arms together to reach our urban inner-cities because one day, they will reach us, in our suburban communities with crime and violence. I mentioned, *"A wise man sees what is coming in the future based on the trends in society and prepares before the trouble arrives."*

Thousands of individuals from the surrounding community came to the Center annually. They came for various reasons. Hundreds of them were mentored and positively influenced over the years.

Deb: It's great to hear how many people were able to be ministered to at the Center.

Paul: Once the community knew we were there, they began telling their friends and families. I remembered our first Christmas Event, over one thousand people showed up!

Demolition of the Sanford Housing Projects

I was invited to officiate over the mortgage signing event for the Housing Project. It was a warm sunny day. Public officials and government leaders from Washington DC were present. The loan was for over $4 million. It was designated for renovation of the housing units. The deplorable conditions of the projects precipitated a deluge of complaints from the residents. Weekly articles in local newspapers and television bombarded the ears of Housing and Urban Development (HUD). This mortgage was a landmark moment to mitigate this major concern for the residents.

Soon after, construction crews began the massive makeover project. New roofs, flooring, and complete paint job began changing the face of this development. About a year and a half after this renovation project, I was shocked when I heard the news; *"The closing and demolition of the Sanford Housing Projects."* This meant the displacement of about fifteen hundred individuals.

Deb: Am I hearing you correctly? After borrowing that kind of money, they just decided to close and demo the place?

Paul: Yes, I was shocked! Social workers and case managers came to our Center to meet with some of the families. We were kept informed of the challenges during the process. Some of the families refused to move. Some retained Legal Aid Counsel and turned down the vouchers to relocate to any community that would accept the tax-payer funded program.

Deb: Paul, let me make sure I am hearing you correctly. You are saying because of the displacement of the people from the Sanford Housing projects, some were funded by taxpaying families to move into this Gated Community?

Paul: Deb, you are correct. This is why the crime rate in the community rose to such a high level. Before going further with the Trayvon Martin story, I would like to lay the foundation of the impact of the FFS on today's youth. It will give you a backdrop for what I have to share.

Deb: I was always wondering why I was seeing so many young people with evil characters on their bodies. I notice you were alluding to various levels of Glory Codes and what it translates into in our society. Can you briefly share what that means?

Paul: In the future, I plan to train coaches on how to help individuals to know their GC and how they can move to the plus side and change their destiny. I will place an *assessment link* on our website for individuals to know their *Glory Code (Level) and where to find help.* This could help stop the next school shooting; suicide or mass murder.

The year was 2010-2011, the real-estate market was still trying to recover from the big housing meltdown of 2008. Landlords were desperate for anyone to rent their homes, townhomes or apartments.

Investors purchased some of the beautiful town homes in the gated subdivision next to mine. They were impacted when the housing market took a dive. Now, they are very motivated to rent to anyone. Some individuals from the housing projects were now able to use their taxpayer funding to move into this community. Anxious, investor landlords were more than willing to receive guaranteed *(tax-payer funded)* Government Section 8 rental payments each month.

Crime comes to a Safe, Gated Community

This once quiet and peaceful subdivision began to be burglarized three to four times per week. Security cameras located at the entry gates did not record any strange or unusual activities. Unknown to the community, they were being burglarized from within. Young men, between the ages of thirteen to eighteen, carrying backpacks and dressed in hoodies were breaking into their homes. They monitored and knew who was home, or at work. After placing a "baseball sized rock" into a pair of football socks, they would smash and grab. Within mere minutes, they could grab x-boxes, jewelry, I-pads, tablets, cash, and anything else of value that could fit easily in their backpacks. With the backpack on their shoulder, they would then walk to their homes as if they were returning from school.

Community Watch to Protect from Increased Burglaries

The Community Watch was activated. George Zimmerman began to patrol the community to protect it and to see if he could find out the source of these crimes. After he made almost fifty phone calls to the Sanford Police Department, they still couldn't ascertain the source of these crimes. One of our volunteers who lived in that community was burglarized using these same surreptitious measures.

Impact of A shattered Glory Code

Boys raised without their dads in the home are 300% more likely to be in trouble with the law. Their Glory Code is shattered. Their light is now turned to darkness. This is why we are seeing many children wearing black clothes, black makeup, demonic tattoos of evil characters, and black nail polish, etc. The brightness derived from their GC is now turned to darkness.

When you know your Glory Code, you know your destiny and impact. People who have reconciled with The Heavenly Father experience a dramatic improvement in their Glory Code. Here are some indicators of how a crushed Glory Code can impact individuals and society:

- The highest Glory Code that can be achieved here on earth is a (+6) GC
- Individuals with various degrees of mental health can pivot between (+5) to (-7) GC
- Danger! Anyone with a (-7) GC will resort to either murder or suicide.

Deb: Thanks Paul. This helps me understand more. I know each level represents the capacity to be influenced to do good or evil; based on the impact of the FFS in their life.

Paul: You are right! These young men and women are very easy to be influenced and radicalized to commit violent crimes. Children yearn for the acceptance, approval, authority, assignment, attention, affirmation, blessing, guidance, leadership, protection, love, provision and prayers from their fathers.

Trayvon, like millions of young men today, was being raised without his biological dad in the home. Boys *(young men)* from divorced or single-parent homes experience increased:

- **Anger** (*Tears, Rage, Rebellion, Hate, Fearful Dreams, Resentment, Anger towards God, Spiritual Leaders and Law Enforcement*)

- **Aggression** *(Directed towards peers and others in authority as well as mothers, especially if she speaks negatively about the father)*

- **Joining of Gangs for acceptance** *(Creating a substitute family and seeking the protection of a strong father figure in the gang leader)*. These young men become easy recruits for radical groups online and in the community. *They will do whatever it takes to join the gang, or radical, political, resistance groups; including murder, rape, car-jacking, burglary, the killing of law-enforcement officers, etc.*

- **Low self-worth** *(Feeling abandoned and rejected these young men internalize their crushed "GC")*. Many have reached a *(-7 "GC")*, resulting in suicide or murder.

- **Exhibit Predatory and intimidation patterns** towards women, girlfriends, and mothers

- **Nonverbal latent hostility** towards their custodial mother *(blaming her for the divorce or not having the father around)*

- **Bullying** of others who appear weaker *(this feeds their intrinsic lack in their "GC")*

- **Drug addiction** and experimentation to anesthetize the pain within, trying to fill the empty void left when their "GC" was trodden on in the separation.

- **School shootings** or terroristic crimes in order to gain glory externally by doing evil acts to fill the internal void. We see this each day in our nation and around the world.

A boy in 4th Grade Tried to Stab His Teacher

Deb: This explains why we are seeing so many young boys bringing knives and guns to school? We publish so many articles in the news today about these young boys who are threatening to stab or shoot their teachers in school. I remembered a news article about a boy in 4th grade, he pulled out a pocket knife to stab his elementary school teacher. This explains why there is so much anger and bullying on school buses and in school. This is why we see so much crime and violence every day on the streets of Chicago, LA, and other high crime cities across our nation. More young men die on the streets of Chicago each year than we have lost in our nation through war. To prove your point, Paul, 90% of them are from homes without dads.

Paul: Deb, you are right. These are just a few of the symptoms that young men exhibit when they experience the separation of their parents, whether it is through a divorce, unwed non-custodial relationships or death of their fathers. Their dads could lead them on the right path through love and discipline. Remember, their capstone Glory Code, *(their emotional life's oxygen)*, comes from their dads.

Deb: Paul, this explains why I notice that in most of these shootings in urban communities, the young men that are shot are usually very aggressive towards either the law enforcement officer or anyone perceived to be an authority figure. Is this the reason why there are so many rival gang authority figures that are constantly being killed, almost daily? I also noticed that crime is up 1100% against law enforcement officers and churches, synagogues *(places of worship)*. This has reached epidemic proportions in our nation. I am beginning to wonder; can we turn this chaos around?

Paul: Deb, this is only the tipping point. The hurt and anger in many of these young men and women goes deep. They usually do not even value their own lives. Their unconscious quest is to fill their Glory Code and will drive them to do anything. Six out of ten people who commit suicide are from fatherless homes and 100% can be attributed to the impact of the Father Fracture Syndrome.

In a balanced family relationship, the very presence of the father in the home; his strength, his voice, and authority, instills a sense of peace, comfort, and protection. The mother's voice and presence brings warmth and completeness to the family. In the case where there is serious dysfunction in the home from either the father or the mother, these patterns would seriously alter and magnify behaviors of rage, anger, and abuse.

In Dad's Absence, Roles in the Family Change

With dad's absence in the home, everyone begins to take on different roles.

Most mothers overcompensate because of the absent father, enabling *(lowering the standards)* the children in areas where they should be firm and maintain structure and discipline.

If the separation or divorce was due to domestic violence against the mother, the boys will be more protective of their moms. If the mother brings another man into the home without first asking their sons for their permission and blessing, this will elevate their resentment, anger, and failure to bond with the new man or step-father in the home.

Without a father's strength, guidance and protection, these young men take on the protective and unbalanced role of aggression against other male or female authority figures.

Authority without Relationship Results in Anger

Law enforcement officers represent the authority of a father, but not the love, guidance, and protection of a father. The officer is perceived, and in most cases, approached with extreme anger, hostility, and aggression by fatherless young men. The very presence of an officer touches the deep wounds within the souls of these young men. Some of these wounds can be traced back to various past emotional hurts, like racial injustice, unresolved authority issues, anger towards their fathers for abuse or abandonment. For some of them, the last memory was seeing law enforcement officers taking their fathers, mothers, grandparents or siblings to jail, legally or illegally.

The pain from the loss of their Glory Code creates a spiral effect. They keep seeking purpose and meaning through all they do, without quenching the deep void of their soul. The Mental Health *(Impact from Their Glory Code)* of one generation determines the destiny of future generations.

Paul R. Benjamin, Sr.

Chapter 10

Trayvon Martin
The Untold Story in Sanford, Florida

Deb: According to our media sources, Trayvon was suspended from school numerous times.

Paul: This is typical of boys who are raised without their dads. Homes, absent of a father, are more likely to be violent and express aggressive behavior. Trayvon came to stay with his dad who was living with his girlfriend in this gated suburban neighborhood.

Deb: This happened very close to your home. Paul, you could say you were on the front lines. Now, you are championing the cause for the fatherless around the world.

Paul: I began to reflect on the words I mentioned many times, "Let us reach the urban fatherless youths where they are before they reach us where we are, in our suburban-gated communities." I heard a still small voice say, *"Paul, you tried to engage the church to help impact the urban fatherless youth. Now, I am going to give you a voice to the nations!"*

Deb: I was distraught when I heard the news of this tragedy in Sanford. So many other urban cities like Ferguson and Baltimore began to implode soon after. Paul, let me know if I am hearing you correctly. *If Trayvon, and these other young men, were not the aggressors in these incidents they would most likely be alive today? Is it the volcanic rage and anger in these young men from their shattered Glory Code causing them to be so angry and antagonistic?*

Paul: Deb, you are right. Report after report reveal this is the key common denominator. I have seen many young men who express this type of rage and hostility towards authority figures or perceived leaders.

Deb: This explains why I see so much aggression in the urban community on the news. With over 90% of these young men being raised without their dads in the home, I can understand their root cause of pain and anger.

Paul: This is why I am reaching and training men to stand in the gap. There is hope. After a season of mentoring some young, and older men, like these, I have witnessed drastic differences in their character and behavior. They became respectful to authority and adopted a healthier way of dealing with conflict, injustice and bad authority figures. Fatherhood and manhood, is not taught, it is **caught** through a modeled relationship with another Godly man. You become like who you associate with.

Dressed in the same type of hoodie and backpack like the young men who plundered the community, Trayvon was returning from a local store when George Zimmerman noticed him walking. He pursued Trayvon and called 911 to report a suspicious character in his neighborhood. Trayvon, while talking with a female friend on the phone, noticed Zimmerman following him. He told his friend, *"let me take care of this 'bleep, bleep' (verbal profanity) person, that is following me and I will call you back!"* In this aggressive move, he and George had a physical altercation, Zimmerman shot him in *self-defense* and the rest is now history. My heart and prayers go out to Trayvon Martin's parents, Sabrina Fulton and Tracy Martin. I pray that The Heavenly Father, *The God of All Comfort* will continue to minister grace and healing to them through this great loss of their son.

500 yards from my Front Door

This national tragedy took place about 500 yards from my front door. Every morning for months, news media outlets camped-out in front. Their TV cameras aimed as if they were at a gun range, waiting for their next target to interview.

Influence of Positive Role Model Mentoring

Deb: This explains why you are on a mission to equip and engage leaders to take the initiative to positively impact their cities.

Paul: One month before this spark event that transformed the fabric of our nation. I was prompted by the same still soft voice, to contact some key regional leaders. We gathered in the north regional ministry center for prayer and strategy sessions. This was a team of seasoned and mature leaders in the city. We noted that certain crimes or key incidents that occurred in various sections of the city weren't unanimously addressed by our team or other ministry leaders. This left those problems to other community leaders in that region to mitigate. Unknowingly, this deepened the chasm and racial divide in the city.

As a team, we agreed that we were not going to isolate ourselves from the issues in various parts of the city. We chose to take *responsibility* and get involved with the entire city. What happens on the East, West, North or South side of our city is our problem, also!

Two months later, this national tragedy exploded in Sanford. We mobilized other pastoral leaders to stand in the gap. When righteous people get involved to positively influence their city, the people rejoice. But if they hold back from serving and leading in the city, it comes to ruin.

We became engaged in key fronts during this season. Our leadership team prayed and became involved in the healing process and events that took place.

US Justice Department Intervention

Deb: I remembered the big media frenzy. Especially when Al Sharpton and Rev. Jessee Jackson came to the city. This must have been challenging to mitigate this type of crowd.

Paul: The US Justice Department sent in The Community Relations Service (CRS). This is a team of people who are committed to facilitating a peaceful outcome wherever there is conflict. They helped by facilitating an open dialogue between the pastors and the community.

Over 30 thousand outsiders came into the City. By God's grace, there were no outbursts of violence, unlike what took place in Ferguson, Missouri and Baltimore, Maryland.

During this long eighteen-month encounter in Sanford, I remembered saying, at one of the press conferences, *"God will turn around this negative event and begin healing in Sanford and to our nation."*

National Initiative "A Mentor for Every Fatherless Youth"

Deb: My husband, Joel, signed up to become a mentor at your event the other night. After hearing the plight of our nation, he decided to get off the sidelines and make a difference. I am so proud of him for taking the initiative.

Paul: Deb, it is great to know that Joel signed-up. The team will give me the sign-up list later this week. We need millions of men around the nation to do the same. This event magnified our initiative *"A Mentor for Every Fatherless Youth."* After mentoring men and youth for over three decades, this national spotlight intensified what I was saying locally and placed a national face to it. National leaders began to add their voice of support to this cause.

Vision: Raise-up 10 + million Godly Mentors

My vision is to see 10+ million men raised up to become mentors to *fatherless youth in America* and around the world. These men must be Godly men, born *male at birth;* Godly husbands who are married to one wife, *born female at birth;* and Godly fathers.

Mayor of Sanford, Florida Champions the Cause…

Deb: I will do my part to get the word out through all of my media channels.

Paul: Thanks, Deb, we need to bring awareness to this urgent need. I shared this vision with the Mayor of Sanford at that time, The Honorable Jeff Triplett. I invited him to speak at two press conferences where I was speaking to pastors and community leaders. I was informing and engaging them to bring fatherless, young men to the upcoming Promise Keepers' Men's Event.

Mayor Triplett was understandingly frustrated with the duplicitous, *double-tongued* religious and political leaders. They said one thing to his face, but when the TV cameras were rolling they said something inflammatory and contrary.

This Vision brought Hope to the Mayor

This vision brought a fresh wind of resurgence and a positive cause that the Mayor could support. He said, *"I think I found a little bit of God again."* Other leaders added their voice of support to endorse and support the cause. The president of Promise Keepers at the time was, Dr. Raleigh Washington. He too, was at the press conference and added his comments of support, along with other leaders. This initiative is part of our global strategy to positively impact communities around the world.

Fundamentally Changed the Fabric of America

Deb: This was a great endorsement for the cause. Why did this *spark event* in Sanford cause such a huge ripple effect in our nation?

Paul: Let me refer back to the story of *Cain*. Remember that in his quest for acceptance and approval, he murdered his brother. The urban youth of today manifest the same spirit of resentment and frustration. Coupled with disillusionment and discouragement, it would take only ***one spark*** to *ignite a national inferno*. When you consider the fatherless factor, school suspensions and about 50% unemployment rate, most could identify with Trayvon. Signs and T-Shirts began popping up around the country at the time saying *"I am Trayvon Martin."*

This tragic event placed a *"face"* on the national *outcry*. This compounded the deep pain of men, women, and youth who were living under the canopy of their crushed Glory Codes. Many, still living in the shadow of past and present injustices, discrimination and abuses, codified a movement that *fundamentally changed the fabric of America.*

Words of Former President Barak Obama Polarized America

Deb: This event began to polarize our office staff. Some of our black journalists began taking sides and slanting their news articles.

Paul: I noticed the same shift in other media. *Our words can produce life or death.* To add more fuel to this national inferno, *former President Barak Obama*, postured and made statements that strengthened this movement. He said *"Nobody understands the plight of these black males"* and *"If I had a son, he would look like Trayvon."* These statements embolden the resolve of, what has now become a national pandemic.

Radicalized, Mobilized and Activated…

Deb: We actually had to increase security at our office. My boss, John, called a staff meeting to address the racial conflict among our media team. He reaffirmed that we are one team and our goal is to report the truth not *fake news*. He cautioned us to lock our cars and leave the office before dark.

Paul: John made a wise decision. Many underserved, angry, disenfranchised fatherless young men across urban America became radicalized and mobilized. Their shattered Glory Codes made them ripe for the picking. Individuals who were victimized at some point, became identified with this cause. The national media frenzy glorified the vicious explosion of crime and violence against whites and law enforcement officers in cities across our nation.

Inflammatory News Hype

Paul: During a press conference, a reporter from one of the national Television Networks mentioned their ratings went up **86%** during their coverage of this event. She said, *"Our network will be shifting focus, by pursuing more inflammatory, and controversial events like the Zimmerman trial."*

Deb: My company also saw a spike in our online views and subscriptions during this event. We even had international readers register on our website.

Paul: The media outlets were not too interested in reporting any of the good and positive things in the community. One of the reporters asked me "Are you with the Dream Defenders *(the group that was stirring up controversy in the community)* or Dream Center?" I responded, *"The Central FL Dream Center, with the youth mentoring program."* She said, *"I am sorry! I was looking for the Dream Defenders."* Deb, I am thankful that we still have a few positive media outlets like yours in our country.

Deb: Thanks, Paul. We seek to report the truth, and to bring hope and healing in the community.

Black Youths Robbed Three White Women

Paul: I appreciate you taking your time to report this mandate to your readers. I know the truth in this article will offend many people. Thanks for being willing to take a stand for truth.

Deb: You are welcome, Paul. We believe in what you are doing. John and our team are all in.

Paul: Awesome! Let me share what happened next and the fundamental transformation impact in our country.

The jury for Trayvon's case happened to be made up of white women. The day following the publicized verdict that George Zimmerman was found (not guilty), three black young men robbed three white women near their homes in the Orlando area. One woman was robbed in her driveway. They were all told, *"You are being robbed in the name of Trayvon Martin."* This urban civilian army of disenfranchised young men and women *became bigger than the US Army*. They felt justified in their acts of crime, looting, vandalism and radical activism.

Deb: I was glad that I was on high alert. Joel called me and made sure I left the office on time.

Paul R. Benjamin, Sr.

Chapter 11

Birth of Black Lives Matter

Paul: I am glad you made it through that season. Now, due of the influence of ***former President Obama,*** the Black Lives Matter movement was also given birth.

This national outcry spurred a quest for restitution which can never quench the wounded heart. Only divine justice and true ***forgiveness*** that comes from The Heavenly Father will bring healing. These angry and vengeful hearts fueled and gave birth to Black Lives Matter, who used words like, *"Pigs in a blanket, fry 'em up like bacon."* The proliferation of their hostility activated angry, young black men and women, fueling their aggression and murder of police and other law enforcement officers across our nation. This is still occurring today. ***This movement also gave birth to Black Privilege.***

Our words can bring *hope* or produce *hopelessness.* The Pope asked one of our regional leaders, *"What is going on with the tragedy in Sanford?"* One of our partners in Kenya asked the same question. The *world* was looking and being influenced by how Americans handled this crisis.

Deb: We received a lot of push back when we mentioned all-lives matter. Hate mail came in and social media comments were mixed, some supporting us and others responded with hate. There was a fundamental change in our country.

Paul: This spirit began to ooze into every sector of our nation. Left-wing, black clergy and other political leaders bolstered the resolve of millions of blacks.

Black Privilege (The Financial shakedown of White America)

Deb: My media friends were buzzing, "Fearful, white pastors are silent when it comes to addressing wrongful actions of radical, black influencers." Fear of being labeled "racist," silenced many whites. Paul, how can you bring clarity to this fear-based leadership issue.

Paul: These leaders are fearful of media and community backlash. Threats of political ramifications, physical violence and damage to property caused them to shrink back from speaking the truth. Some, fearful of death threats against them and their family, held their tongue.

Deb: Before today, I haven't heard about Black Privilege. I only knew about white privilege. I would like to hear how it as impacted our nation.

Paul: Deb, Black Privilege has permeated many sectors of America. The Political/Media, Religious/Church, Business/Sports sectors:

- In the ***Political and Media Sectors,*** left-wing, black leaders can say any inflammatory remark without any reprisal from the media, peers, or the law. They can use *Black Privilege* (BP), the *"race card"* and their power to leverage left-wing media coverage to shakedown white leaders and white businesses *(blackmail, using extortion tactics to slander, or threaten to start a riot or boycott their business, black-lash).*

  They only have to threaten to *black-ball* their company by claiming they used past or present racist remarks or gestures against blacks. Some companies have been known to pay tens of millions of dollars. Others *"pay-up"* before they are even approached, just to be on their *"good list."*

  Dads need to educate their children and the fatherless youths they are mentoring about the goodness of God and the evils in society today. Our nation is rapidly changing before our eyes daily.

Deb: While you were talking, I couldn't stop thinking of Paula Deen. Like many whites from her generation, she mentioned the "n" word in her past. Her price for this was losing her multi-million-dollar TV show and reputation.

Paul: Deb, this is a good example of people who have changed over the years, but if they would like to take you down, all they have to do is dig-up past documents/emails and comments for anything they can use as "racist" against you. Ministering in the urban community, the "n" word is used by blacks against other blacks, some as curse word and for others as their "name."

Deb: Paul, am I hearing you correctly? The politicizing and policing of whites, for their past use of the "n" word, is more about pillaging them financially than the offense of them using the term in their past?

Paul: No one in their right mind relishes derogatory terms slung at them or their ethnic group. *But…* The motive driving this movement supersedes any tainted stigma of the "n" word. It's about, *"Show me the money!"*

This privilege, now, emboldened by the endorsement and presidency of *A black man in the White House,* had many blacks saying *"We don't have to pay our mortgage. We don't have to pay for our, You name it…"* The sentiment was, our black deliverer, *"Moses,"* will now pillage Egypt *(America)* and take care of us, blacks. This began to polarize conservative blacks on the right from leftist blacks. They didn't want to be identified and lumped together with all "blacks." Left-wing blacks received more prominence because they are in league with the left-wing media.

Deb: Wow! I am speechless. This brings new light to me. I now understand the motive behind this entire agenda. Paul, thanks for taking your time to explain this to me. Let's hear about the other sectors propagating this agenda.

Paul: It would take me a month to explain how deep the claws of this agenda impacts America. Individuals who carry clout, champion this lustful, hate-filled and sinister agenda:

- **Jussie Smollett**, In order to create a negative impact on President Donald Trump and his *"Make America Great Again"* movement, this black, leftwing actor, went to the extreme to *fake-news* his own *self-inflicted* hate crime. In doing so, he re-traumatized millions of blacks who were actually *real* "victims" of a hate crime. Earlier, I made a comparison between *lust* and *love*. Remember, lust is *never satisfied,* until death. We have to pray for these people. Only a true, loving relationship with The Heavenly Father can heal their crushed GC.

- *Religious/Church Sectors:* Left-wing, black clergy can openly endorse political candidates and use *Black Privilege* to guilt and leverage money from white clergy. With overwhelming applause from their media partners, black pastors can use vitriol and profanity from the pulpit. Their hate filled speech is targeted towards white America. This stirs up the hearts of their congregants *(many of whom have a crushed GC)* to spawn further division in our communities and nation. White pastors are fearful to speak-up in fear of the left-wing media and physical retaliation against them personally or their congregation.

- **Business Sector.** White business owners are afraid to fire unproductive black employees. Fearful of being labeled, *"racist,"* sued, or exposed on the left-winged media outlets. Many of them acquiesce and keep unproductive employees. This use of *Black Privilege* (BP) had hurt and impacted the stock value and public image of many companies. Some have avoided the media backlash by paying *"hush"* money. Advertisers are threatened, *"If you don't pull your advertising we will boycott or blackball your company."*

- **Sports Sector.** This same pattern carries over in all levels of professional sports. Certain left-wing professional athletes like Colin Kaepernick use *Black Privilege* to his advantage to further divide our nation while mitigating his crushed GC. Some black parents use it in their children's sports and colleges to leverage key positions.

- In the **Community.** We are seeing black mobs protesting various causes *(many of them are funded by the money plundered by the Black Privilege shakedown of America)*. If they vandalize the community and resist arrest for unlawful behavior, it is labeled, *"racism"* by the left-wing media. Lawyers swarm these cases like bees on a hive. Most of these individuals in the mob are from fatherless homes. There is an urgent need for godly men, women, and youth from all races to *rise-up,* get off the sidelines and reclaim our families and nation. Dads of courage are required to positively influence their families and their families in turn would influence society.

- **Blue Lives Matter/All Lives Matter Movement.** We are witnessing the explosive impact from one spark event, *the Trayvon Martin shooting in Sanford, FL.* The unaccepted verdict of *(Not Guilty)* in the trial of George Zimmerman tapped the nerve of millions of people with crushed Glory Codes. Fueled by the left-wing media this movement reached national status almost overnight. The mention of *"All Lives Matter,"* was labeled as *"racist, hate speech."*

With the 1100% increase of murder and violence against law enforcement officers, at that time, ***Blue Lives Matter*** was born. The mention of Blue Lives Matter was also labeled "*racist, hate speech.*" When former President Obama publicly ostracized law enforcement officers, it gave the green light to black individuals (with shattered Glory Codes) to take action and it ignited their already angry and hateful hearts. This is why we are witnessing the increased murdered of law enforcement in cities across our nation.

Deb: Paul, this information was another *eye-opener* for me. Would you be able to connect with some of these clergy and leaders to help bring healing in the community? This kind of stuff is destroying our nation.

Paul: Deb, I have been working on both sides of the aisle. Pastors and leaders who are willing to build a bridge to foster healing have been reaching out to me. Together, we can help to break the *chains* over the hearts of wounded pastors and leaders whose Glory Codes were crushed in their childhood. This will alleviate the anger and hurt that flows from the pulpits to the hearts of their congregants and our nation.

In the vision for Life Centers Global, we would work with pastors and leaders in communities across the nation. We would share strategies to heal this racial divide in the hearts of these leaders. Once broken hearts are mended, they can unite and team up with others to positively impact their cities.

I will give a quick overview later about the Life Centers Global.com Initiative. People who would like to be trained and equipped to join the global team of positive influencers will be able to get more information.

Deb: Thanks, Paul. My husband and I would definitely like to support this vision and get involved. I know my boss is going to support your vision as well. He is all-in. When he reads this research, I know he will publish it on the front page.

"Stop the Church Service Now!"

Paul: The spirit of *"Others owe me. I am a victim!"* Has activated many people with compromised Glory Codes. *"Stop the church service now and collect an offering for me!"* These words came from a young man who infiltrated the worship service of a local church in Sanford, FL. I was driving on the I-4 highway on my way to speak at another church when my cell phone rang. My caller ID revealed who was calling. I said to myself, *"This pastor should be in their church service now!"* Realizing this was an anomaly, I quickly answered. *"Pastor Paul, I need your help! We don't know what to do! A young, black man came into our church service while we were worshiping and demanded that we stop the service and take up an offering, or else! I know you worked with many different young men in the city. I am calling to get your advice. Is there anything we can do to talk him down?"*

I thought for a moment, then, a still small voice (Holy Spirit) inspired me to say, "Tell the young man that Mr. Benjamin from the Central Florida Dream Center will speak with him tomorrow to help solve his problem. Please give him my phone number." At the time, I had no clue who this young man was, or even if he knew me.

The situation de-escalated immediately after mentioning my name to the young man. It turned out that he knew me from the Dream Center and the situation was resolved peacefully. Who knows, without this intervention, this could have sparked another undesired event in this church that was already traumatized by the looming cloud of the Trayvon Martin and George Zimmerman incident. This was another fatherless young man who was in a desperate situation. I was a father-figure and a role model to hundreds of these young men that came through the Center over the years.

Deb: Paul… This could have been a game changer in that church. Thank God, He used you to intervene in this situation. What happened to this young man after this incident? I am anxious to know.

Paul: I called the young man after my speaking engagement. He recognized my voice and was very apologetic for what he did. He was the caregiver for his ailing mother while trying to make ends meet with his part-time job. There was more month than money. After giving some *sound counsel* and guidance for another job this story had a happy ending. Dads and mentors can influence many lives like this young man. Imagine, millions of us can impact lives around the world…

Mayor of Sanford, Florida Car-jacked by Three young men

Deb: This further validates the impact we can all have when we take the time to invest in others.

Paul: The far-reaching implications when we don't reach this generation of fatherless young men, impacts others even the Mayor of Sanford, Florida at the time Jeff Triplet, was car-jacked by three fatherless young men. This is why this mandate is needed to reach and positively influence this generation of men, women, and youth.

Who would be next? I thank God that the Mayor's life was spared. Usually, there would be post-traumatic ramifications from such a tragic incident.

Deb: We are receiving calls from people in the community that are looking for ways to get involved. If given permission, I will have our office staff pass this information over to you.

Paul: Thanks Deb. My prayer is to see hearts and lives turned around and also for the healing of nations.

Deb: Paul, my stomach is growling, let's pause for lunch. This will be a late lunch, it's already after 1:00 pm.

Paul: You and Dawn can go to lunch. I have some business stuff I have to take care of at the office. Let's meet back here by 2:35.7.

Paul R. Benjamin, Sr.

Chapter 12

Waiting for Politicians to Fix Your City?

Deb: Paul, let's pick up where we left off. You mentioned pastors and law enforcement officers are requesting information on various strategies to impact their regions. What are some of the areas they need help?

Paul: I smile when I think about the first single mom that came to the Central Florida Dream Center for help. This heavy-set, black woman about 5'7" came into our office and with an air of expectation and said, *"I am here for my utility assistance!"* I politely mentioned, *"We are not a government program."* She looked startled. After seeing the size of our building and being accustomed to government intervention, she assumed we were a government operation.

I explained we are a Christian ministry that invests part of our donations back into the community. For everyone who receives assistance, there is a work component involved. For every $10 in assistance received, they must be willing to work one hour. Today, the church has relinquished their responsibility to the community and turned over to tax-paying families *(government)*. This results in the *"Egypt affect"* (*Go to the government for help and you end up being slaves to the system.*)

Some pastors are waiting for politicians to meet the needs in their cities; others ignore the problems; while some blame events or circumstances for the condition of their cities, hoping to elect the next politician to fix it.

Several pastors came to my office. They were discussing the blight and impact of crime in their section of the city. They were hoping to bring the needs of their community for the government to clean up. They hoped the elected officials would deal with the drug dealers, pimps, prostitutes and homeless problem in the community.

I politely disagreed. I said, "Gentlemen! We, the leaders and ministers in our city, need to come from behind the pulpit and engage in our community. It is not the government's job. Let me say it one more time, it is **not** the **Government's Job** to address the social ills in our community. It's ours, the church."

The government, through gentrification, and certain law enforcement measures may physically clean up a section in the city without addressing the root problem of the heart and the crushed Glory Codes of these people. Officials are only relocating these broken people to another area of the city, just to repeat the same cycle again.

Deb: This gives me a fresh perspective why so many churches place and shift *(abdicate)* so much of their God-given responsibilities over to the government. This explains why they lack influence in the community.

Paul: Deep down, these young men and women, are looking for a true sense of family. They are looking for authentic men and women who will be Godly father and mother figures, role models who are willing to stand in the gap to show them a better way. It's the responsibility and mandate of the Church to implement Isaiah 58 *(restoring of life and community.)*

Instead of playing the *"racist game"* to distract and divide communities, what if we rolled up our sleeves and began to positively mentor the next generation. Many go on TV and talk about the problems facing our youth in this country, but what if we trained and equipped them to positively impact the challenges facing their community. Rather than complaining to the government to solve our social problems, *what if we*, the faith community, began launching Community Impact Life Centers in our cities to begin holistically mitigating these problems. We will talk later about the potential impact of **Life Centers** *(Community Impact Centers)*.

Deb: This would be great if the churches united and worked together to minister to their cities. I am looking forward to hearing more about the Life Center concept. I would like to have you share this with my pastor.

"Poor Black Children Cannot Afford to Pay Fees"

Paul: Sure, I look forward to sharing a brief overview with your pastor. We need to see a shift of responsibility and address the lack of influence churches have in their cities across our nation. Dads glean leadership traits from what they see other men of influence do. Their children and mentees benefit from the leadership influence of dads. Today, more than ever, we need men of courage and conviction.

I was in a community meeting where a public official addressed a crowd of young black men and women. As he addressed them, he said, *"I understand our black children do not have much money and cannot afford the fees for various youth programs."* My eyes surveyed the room while he was speaking. I observed many of these same young men and women who he was referring to wearing $80 to $90 sneakers. Then, I looked at their faces while this black leader was addressing them. Some of the young men were crouching over in their seats. Most of the young ladies were looking at their cell phones, while others held their heads down, with almost a look of shame and disinterest.

Prophetic Vision Creates a Shift

The media was there covering the community event. After this leader finished addressing the crowd, I was called to speak. After my introduction, I shared the backdrop of the challenges in our city and nation. I addressed the young audience by saying, *"We have the next millionaires in this room. The next generation of business owners are in this room. The owner of the next McDonalds Franchise is in this room."* There was an immediate shift in the atmosphere of room. The young men immediately sat up from their slumped position and paid attention. They held their heads in anticipation of what was going to be said next. The young ladies stopped playing with their cell phones and looked-up, as if to say, *"Could I really be the next business owner or millionaire?"*

Deb: What a contrast of vision and leadership influence. This helps me understand how these leaders can keep entire regions hostage to their small thinking and vision. Paul, thanks, for being a catalytic leader in this generation.

Dads need to Have the Vision to Ignite Hope

Paul: Thanks, Deb, to God be the glory. I was able to share our three-pronged strategy that we implemented at the Center; *Spiritual, Social and Economic = Renewal.* The entire expectation level changed in the building. After my 10-minute speech, leaders asked for my business card.

Deb: That was great. You spoke to their potential. Now, could you tell me more about the three-pronged strategy you just mentioned.

Paul: I will give a brief explanation:

Spiritual - Leading people to a personal relationship with The Heavenly Father,

Social - Ministering holistically to the social ills in the community and

Economic - Sharing principles to develop multiple streams of income. This leads to *Renewal* in lives and communities.

Deb: Paul, this is awesome! If churches would get behind this key principle, we could see cities transformed.

Paul: Today we need parent figures, men and women, who will call forth the potential within our youth and speak words of hope, inspiring greatness and reminding them, *"God **spoke** the world into existence."* I am mobilizing and training a team who will Teach, Equip, Engage and Encourage leaders and influencers to impact their cities and nations.

The Degree of Your Influence Gives Weight to Your Words

Deb: I am glad to know other leaders will engage in this cause. Now is the time for us to unite and turn America back to God.

Paul: This is why we need to get this urgent message out to the world. The degree of your influence gives weight to your words, locally and nationally. For example, the words a father or mother speaks to their children or family; the words a mayor speaks influences his or her city; the words a President speaks, influences and affects the nation. Now when these words and actions are given national and international media coverage, it has global ramifications.

Youth, seeking to quench the vacuum in their *Glory Code*, are easily influenced by the words and actions of leaders. As the potter molding clay, leftist leaders leverage the anger and pain in today's fatherless youth. They are pliable and can be easily influenced to do good or evil. *Who, will invest their time to be the influencer?*

The Word Father Means Source. Who's your Source?

Deb: We need to seize this opportunity to be positive influencers for today's youth.

Paul: Amen, Let's do this!

The word father means source. Who is your source? Who are you receiving your information from? Whose voice are you listening to? Whoever you listen to and obey, you will be under their influence.

Whatever is in your heart, *good or evil,* will ultimately influence your thoughts. Your thoughts will influence your words. Ultimately it will dictate your actions. What you think and believe in your heart, that is who you are. Private beliefs *(your core values and world view)* will become your public practice. Dads and mentors need to know that they are key influencers in the lives of young men and women. They may be the only book *(lifestyle)* these young men and women are reading.

Words Spoken, Cannot be Retrieved

Deb: After hearing this information, I am self-conscious of my actions.

Paul: I too, have to constantly be reminded that my lifestyle is to reflect the character of The Heavenly Father. *Words that are spoken, whether truth or lies,* **cannot,** *I repeat* **cannot,** *be retrieved from the hearts of the listeners.*

The media plays a key role in how events are perceived and received. Whatever you affirm and promote, *good or bad,* you get more of. Millions of fatherless youth are yearning for the affirmation and approval of their fathers to quench their crushed Glory Code.

So, when a fatherless youth sees that he or she is being acknowledged by the news media for committing a crime, guess what? They become motived to commit more crime. Soon, others follow in their footsteps. Gang members, in the same fashion, glorify their crimes and time spent in jail or prison as honor and respect. The greater the crime, or time spent in jail, the greater the glory. Fatherless young men find false glory by committing various levels of crime to gain approval and acceptance of the gang leader.

How often do you see positive news on TV about black or Latinx young man? However, you can be certain, there will be news showing how many of them committed a crime or were shot in gang-related violence. This further justifies their dark glory from the Enemy.

A glass *half-full* with "*dark-water*" *(crime, violence and abuse)* can be transformed by pouring "*good, pure water*" into it. In time, this glass, will be filled with "*good, pure water.*" The "*good and pure water*" will always *replace or displace* the bad water. The same principle is true about a loving, mentoring process. In time, "*dark hearts*" and lives will be transformed into loving, *Christlike* character. This will only be possible if Godly men and women invest their time to pour the *"good, pure water"* from The Heavenly Father into the lives of this generation.

We do not have a Racism Issue, only a Sin Issue

Deb: I notice more negative news than positive. It is sad though! People like the buzz of bad news. The media keeps them hooked on negative and fake news. It's big money for their networks. We receive mail from some black clergy when we report a crime that was committed by a black, young man. They claim it is racist when we publish these articles. Paul, what do you think?

Paul: Some clergy are more concerned about the external image of blacks in the media than their internal character. We do not have a racism issue in America, we have a sin issue. Not walking in the Love of The Heavenly Father is the issue.

At this point, as you read along, you might think this guy is crazy, contemplate closing the book and want to forget about reading the rest of the story. I implore you to stick with me to the end.

Deb: I never thought of it before as a sin issue. It was always addressed from a racial context in our media room and in church. This makes sense. Everything goes back to the original sin issue with Adam. I forgot, this is just one of the symptoms of the FFS.

Paul: Every situation I address should be viewed through the prism of the "Father Fracture Syndrome. During all the events that occurred in our city, I was asked to sit on many race- relations panels to discuss the issues in our city and nation. Many of the leaders on the panel focused on past and present racial and cultural issues between blacks and whites. Some spoke about the injustices during the days of slavery. Others spoke of current day injustice with law enforcement officers. No one took it back to the source to address the root of the problem, the heart, from which all the issues of life emanate.

Remember the farmer's story. We always have to go to the source. We all came from one Earthly father, Adam. So, we all share the same bloodline. Even though we may look different on the outside, *(What a wonderful Heavenly Father He is, to create us in so many beautiful external colors, cultures, and sizes to show His Glory)* but on the inside, we all look alike. We all share a linked and common DNA that leads us back to one source, Adam, our Earthly father.

We have all been impacted by the *Father Fracture Syndrome*. The only difference we now have is the DNA of which father (source) we choose to obey and serve. Our words and actions reveal which father we are truly being led or driven by. If we are led by The Heavenly Father, we speak His words and act the way He commands us. If we are being driven by the father of lies, *(fake news)* lust, hate, revenge, and racism it will be reflected in their actions and words.

Am I being led or influenced by the Devil?

Some would say, I am not being led or influenced by the Devil. I follow and am being led by the Heavenly Father. I am a Christian, great! I would like to ask, are your words and actions lining up with that of your Heavenly Father?

The Apostle Peter once spoke some words that did not reflect the heart or will of The Heavenly Father and the Lord rebuked him saying, *"Get behind me Satan! You are offensive to me, for you do not regard nor understand or speak the things that are of God, but you speak those things that are of mankind and your culture."*

Our words reflect which father *(source)* it is coming from. Words originating from the Heavenly Father produce love, life, righteousness and peace. Words from the father of lies, the Devil, Satan, who is here to steal, kill, and destroy, produce discord, conflict, hate, murder, racism, and disrespect for each other.

Our actions also reflect the same principle. Again, the Apostle Peter used his sword to attack and cut off the ear of a man. The Lord spoke to him and told him to put away his sword. We do not fight the spiritual battle of life with physical weapons, but with spiritual ones by speaking His Words that He has given us to speak. He said if the enemy abuses or curses you, you should bless them and even feed them if they are hungry.

hen we yield to Satan, the father of lies and murder, we are driven by him and implement his agenda in our homes and society. Just look at the amount of domestic violence, divorce, murder, crimes in schools and the community and we do not have to guess which father is the source.

The Character of The Heavenly Father

Let us look at the *Character* of The Heavenly Father and His people. His children who choose to accept, embrace and obey His voice reflect the foundation of His heart which is, Love, Righteousness, and Justice.

In the comparison between Love vs. Lust, Love paid the ultimate cost to bring about good for others. He said that love is the fulfillment of the Law. He gave one key command for His children to live by, to walk in His Love.

What we Call Love

Before I share what love is, *let me share what we call love in our nation.* When we use the word, I love you or I am falling in love with you, what we are actually saying is, *"I like you when everything is going good between us. You make me feel happy inside. I like your body or you turn me on."* This type of love is based on our sensual feelings and emotions.

The other type of love we talk about is the love of Earthly parents for their children. This kind of love is stronger, but not perfect. Even parents, when certain things happen, can walk away from their children. Today, we are witnessing parents killing, selling, trafficking, abandoning and abusing their children in all forms of depraved ways known to mankind. Likewise, we witness children doing heinous things to their parents; murder, stealing, elder abuse, abandoning them to senior facilities and never checking-back-in to see how they are doing.

The Love The Heavenly Father commands us to live by, only comes from Him. This kind of love is given and made available to us at the moment we accept the perfect gift of His Son when we invite Him to come into our lives and ask Him to become our Lord and Savior. He is Love personified. Apart from Him, we cannot walk in this kind of Love. The Heavenly Father would not command us to walk in this kind of Love, if He first did not download His *(released His Love within us)* Love into our hearts at the very moment we choose to be reconciled and come back into relationship with Him.

Love is a Choice, Feelings are the Result

Love is a choice, not a feeling! The result is the feeling of peace, joy, wholeness, and serenity that exceeds the understanding of our natural mind or emotions. This kind of feeling can only be experienced when we choose to obey The Heavenly Father by walking in His kind of Love. In doing so, our lives will be transformed, as will our families and the world. This is why we are commanded, not *suggested* to **Walk In Love.** It is His breath in our lungs and His Spirit that gives us life. When we choose not to Love, it demonstrates that we are still walking in disobedience and rebellion like the other father, the Devil. The Heavenly Father took it even one step further, He commanded us to love our enemies.

(People we hate because we disagree with their political views or because they hurt or abused us.)

Deb: At this point, people might be thinking, "What? You mean He wants me to love and forgive those people who hurt me, abused me and speak evil of me?"

Paul: Yes! Remember, the first Season of The Father, Passover? Jesus died so we can receive the gift of forgiveness and be reconciled (reunited) with Him. If you have not asked Him to forgive you yet, there is nothing that you have done that He cannot forgive. He didn't come to condemn you, but to reconcile you to His Dad.

Knowing that you may be living with a crushed Glory Code, *(from abuse and hurts from the FFS)* He is longing to heal you. He once told a woman who was caught in the very act of sin, *"Go, and sin no more."* He said this because of His great love for her. Just penning this line, I feel His Love and compassion towards you. It is so vast no one can ever understand the depth of His Love for us. I encourage you to accept His invitation to be reconciled into His Loving arms. He is waiting and longing to welcome you. He shared a short invitation letter in the Bible *(John 3:16)*.

Walk-in His Love. Do what He Modeled.

When we live and walk in His Love, we will do what He modeled through His Perfect Son. He said, *"I do all things I see my Father do. The things that I do is the Father doing it through Me."* Our example of how to walk in this kind of Love was modeled by His Son Jesus. He was abused, beaten, cursed, rejected, hated by religious leaders, and experienced racial bigotry. Before He died on the cross, to satisfy the ultimate justice that was required, He said these final words, *"Father, forgive them, for they know not what they do."*

This powerful act of obedience, along with these powerful words of forgiveness, forever released us from the commanding grip of sin and slavery to the father of lies and death, the Devil. Now, those who are back in a relationship with The Heavenly Father are given the authority to overcome the lure of the enemy who works through the desires *(lust)* of our flesh.

They now have the choice to use this authority and power to first yield to the will of their Heavenly Father. They can then use His words to bring life, healing, and reconciliation or operate through their fleshly lust and desires motivated by the father of lies, just like Peter did. This is why we hear so many people saying, *"I am spiritual, a believer, or a Christian"* but their words and actions are just like the Devil.

Paul R. Benjamin, Sr.

Chapter 13

The Audacity of Unforgiveness

Deb: This is a new understanding of our duplicitous nature. In one breath, we can glorify the Enemy or The Heavenly Father by our words. Thank God for His grace and love to endure our mess for a season.

Paul: Amen, Deb! I am a recipient of His love and grace. During a lawsuit with our former tenant, I had a choice to make. Am I going to walk in bitterness and unforgiveness towards our tenant who owed us multiple thousands of dollars, or choose to walk in the character of my Heavenly Father and forgive? Not to mention, we had lost hundreds of thousands in lost revenue.

Because I love my Heavenly Father, my desire is to please and obey His commands. He requires us to forgive those who abused and caused us pain. How could I have the *audacity not to forgive*! My decision was easy. Just as love is a choice, **forgiveness is a choice**, a conscious act of obedience, governed by our will.

Praying for your Enemy

During our lawsuit, my tenant's daughter became seriously ill. When I found out, I went next door and offered to pray for him and his daughter. He was shocked at my offer to pray for him and his family in the midst of our court battle. After regaining his composure, he said, *"Yes! Please pray."* After praying for him and his daughter, I blessed them and returned to my office. He didn't know The Heavenly Father said that our only "Enemy" is Satan, not people. However, Satan works through yielded people to accomplish his covert agenda.

I have free will. I could have chosen not to forgive my tenant. This would have broken relational fellowship with my Heavenly Father, who said, *"We cannot talk or communicate with Him until we make it right with the person that hurt or offended us."* *(They, too, are made in His image)*. Only then, can I communicate with Him and have our communication restored. He forgave me, so I, too, can have the *power to forgive others.* By not forgiving I would have chosen to join Satan's rebellion against the Heavenly Father. I would have chosen not to be at the *Father's Family Table.*

Unforgiveness today is the ulcers of tomorrow...

Deb: That was a precious moment. I don't know if I would have had the courage to do that. Tell me, how did this story end between you and your tenant?

Paul: The Lord inspired me to stop the lawsuit, release him of the debt and ask him to vacate the building. I called our attorney and notified my tenant of my decision. The year was 2006. I asked the Lord, *"In return for the thousands I released and forgave my tenant, I would like for you to heal his heart and woo him to yourself so one day I can receive him as a brother in Christ."*

Deb: This is a unique concept! Asking God for a *Return On your Investment (ROI) (forgiveness)*. Keep me informed how this goes.

Paul: Sure, Deb, I will let you know what happens. People don't realize there is a Return On Investment when we forgive and release others for their acts of injustice against us. The *ROI* can take on many forms. The Heavenly Father would like to grant them their ROI. In my situation, I requested for my tenant to become my brother. The first ROI is a sense of peace. For others it could be the restoration of a broken family relationship, a restored job with back pay, etc.

2016 Pulse Night Club Shooting in Orlando Florida

Deb: A thought just came to mind regarding the mass shooting in Orlando. When I received the news, my prayers went out for the families of the 49 people killed. We did a cover story on this tragic shooting.

Paul: I prayed with a family that lost a loved one in this tragedy. The gunman who planned and executed this human slaughter had a crushed (-7) GC. When I heard the victims' names that were killed in this horrific incident I was surprised. As the names were scrolling on the TV, I instantly realized 75% of the names were all *Sephardic Jews (Latinx Jews)* from the Kissimmee, Florida area. I began hearing names like; Hernandez, Fernandez and many other "ez" ending names. These are all Sephardic names that were cover-up to protect their identity.

Six out of ten young men in the *Latinx* community are being raised without their dads. They don't know their true identity. Their ancestors were part of *"the forced ones,"* the Jews that had to flee Spain. They were told *"You will be killed if you don't convert to the Catholic Church!"* Entire generations were forced to hide and deny who they were. Their sons and daughters grew up without knowing they were part of *"The Chosen People of The Heavenly Father."* The head of the Latin Kings Gang is a Sephardic Jew. He doesn't know the power and influence of his legacy.

Deb: I didn't know this. I have *Hispanic* friends with these Sephardic names. What I am hearing is, if these people knew their heritage and legacy, it would have impacted their destiny?

Paul: You are right. Dads are commissioned to pass on to their children the knowledge of who they are, as well as the power and influence of their heritage. Not knowing your tribe or God- given purpose, can destroy your destiny. In this case, their tribe is called the people of the *"Book-Torah."* They were the ones who penned the Words that came from the heart of The Heavenly Father. He spoke it and they wrote it.

Their homeland is the Negev in Israel, the place where Abraham and Isaac lived. Today, it is set-aside and waiting for them to return home. I am part of a team of leaders who are trying to reach and impact these young men and women with the knowledge of their people and their purpose.

Deb: I know this was a controversial, gay nightclub. Did you and the clergy get involved with this tragedy like you did in Sanford?

Paul: Yes, the *"Band of Brothers"* *(a team of pastors that pray and fellowship monthly in the region)* gathered and held a special prayer vigil for the families and city. This event was held at First Baptist Orlando. Hundreds of people attended, including some families of the victims. There was a national backlash. Pastor David Uth, the senior pastor, received hundreds of letters of hate mail and emails for hosting this event that represented the homosexual community. We shared the love of Christ with the people and prayed for their families. The Heavenly Father loves them and desires to heal their crushed Glory Codes. He doesn't want anyone to perish, but that all would come to know Him as a Loving Father.

Deb: Paul, that is sad to hear. God loves people, but He dislikes their sin. All too often, we attack the person and not the Enemy working behind the scenes through their crushed GC. I am glad we have leaders out there like the *"Band of Brothers."* This world can be a very cold place.

Homosexuality & Lesbianism, Same-Sex Attraction, Gender Identity Confusion

Paul: The impact of the Father Fracture Syndrome on dads and families is overwhelming. It brings tears in my eyes as I feel the love *of The Heavenly Father towards his people.*

I address the painful symptoms of the broken and tattered Glory Codes of children, who are now adult men and women. Inside, a little boy or girl is longing to experience the true love and affirmation of a dad, like The Heavenly Father. Many never fathomed it possible to experience the healing touch and seal to their GC by The Heavenly Father.

One touch, one word or one act can either positively or negatively impact the life of a child. The affirming touch and words of a dad or mom can bring warmth, love, and healing in a child's life. There are still may wounded adults longing to have their GC healed.

Today we are witnessing the negative impact from the crushed Glory Code in the lives of so many men, women, and children. Their physical, sexual and emotional lives were violated by a dad, mom, stepdad, stepmom or another authority figure. Some of these authority figures may include: family members, clergy or neighbor. Later in life, it could be abuse from a spouse, boyfriend or girlfriend or even the result of a violent, criminal act.

Can You Mentor Me?

Deb: We see so many painful news stories in our office. It seems to never end. My heart is stirred to make a difference.

Paul: I can identify with wanting to make a difference. I received a knock on my office door. It was a young man asking, *"Can I please speak to Pastor Paul?"* I answered, *"I am he!"* He quickly introduced himself, *"I am Harry (not his real name). I was sent to be mentored by you."* I was surprised! Two days prior, I had asked the Lord, *"If you want me to launch a mentoring and community impact center in the most violent part of the city to send me a man from that part of the city."* Here, standing in my doorway, was the man.

Deb: As you shared this, I was thinking to myself I wish my prayers had such a quick and direct response. Sorry for interrupting you, I couldn't hold that one in. Okay, I am anxious to hear the rest of the story.

Paul: I thought the same thing, too. I was shocked at the quick response.

He lost his Manhood (innocence) at 6 years old

Paul: Harry was from the section of town I mentioned in my prayers. When he was six years old his dad sexually abused him. He told him, son, this is how I show my love for you. At this point, in 2001, Harry was living a homosexual lifestyle and having sexual relationships with various men and pastors in the city. Many boys and girls living in the LGBTQ+ lifestyle were sexually abused by a father or mother figure.

What the Father Affirms is Activated

Harry didn't realize what a father affirms and approves is activated; and what he disapproves and devalues, begins to be de-activated in the life of a child. His dad affirmed and activated the principle that his love and acceptance were sexual. Every time Harry had a homosexual relationship with a man or pastor, he felt approved and accepted. The Heavenly Father has the highest seal of approval and affirmation in the universe. His power and authority can Reset, Restore and *Renew* even the most crushed Glory Code in the world.

The Authority to Break, Bless, Build and Renew

Knowing Harry's crushed GC was at a (- 4) level, I anointed his head, hands, and lips with olive oil and prayed the Father's Blessing over him. Harry began to tear up. He said, *"No one ever prayed for me like that before."*

Deb: I am still drying the tears from my eyes. I am now picturing the many 6-year-old boys who were abused and sealed by this same marred image. Today, many of them are *sexual predators* instead of *protectors*. What happened after your blessing?

Paul: One week later he came to my office and said, *"What did you do to me? I am not able to return to my previous homosexual lifestyle!"* He said he no longer had the same desire. I explained that The Heavenly Father Loves him and had begun a renewal process and is healing his crushed Glory Code.

Harry didn't understand. My blessing came into alignment with The Heavenly Father's Words of blessing over his life. The power of this blessing *(the seal of The Heavenly Father)* broke the effect of the initial seal from his earthly dad over him. This launched the renewal process, moving him from a (- 4) GC to a (+ 5) GC. It takes time to renew the crushed GC of anyone who has been violated by significant male or female authority.

Deb: Paul, that's awesome! This gives me hope for others who have been abused.

Paul: Today, many men and women are still struggling with their sealed identities initiated at the time of their abuse. The Heavenly Father is waiting to break off every wrongfully sealed identity. If anyone is willing to embrace His touch, He will bring healing and renewal to their shattered Glory Code.

Deb: Some of my friends living in this lifestyle thought they were stuck. I am encouraged there is hope for them.

Paul: I also caution girls and women to guard their hearts from being crushed further. Dads need to let their daughters know; *"guys"* use the words *"I love you"* to get sex. Girls who are looking for the seal of approval and acceptance from a male, "dad-figure," acquiesce and surrender their virtue to multiple males. Some, even turn to other women, seeking to mitigate their (-4) GC.

Incestual Relationship with dad

Deb: This reminds me of the child movie star, Mackenzie Phillips from *"One Day at a Time."* She was raped by her rock star dad, John Phillips. He told her it was love just like Harry's dad told him it was love. Mackenzie and her dad engaged in a 10-year consensual, incestual relationship which continued while she was married. This heinous relationship stopped after she became pregnant. With the uncertainty of who fathered the child, her dad paid for the murder *(abortion)* of her baby.

We need dads to be a Dads like The Heavenly Father. Paul, I am 100% with you on this mission to raise up a generation of great men and dads! Information like this makes me sick to my stomach.

Paul: My heart and prayers are with Mackenzie Phillips and the millions of girls and women like her. Unconsciously, she, and many others, are seeking to fill the chasm in their heart. This void is never fully sealed until these girls and women experience renewal that only comes from *The Heavenly Dad.* His authentic Love will heal their crushed Glory Code. Many retirement age women are still looking to fill this void in their lives. This is why I am on a mission to equip and engage men and women around the world to stand in the gap to help facilitate healing and renewal to this generation.

I have the Homosexual-Lesbian Gene

Deb: I am charged up with a new fire! Interviewing you is unveiling layers of the "FFS" that motivates me to make a difference.

Paul: When it comes to sexual identity, *the "FFS" has a far-reaching impact.* Words of dads and moms begin to mold and shape the psyche of the baby while in the womb. The baby's intrinsic Glory Code is being shaped by their words and gestures. The words we speak are spirit. People don't realize that they are spiritual beings. Words spoken from the conception of the baby, positively or negatively, shape the emotional identity of the child.

One of the biggest lies told to children and adults struggling with their sexual identity is, *"You were born with the 'gene' and you are pre-disposed to be this way."* The source of this lie is the father of fake news, Satan. There are ***only two sexes***, male and female. No one is born with a *"homosexual or transgender gene."*

The Government or any paid *"Scientist for Hire"* can conjure up a law or *"scientific paper"* to say whatever fake news they would like to espouse about *"being born with the gene."* But…

The truth is scaled by The Word of The Heavenly Father and this trumps everything and everyone in the universe. His Word said, and is forever affirmed, He made male *(man)* and female *(woman)* and the two of them shall multiply *(give birth to children)* and fill the earth.

Deb: I have some friends who are conflicted about living this lifestyle. Some say they are Christians and are attending church. They are accepted in some churches. However, in others, they are not allowed to serve in any leadership roles. They are accepted as individuals. Yet what they are really yearning for is approval of their lifestyle.

Paul: The Heavenly Father loves everyone. He wants all those impacted by the FFS to come to repentance, reconciliation, and relationship with Him. He said to the woman caught in her sin, *(adultery, homosexuality, LGBTQ+, lies, fake news, stealing, crime, etc.)* *"I forgive you. Go and sin no more…"*

When anyone is truly repentant and sealed by The Heavenly Father, they will be able to walk in victory from their past lifestyle. Millions have been renewed and sealed. Now, they are living a new life and in their true God-given identity.

Deb: Bruce Jenner, because of his crushed Glory Code, changed his sexual identity to *Caitlyn Jenner (Transgender)*.

Paul: His actions impacted his family and millions of children across America who looked-up to him as a role model.

Boy Scouts of America, a once trusted organization, that stood for character and courage, succumbed to pressure and allowed homosexual leaders to influence boys. Their financial bankruptcy was not the only tipping point, but, the "moral bankruptcy" of the leaders, and sexual abuse of the boys who were looking for a father-*figure role model*. We are praying for these leaders.

Passionate Need for Approval & Acceptance

Deb: Thanks, I get engaged in our storyline and I need to remember, we need to pray for these people.

Paul: Amen, Deb! The passionate and fervent desire for approval and acceptance is so important in quenching their GC, people in the LGBTQ+ lifestyle will go to any length to fill this void. That's why they went to the extreme to twist *(hijack)* the word *"gay"* to represent their lifestyle choice. The word *"gay"* connotes a sense and feeling of *joy, peace, and happiness*. These are all the emotional feelings they are seeking to fill the void in their Glory Code. An external word does not fill an internal void in the heart. People can change a word, but only *The Heavenly Father* can change your nature…

My prayer is that every person struggling with their sexual and emotional identity would come to the revelation of the true Love of The Heavenly Father to heal their hearts. Jesus reflected the heart of His Father. In John 8, He said, *"Let him that has 'no sin' cast the first stone."* **No one can cast a stone!** The Father said, *"Go, and sin no more."* He knew that this Lifestyle is a choice, not a gene. *Fake news* from the Enemy tells you, *"It's a gene."* *(something you were predisposed to, without your choice),* but this a lifestyle choice. Victory and healing can be found in a healthy renewal of our GC in an authentic relationship with The Heavenly Father and with the help and encouragement of authentic, Godly people.

Deb: My heart cries out for so many people. Some of whom, are my friends. Paul, every topic we touch just seems to validate this mandate to bring healing to nations. We need people to know the impact of the FFS and how to minister healing.

20 years of Gripping Fear before burying My Son's Ashes

Paul: Many people don't understand the impact of the FFS on individuals and society at large. Rage and violence shape the actions of many walking under the influence of the Enemy. Matthew Shepard, a 21-year-old homosexual college student was violently beaten to death in 1998 because of his lifestyle. Due to their sons' violent death, his parents feared it would be unsafe to have a formal church funeral.

Matthew's parents kept his ashes for 20 years until Rev. V. Gene Robinson, the first openly Homosexual Bishop in the Episcopal Church, agreed to perform the funeral ceremony. The pain and anguish expressed by his parents was as if their son was just murdered the day before. The Heavenly Father is reaching out to all of us. He wants us to bring our hurts and pains to His loving arms. He is waiting to forgive and heal our crushed GC in His presence.

Deb: As a mom, I can identify with these parents. I remembered when the news of this story came into our news room.

Paul: This was a vicarious funeral for many parents who didn't have a formal burial for their children who were victimized for living this lifestyle.

O.J. Simpson's GC Was Crushed

Deb: I remembered you told me that O.J. Simpson's "GC" was crushed to a (-5) level when he saw his father with another man in a homosexual relationship.

Paul: Yes, we did discuss this during dinner. Growing up in a divorced home which crushed his "GC" was further demolished when he found out that his dad was living a homosexual lifestyle. In urban America, this lifestyle is also called *"the Down-low."* Having being raised by his single mom and separated from his dad had a profound effect on his mental health, like so many youths today. Actors in Hollywood are impacted by the "FFS." Many reveal the symptoms of their crushed "GC" in their politically charged tirades on TV, fueled by the leftwing media. Remember, *our words reflect what is in the heart...*

Deb: Let's keep praying for all of them. I used to like looking at the Oscars. Now, it is laced with venom and leftist innuendo.

Deb: I am glad you took some time to mention this. States are making it a crime to address this subject with parents. When we send our children to government schools they are influencing our children based on their own crushed GC.

Are their only Two Sexes?

Paul: This why I stress the importance that dads need to model and train (teach) their children at home. The school system will often contradict the values taught at home. Parents that home school their children, produce the most sought-after graduates by corporate America.

Deb: Paul, the damage being caused in this generation of parents will reverberate to future generations.

Paul: You are so right. Mike, one of the boys that was in our after-school, mentoring program was molested by multiple men. His single mom, Tasha, was also the product of sexual abuse as a child. Her revolving relationships exposed Mike to many abusive men.

Deb: This story was a tearjerker. My heart goes out to boys and girls like Mike.

Paul: If I said yes to every boy or young man that wanted me to be their dad, I would need a house the size of a mall.

Deb: This one breaks my heart. Paul, I don't know how much more I can take today. Lets' call it a day. If you and Dawn are free tomorrow morning at 9:01.5 am we can meet for breakfast at our usual place. See you there...

My son feels and thinks he should be a girl

Paul: I received a call from a couple, Joe and Mandy. They were concerned about their 10-year-old son, Randy, who was struggling with his male, sexual identity. I immediately asked his dad Joe if he wanted a baby girl when Mandy was pregnant. There was a long pregnant pause on the phone. He said, *"Paul, now you mentioned it, that was all I spoke about from the moment my wife became pregnant. When the sonogram revealed that the baby was a boy, I was disappointed. In my spirit, I didn't accept my son from the womb"*

After sharing the key principle of the power of his words and actions, Joe realized the impact his rejection had on his son, Randy. He didn't realize that he, as the dad seals the physical, sexual and emotional DNA in the life of his children. Joe and Mandy understood that Randy's GC was crushed in utero by their words and actions. I prayed with them and shared how to address this symptom to *bring healing over time…*

Millions of dads and moms are walking with crushed Glory Codes. Many are at (+2) to (-2) GC. They cannot give what they do not have. Now, we are seeing parents waiting until their children are *old enough* to decide if they want to be a girl or a boy.

The Heavenly Father made only two (2) sexes in the entire world, male and female. There is no other plan or change. The father of fake news, has used broken dads and moms with crushed Glory Codes to propagate the lie, *"You are what you feel or think."*

10-Year-Old Boy Sexually Abused by Multiple Men

As I mentioned, 70% of boys and girls that are sexually or physically abused are raised by single moms and their live-in boyfriends or stepdads. Mike, to help fill the void in his Glory Code, told the children at the Center that Mr. Benjamin was his dad.

Would you be my dad?

One day, while in my office, 15 children came to me. *"Mr. Benjamin, come! Come! Mike, is telling everyone in front that you are his dad."* I knew the cry of Mike's heart. He needed and desired a dad in his life, especially one with the stability and character he witnessed in me.

When I arrived in front, there were about 10 boys and 5 girls anxiously waiting in a circle around Mike, who at this point, was hanging his head in embarrassment from this tribunal. With all eyes upon me, like a jury affixing their eyes upon the judge awaiting his sentence, I told the group, *"I am not Mike's dad, but I am his father-figure mentor."*

Today, there are millions of boys and girls like Mike who are yearning for the love of an authentic father figure or mother in their lives. What they are really saying is, *"Would you be my dad?*

"I would like to be in Jail with my dad"

I was invited to speak at Hamilton Middle School in Sanford, FL. At the time, 70 - 80% of the students attending, didn't have a dad in the home. It reflected in their behavior and grades.

I took a few men from our team with me. I asked one of the 7-year-old girls what she would like to be when she grew up? She replied, *"I would like to be in jail with my dad."* My heart was touched along with all the other teachers and the team members who were there with me. The cry of this little girl is the cry of millions of little girls and boys looking for their dads to heal and seal their GC.

Chapter 14

A Snow Dad is Better Than No Dad

With a huge smile on her face, Deb enters the room.

Deb: "Oops! Sorry guys. It's 9:02.7 am, that makes me 1.2 minutes late."

Paul: Ha, ha, Deb! Point well taken. This is good. I now have a new student.

Deb: I thought I would humor you and Dawn. This interview has some heavy content. I need to amuse myself to keep from crying or getting too *fired-up* at times. I saw Dawn smiling, Paul lets' pick-up where we left off, before she gives both of us the *"look"* to move it along.

Paul: I, also, try to keep things light by humoring myself. In the movie *"Jack Frost,"* a young boy's dad *(Michael Keaton)* died in a car accident on Christmas Eve. Several weeks before his tragic death, he presented Charlie, his son, with a harmonica as a gift. He told him, *"Son, if you ever need me, all you have to do is blow on the harmonica and I will come to you."*

As part of their Christmas tradition, Charlie and his dad always made a *"snowman."* One year later, on the anniversary of his dad's death, Charlie with tears in his eyes, decided to blow his harmonica. To his disbelief and surprise, the spirit of his dad entered the snowman that he made days earlier. The snowman came to life. It was his dad, the "snowman."

After a period of fun events and activities with his dad, including attending one of Charlie's hockey games *(which his dad missed almost every game while he was alive)*, the temperature in their city rose and the snow began to melt. In a desperate effort to save his *"snowman dad"* from melting, the school bully, Charlie's arch-enemy, who himself didn't have a dad, came to the rescue. Charlie was trying to lift his *"snowman dad"* into a truck to relocate him to a colder climate to avoid him from having a *"melt-down."* This young man, his arch-rival, now, his buddy in the quest to save his *"snowman dad,"* said, ***"A snow*** *dad, is better than no dad!"* Today, most fatherless young men do not care about the *race or ethnicity* of their male father-figure mentor. The only cry of their hearts is, *"Will you be my dad?"*

Deb: I am tearing up just hearing this story. We can avoid a *melt-down* in the lives of fatherless young men if we get Godly men to stand in the gap.

Paul: Amen! You are on a roll Deb.

Deb: I am trying to keep up with you. On a serious note, this validates your message. Dawn is smiling in agreement.

Dads are not born, they are made...

Paul: Tonight, is our *date night*. She knows I can get carried away when I start making puns. Now, you are doing the same. This could make for a long day. We need to end our interview session by 3:54.8 today. We need to get ready for our dinner engagement.

Deb: Joel and I need to get out more and have these date nights. Our children are older now and they can take care of themselves. Maybe we could do a double date with you guys sometime?

Paul: Sure, Deb, we love to. I will let you ladies work out the details.

Let's get back to Charlie. As he blew the harmonica to call his dad, I too, am blowing a symbolic harmonica calling men of courage to step forward and stand in the gap for this fatherless generation.

Dads are not born, they are made! They are molded, shaped and sealed by another man... It takes courage from God to step forward. Real men are forged on the anvil of truth in God's Word, into the image (character) of His Son, Yeshua, who is the expressed Character of His Father.

Deb: As I promised, I am on board. I will get this out to the masses. Together will sound the alarm.

Fractured Men, Husbands, Fathers, Marriages, and Families

Paul: We are witnessing the culmination of generations impacted by the Father Fracture Syndrome:

- Broken boys become broken men.
- Broken men become broken husbands.
- Broken husbands become broken dads.
- Broken dads raise broken children and families.
- Broken families produce broken societies.
- Broken societies create a broken world. *Are you prepared to help break this cycle in your family and society?*

The Power of Positive Influence

Jim, a young man I was mentoring, was raised without a dad. His dad would pop in and out of his life from time to time, never being a positive influence. After our move to a new location, we had lost touch with each other. Jim began to revert to some of his old ways. He and his girlfriend were on the verge of selling illegal drugs. Just in time, The Heavenly Father reconnected us and we re-established our mentoring relationship. With positive influence and guidance, Jim broke off his unhealthy relationships and embraced the true purpose his Heavenly Dad created him for.

Today, Jim is married, and working in corporate America. He and his wife are actively involved in a local church. He is now giving back by being a positive mentor, influencing other young men.

Men need other Godly men to positively influence and sharpen *(build-up and hold accountable)* each other. Only about *one in twenty* men have a male friend that they can depend on. Men need an older man to pour into them, a peer friend for brotherhood and a younger man they can in turn pour into what they have learned. If we continue to short-circuit this process into authentic manhood, millions of young men will continue to ask the same question *"Am I a real man?"*

Deb: This was great timing! This validates the impact that Godly men can have in the lives of fatherless young men today. Imagine if Jim hadn't re-connected!

Sperm Donor Dad and Tax Payer Dad

Paul: There is an urgency! In many cases, it could be the difference of life and death, prison or poverty. The time is now!

The *"war on poverty"* launched by former President Lyndon B. Johnson in 1964 greatly damaged men and the family structure. This system was covertly designed to dismantle the value of dads, marriage and the family structure. ***Clandestinely implemented to transfer dependency*** and control of indigent families to the government. It rewarded and encouraged women to ***not get married*** and depend on the man *(dad)* to be the primary income earner in the family. Rather, it encouraged and rewarded her dependence solely on the government. The government in turn ***pillaged working tax paying families*** to pay the bill. Now, these single moms only needed men as sperm donors. Children born into this system allowed these moms to leverage more income from the government, their new *"dad,"* hard-working families.

Deb: This program did help many families who used it as a hand-up during a rough patch in their life. For some, it became a hand-out and way of life.

Paul: Money only magnifies and multiplies who you are. For many millions, they were not able to escape the economic trap.

Jump out the window

Paul: Recipients of this program were subject to accountability. Single mom recipients in urban communities had surprise inspections from government *caseworkers at midnight.* They were threatened that, *"If a man (dad) was found in the home, they would lose their welfare support."* Dads would *jump out of the window* to avoid his family losing their welfare.

Many of them literally never got married because if they did, they would not qualify for the government benefit. This sent a clear message to dads; Abdicate your role in the family and the responsibility will shift to tax-paying families, (government). This strategy was inspired by the Enemy.

Ultimately, the positive influence they could have had with their wives *(baby mamas)* and children, was now turned over to a government social worker. Today, 9 out of 10 children in urban America are growing up without a dad in the home *because of this covert strategy.*

Dads abandoning their Role

Deb: This is sad. I know in the 60's many black men were discriminated against in the marketplace. If they were fortunate enough to find work, their wages were half that of their white counter-part. This explains one of the reasons their families were easily enticed to depend and succumb to the government system of control.

Paul: These dads became servants to the *"Golden Rule: The one who has the Gold (Money), Makes the Rule." In this case, it's the government.* Dads began relinquishing their fathering role, knowing that they were only needed to be sperm donors to the baby mama. Over the decades, this became the game plan.

When a teenage girl becomes pregnant, she is trained how to implement the game plan. Generationally, they are conditioned to go to their *"**tax-payer dad**, the government."* They, in turn, will plunder working families to pay higher taxes to keep control over these families in the system.

The tax-payer dad provides money for *Food, Housing, Utilities, Medical, Dental, Transportation and Special Education Programs.* They will even pay for murder (abortion), if the teenage mother wants to end her child's life.

Deb: Paul, I looked up, *"The War on Poverty."* After 5 decades, and ***22+ Trillion Dollars*** later, the tax-payer dad is still footing the bill. It seems that the government has created a greater number of people who are now ***slaves to this system***. It's sad. As a tax-payer, I have no real say in how my taxes are invested in these programs. What is the return on investment?

Paul: Deb, I am glad you asked. Here is just a brief report of how the 'Tax-Payer Dad's' Family is doing and what social control (welfare) has produced in our nation.

- The quickest way to **enslave** a segment of society is to remove the *dignity and glory of work*. This removes one's purpose, hope and a sense of destiny.

- By removing the father (honor and value) from the family, it sparks a spiral emotional effect resulting in daughters looking for love in all the wrong places. This leads to the *highest number of unwed pregnancies and murder* (abortion) of children.

- Just like drug dealers, *"the system"* only gives you enough to get you hooked on their product. Before too long, you are dependent and want more to get through the week. These families desire more income, while trying to *stay off the payroll* (by finding a job). To *avoid being kicked-off the welfare-roll* they will often turn to illegal enterprises like *selling drugs, trafficking, gambling, car-jacking,* and some have been known to choose more honorable trades *"off the books."*

- These illegal and criminal activities increase the number of arrests. African-American men represent *the highest percentage of the jail population.* Some of their sons and daughters meet them for the first time in jail.

- The added stress in the home correlates to the increase of domestic violence, sexual abuse, *mental health, and substance abuse* in America.

- In fear of *being kicked-off the welfare-roll,* a healthy "work ethic" is not cultivated. This fear cripples many who already lack the skills to obtain and maintain legal, gainful employment. They are proficient at working the "system" and are conditioned to think of it as their way of life. This produces the *highest un-employment rates* in cities across the nation.

- *70% of these children/students find it easy to drop-out of school,* as there is little value for education. After all, most of their parents never obtained an education higher than the 6th Grade.

- Over time, this way of life produced a sense of "entitlement." Many recipients became unthankful and ungrateful, demanding more from their Tax-Payer Dad, working families, the government.

Deb: Paul, this is a sad commentary of the demise of a generation.

Paul: You are right. Let us consider numerous churches in the urban communities are funded, in part, by families who are being taken care of by the *"tax-payer dad."* Many of the same pastors were also raised by their single moms and the *"tax-payer dad,"* *(government).* This is the reason so many of them believe that the solution is *"more tax-payer (government) intervention programs."*

In urban black communities, 8 out of 10 children are born to unwed, teen moms. In Latinx and white communities 5 out of 10 children are born out of wedlock. This further feeds into the demise of the family structure. Way too often, the teen mom doesn't know who is her baby's daddy.

Deb: This explains why so many of these families are encouraged to stay on the system. The church supports the same mentality because they benefit from it. I sense that you could keep listing more things from this failed "system."

Paul: Deb, you are right. The question should be, what if this ***"system"*** is successfully designed to accomplish exactly what it has...

"Millions of poor people, loyal and dependent, on the leftist, political agenda. After all, they need to control the "poor" so they can pillage, **"we the people"**

Political Profiteering from The Poor

Paul: This is why we have to wake-up the sleeping giant *(the church)* to the reality of these principles.

Government, (social welfare), programs, instead of promoting and encouraging marriage, and the moral significance of family, encourage and reward single moms to stay single and dependent on the *"Tax-payer dad" (government)*. Children are growing up with this poor economic model and it is compromising the morals of family.

There is an undercurrent in many urban communities. *Called "Spiritual Marriage." This, too is impacting the family image.* To avoid the appearance of *"shacking-up,"* some couples are having *"spiritual weddings."* This is a front. It is an effort to appear respectable before the church community. *The woman remains single in the eyes of the system* to avoid losing her welfare benefits, but the church recognizes her as married.

Today, many seniors are, also, adding to the moral decline of society. They are doing the same thing, in fear of losing their *social security benefits* from a deceased spouse.

Leftist, political leaders capitalize on this principle of *"economic slavery to the system."* Every election cycle they dangle this *"economic carrot"* before those who are dependent on it. They use statements like *"If you don't vote for me, your welfare benefits could be cut."* They also pay certain clergy to keep speaking the same message.

Deb: This is sad. It's the largest slavery system in the world...

Paul: This is a great place to wrap up. I see Dawn giving me the "look" which means its time. We need to leave soon for our date-night. We will schedule to meet with you on Monday at the same time. Have a blessed weekend.

Deb: I saw when she looked at you and realized the time. I am glad to end for today, I was getting a little agitated with this subject. Just seeing how the Enemy can use people to accomplish his agenda opened my eyes to a new realm. See you guys on Monday.

Chapter 15

"Poor Privilege"

Paul: Morning Deb! How is my favorite journalist today?

Deb: I am blessed! Joel and I spent the weekend at Ormand beach. I used the time to work on my tan and reflect on our last topic. How was your date-night last week?

Paul: Dawn and I enjoyed a quiet evening. We had dinner and walked at Disney Springs. She got a chance to clock her 2.4 miles on her app and I burned off part of my dinner in the beautiful 70-degree weather.

Deb: That sounds wonderful. Joel and I would like to join you guys next time. Maybe we can do dinner and a movie.

Dawn: You are talking Paul's language! He loves his action movies. However, so many of them are rated "R" for profanity, it *"turns him off."* It's too difficult to sit through the obscenities. It is, also, difficult for me to find a good chick-flick for the same reason.

Deb: I feel the same way. For now, we will stick to dinner and a cool walk. Okay, Paul, let's pick up where we left off. You were about to address the impact and motive of the slave system.

Teach Them How to Own the Entire Lake

Paul: When I turn on the TV, there it goes again! Another infomercial or commercial, "Please send $20 per month to feed a hungry child," or I may see the other one, "One in 5 children in America will go to bed hungry tonight, but for only $19 per month we can help stop hunger." I never see a commercial for, "Help us provide jobs for the poor." Five years later, I see the same children on the TV program, without any change in their appearance or their blighted community.

America is the wealthiest country in the world. We throw away billions of tons of good food every year.

Deb: It's funny that you mentioned this. I see the same programs and wonder to myself, "Why aren't these children looking better and prospering after all of these years?"

Paul: Don't get me wrong! I have no problem with a good organization asking for money to help feed poor and hungry children. I have personally given or invested in some of these organizations. The principles we teach from The Heavenly Father are:

- ***Give a fish*** *(take care of the immediate need).*

- ***Teach them how to fish for themselves*** *(equip them with the education, resources and career training/entrepreneurship development to provide for themselves and family).*

- ***Teach them how to own the entire lake*** *(they can feed their families and provide opportunities for their village).*

Deb: What a contrast! This is a concept I can buy into. This could change the world.

Our Feeding Program is Successful. We Went from Feeding 200 to 1,500

Paul: Many people, some with good intentions, cripple the poor by only giving them a fish. I was speaking with one of my pastor friends in ministry. He said, *"Paul, our ministry is growing. We started off feeding 50 people per week then it jumped to 200. Now we are serving 1,500 per week. Praise, God!"*

I politely asked him this question, "Tim, would your donors/investors count your success by how many more poor people you can feed or by how many poor people you can move **from Poverty to Prosperity?**" Tim held his head down for about 60 seconds, it felt like five minutes to me. Then he said "Paul, you are right! We were so caught-up with free food give-away and the excitement of seeing the long lines of people that we didn't realize we were not helping, only hurting them. How can we rectify this problem? I shared with him some key principles and ways to address his newly found concerns.

Deb: My eyes are now open to this problem in the community. Reflecting on the church ads that read, *"First Church is having a free food give-away on Thursday. Bring* *your friends and family."* I see very few churches teaching people how to fish for themselves and to change their destiny.

Paul: For over thirty years I have worked with families from all spectrums of society. I have seen the negative impact upon multiple generations who are dependent on the *"Tax-payer dad."* This is now ingrained in the culture and passed down from mothers to their children. It is now their *"birth-right"* and now, these are their expectations:

- *"From birth, I have the right to be supported by my "Tax-payer dad."*

- *"Tax-payer dad" will pay for my food, clothes, medical, dental, schooling, transportation, medication and housing."*

- *"When I have more children from a "sperm donor dad," my "Tax-payer dad," will pay me extra money per child."*

- *"I will get my child diagnosed with one of the many mental diagnoses such as Attention Deficit Disorder (ADD) or Bipolar Disorder, and "Tax-payer dad," will pay even more!"*

Deb: Wow! Paul, what a mess we have created. A generation raised to be continually programed to be slaves to the government system. How can we help to break this vicious cycle?

Work for your Food: The Principle of Gleaning

Paul: Deb, it is sad. The Heavenly Father said, *"We would **always** have poverty issues in the world until His appointed season."* He knew the far-reaching impact of *The Father Fracture Syndrome* on families and society. He, also, knew that individuals and families need an *opportunity*, or *"a cause, so to speak,"* to show, or *"activate their compassion gene,"* to help and serve others. Otherwise, we would become even more *"self-centered."* That's why He established the principle of *"Gleaning"* (*The* ***Opportunity*** *for the poor to* **work for their food** *and if they are not willing to work, they shouldn't eat from what others have worked for)*. This key principle was first taught to the Jewish people and passed on to us through the Torah and the Bible. These principles create a healthy work ethic that brings glory to the Heavenly Father. He knows that work helps to cultivate a healthy Glory Code.

Deb: I never knew this key principle. This explains why some people who are not working seem to have more issues and problems than others. They have a sense of purpose and accomplishment.

Paul: That's right. Work brings glory… and the rest, is another story! With a smile on her face, **Deb responds,** "You just had to get a little pun in there, didn't you?"

Paul: *Yep, I couldn't help it…*

Bitter Dads, Angry children. No child without a Mom

Deb: I see so many articles come across my desk laced with bitter divorce cases. It seems so hopeless.

Paul: After a divorce or break-up, some hostile, angry dads choose not to get remarried. They, however, choose to play the field *(fool-around)* and start having *"friends with benefits."* This sends the wrong message to their children. Children thrive in a two-parent home with a female mother and a male dad. The mother brings warmth and gentleness to the family. Both dad and mom contribute to the healthy vitality of their children's GC. After a divorce, if their custodial dad alienates them from their mother, and instead, bring random women into their lives, it breeds anger and resentment in the hearts of the children.

"No child without a mom." The value of motherhood, and fatherhood, reflects the complete character of The Loving, Heavenly Father. Today, there are numerous men who have grown-up never knowing the warmth of a hug from a loving mother.

One of the roles of husbands is to love, serve and honor their wives. The emotional health, and GC, of their children depends on it. The tender warmth and gentleness that a mother was meant to bring into the family, emanates from The Heavenly Father. She was designed to reflect part of His tender character to His children. Families are incomplete without a mother's love.

Deb: You were just talking about my mom. This brings tears to my eyes. After all of the verbal abuse from my dad, my mom still showed us her tender love and compassion.

Paul: This is why one of the key roles of a dad is to protect his wife. Not only physically, but emotionally. This helps to protect her Glory Code so she can model who she was created to be; warm, tender, caring, gentle, entrepreneurial, and breath of fresh air. Her role is to be a sweet aroma to her family. Deb, when your dad was being verbally abusive to your mom, he was in essence crushing her intrinsic nature. Praise God, His Word, on the inside of her, was greater than the abusive words of your dad.

Deb: This further validates your mandate to help men become transformed into the character of Christ.

Men Looking to Marry their Mothers

Paul: Men who were excessively pampered as boys by their mothers tend to look for the same attributes in their wives *(mom)*. They often place unrealistic expectations on their wives. They expect them to clean up their messes, pick-up their dirty clothes off the floor and cook as their mom did., etc.

Men, our role as husbands, is to love and serve our wives like Christ (In the character of The Father) loved and served the Church, His Bride. As husbands, we are not just loving our wives, we are loving our children's mom. So… we are really loving ourselves. Dads, when we show warm, loving affection to our wives, we are solidifying and helping to seal our children's Glory Code.

Peace with a Price

Men *(husbands)* want, and look forward to, the pleasure of sexual intimacy with their wives. Sometimes, to avoid rejection from their wives in the bedroom, men will avoid discussing and taking a stand on important issues that may lead to conflict with their wives. So, they keep their peace *(hold their tongue)* in the home so they can have *piece in the bedroom.*

Men, our wives are looking for our leadership, not just "Yes, men." Remember what happened to Adam. We are still paying the price today, for the "piece" Adam had in the garden…no pun intended.

Deb: Dawn, he is at it again with the puns…

Dawn: Deb, it's your turn, you give him the look!

Paul: She is another punster, just like me…

Girls looking to Marry their Dads

Paul: Dads play a very important role in their daughters' lives. They are looking at how you love, serve and protect their mom.

Men, don't stop courting your wives soon after marrying. We need to model a healthy, on-going, dating relationship with our wives. After all, one day our daughters will marry a man just like us. We need to still open the car door for our wives, like we did during our courtship.

Despite what some women are saying, (those in the women's liberation movement who condemn traditional marriage and the role of men in marriage) authentic women, (those with renewed Glory Codes) still desire to be treated like queens from you, their king. At weddings, I encourage new husbands by saying, "Keep the courtship in your marriage and your marriage out of court!"

Deb: Amen! I am one of them. I enjoy being treated like a lady. Joel opens doors for me. Dawn, does Paul open doors for you?

Dawn: He sure does.

The Father's Blessing Seals the GC

Deb: I've heard you say multiple times the importance of the father's blessing. My dad didn't bless us. Paul, why aren't more dads blessing their children?

Paul: Jewish dads were commissioned by The Heavenly Father to bless their children. This was not a Jewish blessing, but The Heavenly Father's Blessing. It was ordained for dads to impart His Heart and Character to their children from generation to generation. The increasing influence of the "FFS" has diminished the intended legacy of this blessing. Today there is a new resurgence and a slow awakening within the hearts of dads pertaining to their divine role in their families.

Deb: Thank you for sharing. I never knew this principle.

Paul: Many Christians, by their actions, forget that the Bible is a Jewish Book. The principles from The Heavenly Dad are all outlined within its pages.

I was mentoring Bill, a 42-years old man, who was on his 5th marriage. His dad, Frank, was in his 6th marriage. Bill never had a balanced, male role model in his life. Just like his dad, Bill went from one dysfunctional relationship to another. He was attracted to women who had crushed Glory Codes like himself.

After a conversation with Bill about his dad and his family issues, I asked Bill if he wanted me to pray for him? *"Yes, Pastor!"* He said. I prayed the "Father's Blessings" over him as Bill had never received his dad's approval and blessing. After placing my right hand on his head, I prayed. The Heavenly Father began to do a mighty work in Bill's heart. He couldn't go to work for two days. He was in a daze *(some would call it "being drunk in the spirit").* At the end of the second day, his wife called me to ask, *"What have you done to my husband? He has been so peaceful, but he's been in this fog-like state for days now. He needs to go back to work!"* I told her, *"I prayed the Father's blessing over him. The Heavenly Father is doing a deep, generational repair."* There are many men like Bill in the world. They are yearning for their dad's blessing and approval.

Deb: Do all the men experience what Bill did when you prayed the Father's Blessing over them?

Paul: Every person has a different experience. The Father knows and ministers to the various crushed areas in their GC.

The Voice and character of the dad

Paul: A dad's voice, and his actions, sets the tone in the home. It can instill either a sense of peace or fear and discord. In homes with fear and discord, children will perceive their Heavenly Father through the same ***fractured*** lens as they viewed their earthly fathers. This was the type of dad Bill grew up with. When Bill read his Bible, all he heard *was the angry voice of his dad*. Children flourish when their dads listen to them and validate them.

Did the face of your dad reflect acceptance or disapproval?

Paul: The facial expressions of dads will either convey approval and acceptance or rejection and disapproval.

Growing up, Bill never saw or experienced a warm reception from his dad. His father's countenance was mostly one of disapproval. He felt that he could never do anything right. He thought that God was the same way with him. He said to himself *"God would never approve of me, regardless of the good I may do!"* Many men *(and women)* carry these same thoughts and behaviors into their current relationships, marriages and families. As a result, their children will feel the same way as Bill did, never experiencing acceptance.

Consequently, girls who grow up with this kind of father, have an unhealthy perception of men, relationships and The Heavenly Father. In their search for approval, many women acquiesce to abusive behaviors from their husbands not unlike what they experienced from their dads.

Deb: This gives me greater understanding for men like Bill. My heart, also, goes out to women who remain in abusive relations (*finding a man just like their father*). I am still hearing my own father's negative voice in my head. Let's move to a different topic. I need to replace my current thoughts.

The arms of dads: Love & Embrace or Abuse & Punish?

Paul: Sorry, Deb, some of these topics will stir-up emotions in you and many other people. When this information becomes **revelation**, a deeper level of healing can occur in the GC.

I speak to you now about your dad's arms and hands. Did they embrace you with love or did they punish, abuse, molest, reject, or embrace you? My heart, and The Heavenly Father's heart, is broken for all of you who were abused at the hands of a dad or father-figure male.

If you were one of them, I will stand in proxy on their behalf and ask you to please forgive me. I pray for the healing touch that comes from The Heavenly Father's Glory Source to soothe and heal your heart right now as you read this. May the crushed state of your Glory Code be renewed. May your image of The Heavenly Father be renewed. I decree a brand-new relationship is being established between you and your Heavenly Dad. He yearns to bring you His Love and Peace through a healing relationship with His Son.

Hands that Heal

The hands of a dad are to lead, guide and defend. The strength of his arms should provide warmth, comfort, protection and deliverance. His right hand represents his righteousness (*the strength to do what is right*). When The Heavenly Father refers to His strong Right Hand *(Arm)* that redeemed *(purchased and rescued)* us out of Egypt *(the world of sin, pain and bondage)*, He is referring to His righteousness. His Son, Yeshua, Jesus, is His Right hand of righteousness.

When you reflect on the hand of your dad, He wants you to replace the past image of hurt and abuse with a new one. His glorious right hand, His Son, paid the ultimate price to bring healing and renewal to you.

Dads, you should not use your "hands" to discipline your children. Your hands are to guide and show loving affection. Due to the "FFS," many authentic roles and functions of fatherhood have become distorted. When you extend your hands in a gesture to hug your child, will he or she embrace you or retreat in fear? Unsure of your intentions, your child will always be conflicted between your motive and action.

Deb: Paul, did the Heavenly Father institute discipline because of the FFS?

Paul: Before the FFS, there was no need for discipline. Now, His children, those who have chosen to be reunited with Him, He disciplines. Godley dads need to follow His example when disciplining their children.

Conversely, punishment is for those who are still rebelling against His Loving call to be reunited with Him. They are reserved for His wrath. Discipline is like a loving Shepherd with his rod, guiding or prodding his sheep onto a safe path to keep them from evil. *The Enemy* is waiting to steal, kill and destroy.

Father-Rohi *(Shepherd)* is another character trait of The Heavenly Father. He leads us and protects us. He will prepare you a table in the presence of your enemies. *This is to help you forgive and be reconciled around the Fathers' Table of forgiveness and healing. (He will lead, feed and provide for all that you have need of in life)*.

The Heavenly Father models loving *(not angry or hurtful)* correction and discipline. Some dads may choose to use a thin bamboo twig, like what my dad used on my rear assets. Others may use a paint stirrer or their leather belt.

King David said, *"Your rod and staff, they comfort me."* Dads who love their children should discipline them to keep them on the *(right)* righteous path. King David was saying, *your "rod"* of discipline (not abuse) and your *"staff"* (of strength, guidance and courage) will lead and guide me all the days of my life. This brings me comfort.

Deb: This image of a Shepherd reminds of the picture I once saw of Jesus. He was holding a perfect little lamb in His arms. Sometimes, the child in me yearns for a hug from my dad.

Paul: Deb, you and so many people, long to have a renewed, healthy image of a dad. Marred by the FFS, many dads don't know how to show their children the kind of love The Heavenly Father intended for them to experience.

Chapter 16

Society Shifts to the Far Left

Deb: Knowing that my father was a product of his environment and recognizing he was abused by his dad, I now have a sense of sympathy for him.

Paul: My heart goes out to you and the many children *(and adults)* whose image of fatherhood has been blemished in this process. Because some parents abused the concept of discipling their children and went to the extreme, like burning their hands on the stove or other forms of cruel and unusual punishment.

Some government officials, in an effort to help, have *moved far left*. Some states have even banned all, or most forms, of parental discipline. It is now labeled abuse; and when parents are not allowed to maintain structure and discipline in their homes, it will result in anarchy and discord. When children then get into trouble with *"The Law,"* these same government officials will discipline and punish them for you by placing them in jail or detention centers. When they have finished *punishing your children* they will send you a bill and ask you to pay for their parole. Remember, whatever is eradicated from the family structure, *society **will** have to foot the bill and pay the price.*

Deb: Paul, you are right. I have seen a news stories where teens knew that their parents couldn't discipline them. They held a late night party, against their parents' wishes and got into trouble. at One young man got drunk, crashed his car and killed two of his friends.

Paul: Deb, what a horrific story! These are just some of the ramifications from removing balanced, loving discipline from the home.

Disillusionment leads to Discouragement and Lost Love

Natural affection *(love) is being lost due to disillusionment and discouragement* in the hearts of men, women, and youth in our society. They are impacted by the Father

Fractured Syndrome. The love of many with a shattered GC will grow cold and indifferent. Without hope of ever experiencing the true love of a dad, they lash out toward other family members and society. As I mentioned earlier, what is not received and settled in the home, society will pay the price, physically, spiritually and financially. Just examine a few quick examples of the ***cost to society, or tax-payers.***

Forced Investor, the High Cost to Mitigate the FFS

Deb: I often get frustrated when I see the amount of my tax-dollars being abused by the government for programs that are ineffective and wasteful. Just think about it, we are all paying daily for the FFS.

Paul: This is just a short list of what every tax-payer (*Forced Investor*) pays annually:

- Billions of dollars each year to incarcerate fatherless youth

- Billions of dollars each year for mental health therapy for fatherless youth

- $22+ Trillion in welfare programs resulting in millions of fatherless homes.

- Billions in property damage by youth

- Billions in legal fees for youths without dads

- Billions of dollars each year to abort *(murder, slaughter)* babies (80% of these girls who murder their children are from homes without dads).

- Billions of dollars each year for counseling to help girls, ladies and even the *baby-daddy* after they murder (abort) their babies.

- Billions of dollars each year as our government sends payments to other countries to implement these same failed policies in their countries.

- Billions of dollars each year on families who are entering America illegally by breaking the laws of our country.

Look at your *paystub*, this is only the short-list of bills your *forced-taxes* are paying for. The impact from the FFS cannot be solved by just taking the hard-earned money from families to pay for the cure of these symptom. This is an unbalanced approach to address this core problem. This is what I call being a ***Forced Investor.*** Every tax-paying individual or family in America is a *forced investor*.

Deb: OMG! Wow, Paul, these numbers are staggering. This is only the short-list? I don't want to see the full list. This explains why our government has such a high deficit. I think it is around 20 plus trillion now. Paul, I never heard that term before.

Are you a forced investor?

Paul: Deb, you are right to be shocked. The value that authentic dads bring to the table can go a long way in mitigating this major symptom from the FFS. I mentioned that we *are forced investors.*

As tax-payers, we cannot decide or have any say in what the government officials use our tax dollars for. They create laws and fund projects that may not reflect our Core Values. When they need more money, they raise our taxes.

Deb, this is what I call a **Forced Investor** (Someone who doesn't have a say in how their hard-earned money is squandered, aka, invested) with little or no positive impact in the lives of individuals, families and society at large.

You can be an Intentional Investor

This is why I encourage people to invest their money intentionally into programs and organizations that are helping to effectively mitigate these symptoms by addressing the root cause. This will bring about long-lasting solutions that will change the fabric of society. Now, you will be intentionally investing in what you believe in. Just like I mentioned to the pastors, we need to intentionally impact our communities. Remember, we don't invest in companies, we invest in people. So, know the people behind these companies. Their character will count in the long run…

Deb: I never thought of this before. So, when we vote to elect someone with an agenda that doesn't reflect the character of The Heavenly Father, we are really perpetuating a corrupt and broken system of *"Forced Investing,"* which impacts all of us. My vernacular is constantly expanding when we get together. I now feel more equipped to be a true ambassador for this cause.

Paul: The unraveling of the depth and far reaching entrenchment of the "FFS" will take us a lifetime to mitigate. We are required to do our part in the time we are here on earth. To whom much is given, much will be required of them.

Paul R. Benjamin, Sr.

Chapter 17

Purpose, Plight, and Pillage of Humanity

Paul: The purpose, plight, and pillage of all humanity hinges on the battle for the heart of mankind. *The father, to whom you yield your heart and obey, is glorified by your lifestyle.*

If you choose to yield your heart to do unrighteous things, thus glorifying the father of lies, deception and murder, the Devil, you will spend eternity with him. Forever separated from the blissful, peaceful and glorious presence of The Heavenly Father and His Family.

The *Principle of first Impact:* Whoever puts the most in, *will ultimately* get the most out. A dad's role is to positively influence the heart of his children. Even from the womb, the power of dad's voice begins to shape the GC in the child. His words and actions leave a life-long impression in the heart of his children. He can build and seal a positive image to enrich their GC or he can shatter their GC by being a negative influence by his words and gestures.

Dads need to teach their children how to guard and *protect their hearts from negative influences.* The heart is the central processing unit (CPU) of the soul. This is where the hurts and pains of life are influenced. It's also the central processing zone for our Glory Code. This is a delicate place where moms and dads can crush or codify the renewal of their child's Glory Code, with the dads providing the capstone seal.

The (CPU) is where we gage the Glory Code level. Parents, who are in tune and equipped with this knowledge, can sense and positively influence their child's GC. Glory Code levels can range from a (+6) to (-7). Knowing the key factors in the life of a person, you can identify where their GC is on the scale. This could be the difference between life and death.

Deb: Paul, I haven't heard the term (CPU) since I left high high-school. It validates how important our lifestyle and words are upon children and future generations. As a mom, I need to engage in my children's lives. I would hate to think I missed some key indicators in their GC that I could have caught.

Paul: Deb, as parents we can't be everywhere or do everything for our children, but we can mold and influence their hearts to cope with the negative impact of our society that we all have to live in. Some children raised in homes where their dads are absent manifest some of the symptoms of their crushed GC in school. Here are just a few ways some of these children act out:

Yearning to fill the silent, unknown void in their crushed GC, some children manifest anger and hate toward others, especially those from well-balanced, intact, heterosexual homes. Many are longing to have a true sense of "family life" that The Heavenly Father intended. Some bully younger children. I remember when my children were in school. They were picked on by students who didn't have dads at home. My heart goes out to these children.

Parkland, Florida School Shooting Tragedy

School Shootings. Children who reach (-7) in their crushed GC will either murder or commit suicide. They usually shown signs long before they get to this point. First, I would like to pause and pray for the families who lost loved ones in the Parkland School shooting massacre in Florida. It's one of those societal ills *(unresolved GC issues in the home that affects society)* that we are paying for today. As I mentioned, what is not resolved in the home, *society pays the price.*

Principles applied correctly can save millions of Lives

This is why I am making this information available. If we can save one life, it would be worth it all.

After every school shooting, we find out about the child's relationship with his dad. 90% of those who initiate this heinous act, have a (-7) GC. 100% of school shootings are executed by a young man with (-7) GC. The mental health of children with crushed Glory Codes goes deep. This is why we need to teach, equip and engage healthy balanced men, women, and youth to intervene before these tragedies. *(This is another all-day seminar)*.

A precursor to such tragic events would be displayed through defiance of authority in the home, at school and even against law-enforcement officers. Children with a crushed

GC display these symptoms. Girls will even cry out for help by cutting themselves. Some will use social media to share their feelings of pain and anger.

Truancy or school dropout rates are off the chart while cyber bullying and school gangs permeate all sectors. Peers with shattered Glory Codes identify with each other and join various suicide pacts or radicalized movements.

Health issues, heart disease and even cancer are just some of the manifestations from walking in unforgiveness resulting from a crushed GC. Many children exhibit increased health problems which stem from relational issues with their dads. They don't know the *"why"* for their marred GC.

Deb: My heart and prayers are with the parents that have lost children in all of these mass shootings. If only someone knew the GC level of these shooters before they acted out. I know you can't go too deep in this subject, but we need you to train leaders how to identify some of these key signals. This can save many lives.

Guns or (-7) GC Last stage in Mental Health Depravity

Paul: Deb, you are right. Helping leaders learn how to identify some of the symptoms will save lives. Teachers are already overwhelmed with class sizes and students that bring their anger and behavioral problems on to the school bus and into their classrooms. This will be one of the initiatives we will begin to mentor families (husbands and wives) how to impact students in school.

National Outcry of the Left

The national leftwing outcry about guns and "gun violence" immediately followed the horrific *Parkland Florida School shooting* incident. Leftist political operatives in partnership with the fake news media attacked guns citing them as the root cause. The news coverage dwarfed the death of the children, and the pain of their parents, subverting their trauma for the expediency of eradicating the second amendment rights of all law-abiding citizens.

Shootings in El Paso, Texas Wal-Mart & Dayton, Ohio

Deb. Paul, you are so right. While we have been talking, I received a news alert of another mass shooting in El Paso, Texas at Wal-Mart and another shooting in Dayton, Ohio. I guess, based on what you have been telling me, both of these shooters were at a (-7) Glory Code level. Just like you said, the leftist political operatives and the fake-news media are already blaming guns again.

Paul: Deb, let's pause and pray for these families who have lost their loved ones in this tragedy. It's amazing, this type of shooting is always by someone with this Glory Code level of (-7) and yet all the blame goes to the gun or its manufacturer.

Deb: Are we supposed to believe that these *leftist leaders* love and care about us? When they sponsor and pay for the murder and slaughter of over a million children (babies) per year? These same people who commit such atrocities express shock when a (-7) GC shooter murders innocent people. Is murder by someone wearing a white coat using *forceps* different from the murder by someone with a *gun* wearing blue jeans?

Out-ward Acts Reflect In-ward Pain

Paul: Deb, you are right. In a society where there is **no value** for "life" from childhood creates a mindset that **no "life" has value.** This is why we need to mobilize godly dads and families to stand in the gap to positively influence this generation. Just like the farmer's story, the leftwing media and political pundits hijack these tragic incidents resulting from a young man with a (-7) Glory Code. The Mental Health Level (MHL) should have been evident to those around him.

The threat, Young Men with (-7) Glory Code

The Parkland School shooter, Mr. Cruz, like so many fatherless young men had exhibited behavioral problems until finally, his Glory Code level reached (-7). At this point, his life and the life of others didn't matter. He committed the outward act of violence, to reflect his inward pain. Today, the Mental Health level (MHL) for millions of fatherless young men and women are bordering on dangerous GC levels. Let's reach them, before they reach us! Youths with (+1) to (- 4) GC levels are more likely to be involved in cutting, school drop-out, gangs, crime, drug abuse, and a plethora of other symptoms.

These young men and women are very easy to be *radicalized by left-winged groups.* Many of them get paid to perform *staged radical protests* at conservative community events. They are even lured into holding entire shopping malls hostage, like the two young men that were recruited from urban America to join the gang that held the Kenyan shopping mall hostage in 2013.

Deb: Based on this information, none of us are really safe! Every day we are surrounded by people with various GC levels. If I ponder on this fact, it would make me depressed. I thank God His Angels watch over us.

You may know someone close to a (-7) GC

Paul: Deb, you are so right. It's only by God's grace we are still alive. Every school shooting is a result of the ***deep-cry*** of a wounded heart. Daily, the unsuspecting public, our *children in school, mothers, fathers, sisters, and brothers* are vulnerable to the mental health levels of anyone with a (-7) Glory Code. They will either implode, by committing suicide, or explode, resulting in *mass shootings, bombings, death by law-enforcement, drunk driving* and many other expressions of their pain.

Your GC Determines your Mental Health Level

Do guns murder people or individuals with a crushed (-7) GC? Cain, who had a crushed (-7) GC, committed the first recorded murder in the world. Did Cain use a gun, a knife, a rock, or his hands? Does it matter which instrument he used or was it the "motive" of the heart?

The Heavenly Father, The God of the universe, said, *"If you have **'hatred'** in your heart towards anyone, **you are a murderer**."* Whatever is in your heart (CPU), *(The storage place for all of life's resolved or unresolved beliefs and experiences, good or evil)* if it is good, from a healthy balanced (+6) GC or evil from a crushed (-1) to (-7) GC, will influence your thoughts, feelings *(emotions)* and actions. I can always tell the mental health of a person by their words and actions.

The Heavenly Father is reminding us that if we love Him, we must love each other also. We are all made by Him, It is His breath of life that is in everyone. One day we will all have to give an account for what we said and how we acted towards each other.

The Ultimate Weapon

Deb: So, Paul, the real, and ultimate, weapon that we need to address is the heart. From our "CPU" all of our GC levels emanate from it. Leftwing operatives have been intentionally addressing the wrong weapon.

Paul: Deb, you got it! By the time you are finished with this interview, you would have a *"Graduation Certificate"* for completing our *"Global Impact Academy."*

This principle is true of every violent act of crime, regardless of the choice of weapon. It could manifest as a terrorist using a car-bomb to crash into a crowd killing 30 people, detonating a bomb attached to his body killing himself and 20 others or using a plane to crash into the world trade center buildings, like on 9-11. It all goes back to the source as a result of the hate and unresolved issues within their shattered Glory Code.

Deb: Thanks Paul, I would place my graduation certificate on my office wall. I am now thinking on a different level. Knowing the "why" makes a huge difference in my thinking. I am now seeing through a different lens.

Paul: You now have 20/20 vision. Let us, as a nation, attack this deadly enemy. Satan has blinded the hearts of individuals that are yielded to him on the left. They are not able to see or understand the truth. If we were to use the same media and political *fire-power* that is unleashed against guns, to *mentor and minister* to the millions of fatherless young men and women, we can make a significant impact in the "GC" levels of this generation. I pray that their eyes and their wounded hearts would be opened to the real truth and Love from The Heavenly Dad.

Bias against Guns

Deb: Understanding the far-reaching implications of the *Father Fracture Syndrome* and its' influence in every area of society, has given me a new perspective. My news articles will take on a new truthful insight and deeper meaning to my readers

Paul: Great, Deb! We can team up. I could help add a Biblical worldview to some of your news articles. Your readers will have a balanced "why" behind the news of the day.

Deb: I would love that! Let me pitch this idea to John and I will get back to you. I am already thinking of some creative articles.

Paul: Thanks, Deb. I am looking forward to partnering with you and the team. I have to make a few important calls. Let's take a 30.3-minute break. When I return we can order lunch.

Chapter 18

Domestic Violence and Child Abuse

Deb: Paul, while you were away for 37.5 minutes, Dawn and I took the liberty of ordering our lunch. She didn't place your order, knowing you don't like your food lukewarm, it must be hot.

Paul: Sorry for being late ladies. One of my calls took a little longer than planned. Yes, my wife knows how I like my food. This is the key reason I eat fast, to avoid eating lukewarm or cold food. I will now order my Atlantic salmon with broccoli and rice-pilaf. I took a call from one of our team members. She just received a call at the center. It involved a domestic violence incident. This was the reason it took me longer on my last phone call.

Deb: When I hear of so many women being abused by their husbands or boyfriends my heart aches for them. My husband Joel is *one in a million*. He treats me like a queen. We need more men like him.

Paul: Deb, does that mean that Dawn and I have to call you Queen Deb?

Deb: Now that you mention it, that would be nice! I don't think this would go over well with Dawn. She is your Queen.

Paul: Okay Queen Deb, I would leave that for Joel to take care of his Queen. My Queen is smiling at us… This is why I am reaching and ministering to men, bringing their crushed GC from (-5) to (+6) through a renewal mentoring relational process. Through the love and influence of The Heavenly Father, they move from being a ***"Predator to A Protector."***

Dan, a young man in my *ranger scout group*, grew up seeing his dad abuse his mom. His dad subsequently divorced her, leaving Dan without his dad in the home. One day, his relative asked him to hold a gun for him. Like a typical teenage young man, he wanted to *show off the gun.*

A Defining Moment

Now armed with this gun, Dan went upstairs to my friend's apartment where she was babysitting my son and daughter. While fooling around with the gun, it went off, shooting her through her neck and killing her on the spot. My son was about *5 inches away* from her when this happened.

"I Have No Son!"

Later, I was called to pick-up Dan from a specified hide-out location. He was waiting for me to turn him over to the police, who, at this point, were looking for him. With his heart pounding and tears in his eyes, I picked-up Dan at the agreed location. While driving him in my white Jeep Cherokee to the police station, Dan asked me, *"Can you take me to my dad's house before I go to jail?"* Knowing that this could be the last time he may get to see his dad on this side of the cold, steel jail bars, I quickly said, "Yes!" We drove up to the house where his dad lived. I knocked on the door, to my surprise, his dad was home. Dan was standing next to me when I introduced myself to his dad. Before I could finish explaining why we were there, his dad said, *"I have no son!"* These were the last words Dan heard from his dad before going to jail. My heart was broken for Dan. It was at that moment I realized that 90% of the young men in my ranger scout group were from fatherless homes.

Deb: This brings tears to my eyes. Like so many of the topics we are addressing. I can't imagine how deep this impacted Dan's GC. My heart goes out to him and the millions of fatherless children and adults in our nation.

Like Father, Like Son

Paul: The family members ultimately forgave Dan for what he did to their daughter and sister. I was asked to speak in court as a character witness on Dan's behalf. Based on the fact that this was an accidental shooting, he was released from jail. Years later, one of my eight sisters fell in love with Dan and they were married. You guessed it! He ended up abusing my sister the same way he witnessed his dad abusing his mom. As a result, their two children were raised in a fatherless home, just like he was.

Deb: That is so sad to hear Paul. You are right, the FFS touches all of us in so many ways. I now understand a little more why so many men abuse their wives.

Paul: We need to reach these men and minister to the *"6-year-old boy on the inside of them." This can bring healing to their crushed GC,* turning them from ***Predators to Protectors.***

Prostitute with Potential

Deb: Paul, I noticed a decrease in the number of marriages across our nation.

Paul: Deb, you are correct. In fear of marrying a predator, many women and single moms remain single. Some may live with their boyfriends without the commitment of marriage which exposes their children to a much higher potential for abuse. This lifestyle presents another set-up for failure.

One day we were having a community yard sale at our Center. Dana, a prostitute in the community, came to see if she could get some free items. Dana, a black woman in her early thirty's, like so many girls and women today in urban communities, was sexually abused by many of her mom's *boyfriends* that had been in and out of her home since she was a girl. In essence, she was sex-trafficked in her own house.

Longing for the authentic love and acceptance of a dad to satisfy her GC, she kept going from man to man seeking to fill the cry of her heart. Incest leads to promiscuity. Dana kept giving-up her ***virtue, for validation.*** Always hoping to fill the void in her life.

Dana approached one of our volunteers and asked for some free items from the 10 thousand SQF area we had sectioned off for the sale. It was filled with everything from books to bikes. Our principle was, *there is a cost for everything*, but, if someone didn't have the money for an item, we would give them *a work assignment to earn the required amount of money* for the items. This is a principle from The Heavenly Father. Many churches and organizations take away the *glory and value of work,* with their ***free, free***, *free* handouts.

Work brings Glory to The Heavenly Father

Dana thought the items were free. Like so many other people in the community, she was accustomed to another organization in the city that left *donated clothes* on a table in their yard for anyone to *freely take*. She said, *"we don't wash clothes, we throw them in the garbage and pick up* ***more free*** *clothes!"*

Jim, one of our volunteers, called me to speak with Dana. I greeted her and explained, *no one is turned away if they cannot pay.* The items she selected were already packed in a box. The approximate retail value (new) was about $150, but used the value was about

$50. In an effort to bring her glory through the value of work, I mentioned to her, *"If you clean and organiz the book display area, we will pay you $5.00 for a half hour of work. We will accept this as your donation for the items."* Her face lit up like a Christmas tree. *"Yes, Pastor Benjamin. Thank you."* Without any hesitation, Dana began cleaning and organizing. I told Jim to call me when she completes her work assignment.

Twenty minutes later, one of my team members said Jim wanted to see me. To my surprise, Dana had already cleaned and systematically organized all the books and items in the assigned area. *"Great job, Dana!"* I applauded her for the awesome work she did. I took $5.00 out of my wallet and paid her *(this cognitive process was important)*. In all labor, there is profit. The physical payment to her said *"work has value."* There was a *glow of glory* in Dana's eyes when she received the money. I told Jim to give her the box with her items. With a huge smile, Dana paid Jim the **$5.00** which she had just ***worked*** for. There was a noticeable shift in her posture and demeanor. We rob people of this process and glory in America with our ***free, free, free*** handouts…

Hope and Gratitude

Deb: You brought dignity to her by allowing her to show that she has value beyond just losing her virtue. Just to think, she could use her *organizational talent as a designer.* Millions of women are yearning for someone to tap into their true identity and bring forth the *beauty that lies within.*

Paul: This was not the last I heard from Dana. One hour later she returned to the Center and asked if I was there. As I was walking towards the side door, there, smiling from ear to ear was Dana. She walked into the Center and said, *"Look at me!"* Wearing the red dress and shoes that she had just *purchased*, she said, *"I would work here anytime!"* Overwhelmed with gratitude for the opportunity, she offered to volunteer at the Center when available.

Deb: This further validates why you must equip pastors and leaders to facilitate change in their cities. By mitigating the growing pandemic of the "FFS" and America's *crippling free handout policies,* we can drastically impact the lives of so many girls and women who are living within one mile of a local church.

False Validation on Social Media

Paul: Deb, you are clearly reverberating the vision. Now, we just need some more great media personalities like you to echo the same message. Girls and women who had their Glory Code and virtue stolen and crushed by men; seek to find *vicarious validation and value* through various *social media platforms*. Their GC level is based on how many *"likes"* they receive on their social posts. Compounded by their dysfunction at home, when criticized on social media, some girls commit suicide or turn to cutting. Some of these girls even post their suicide intentions on social media. Some school girls arrange **suicide-pacts** with their friends.

Deb: We get reports of so many such attempts and reports of these suicide tragedies from schools in our newsroom. Paul, I am glad to know you provide training for churches and couples on strategies to impact students in schools to help mitigate this epidemic.

Lost Manhood to Mom

I recently covered a news report about a single mom who sexually abused her 10-year-old son. This story broke when her son acted out by trying to have sex with a 9-year-old girl in his school. Child Protective Services got involved. We, also, have articles about female teachers having sexual relationships with their young, male students on and off campus.

Paul, I am overwhelmed with all of these sad and disturbing articles that come across my desk. This is why I need to finish and publish the truth about the FFS and the solution. If I can help facilitate healing to at least one person who is willing to see their crushed GC renewed, it would be worth it.

Paul: Deb, my heart goes out to all of these children that are abused around this nation and the world. Just like so many men who became abusers of women after they themselves were raised by abusive dads. Single moms, who abuse their sons, were also abused as girls. 70% of them by their step-dads and other men.

A *wise woman builds her home (nourishes her family), but a foolish woman (verbally and physically abuses) and tears it down.* Moms, and women who have crushed Glory Codes, who have not been renewed will afflict further abuse and pain upon their spouse and children.

Those boys, with their already crushed GC by their dad's absence are further conflicted by the abuse from their moms. These young men, enter into manhood with a flawed and marred image of women.

Their view of women, and ultimately their wives, is now conflicted by their past abuse. Even in their marital bedroom, it is now tainted by these images. Men are supposed to love, serve and protect their wives as their own bodies. When their balanced role and image is impacted, malfunction sets into their marriage. Today we are seeing the manifestation of the various forms of abuse these men inflict upon women.

Deb: Our news room is inundated with the pain and abuse of these men, women and families. I know we don't have time to go into the different nuances of this aspect of the "FFS," but I pray for the healing of these families.

Chapter 19

"Mr. Benjamin, can I work for $35?"

Paul: Deb, if I were to address the depth of each aspect of the "FFS" we would be here for a year. I join you in praying for these families. There is hope!

I was in my office on the weekend when I heard a knock on the door. In the doorway stood 12-year-old Joe. "Hi, Mr. Benjamin! Can I work for $35.00? I need to help my mom pay the light bill. My brother is in jail for selling drugs and I am the only boy left at home to help. She doesn't want me to do the same things my brother did." Joe, a black young man with a short-manicured haircut, was wearing blue shorts and a white V-neck T-shirt. He was sporting a clean pair of brown sandals (flip-flops). As Joe stood in my doorway, my heart was touched with his story and plight. Joe knew you do not come to Mr. Benjamin to ask for money. Rather, you ask "What can I do to earn money?"

Opportunity draws upon Creativity

I quickly thought of various safe projects that Joe, a 12-year-old, could do. We were having a community yard sale. I assigned him the job of holding the *"Yard Sale Sign"* and to help customers to load their cars. Joe did an excellent job. He was warm and friendly with the customers as he assisted them to their cars. His *customer service and hospitality skills* were that of a "5-Star" hotel. I was very impressed with his personality and performance. I thought to myself, what latent potential we have in urban youth, like Joe. This untapped talent is tucked away in urban cities across our nation. We only need authentic leaders to:

- Cultivate what is already within them

- Call forth their untapped potential

- Coach and develop their character for the career opportunities in the marketplace.

We only need people who are willing. We will help activate and develop their skills into a blessed destiny.

Two hours later before the yard sale event ended Dawn and I met with Joe. I counted out *35 one-dollar bills* in front of him and affirmed him on the awesome job he did. He smiled and stood upright, like a son who was honored by his dad. Dawn and I prayed a blessing over him and for his single mom.

Opportunity Zones Championed by Senator Tim Scott

Deb: We need to provide many opportunities for young men like Joe. I can see how your entrepreneurship initiative will help activate the *passion* and *purpose* in young men and women to live out their potential and become economically sufficient. This will move millions from the *"welfare-roll to the pay-roll."* This will change the dignity and destiny of people in urban America.

We received a press release that Senator Tim Scott from South Carolina designed a strategic plan called *"Opportunity Zones."* President Trump endorsed it as a new way to bring businesses into urban cities. This will provide income opportunities for those who are willing to move from poverty to prosperity. Senator Scott, who lived in poverty himself, now from his position of prominence, has returned to be a blessing to his community. This is an authentic leader making a difference. Thank you, Senator Scott!

Changing Mindsets

Paul: We need more Godly leaders like Senator Scott who are on the "Right" providing opportunities, rather than pillaging their communities.

Deb: What a contrast between Senator Tim Scott on the "Right" and Representative Elijah Cummings on the "Left." One *blessed his city* in South Carolina and the other was a *blight and disgrace to his city* in Baltimore, Maryland.

Paul: You are correct, Deb. These are some of the mindsets I address in our cities. Leaders on the Left that "pimp and pillage" their cities and leaders on the Right that "provide opportunities for people to move from poverty by propelling them into prosperity and prominence."

Men like Benjamin Carson on the Right, was raised by a resilient, single mom in urban America. He propelled himself from poverty to prominence to become a world-renowned neurosurgeon, Secretary of Housing and Urban Development. He was also a

Candidate for Presidency in 2016. Leaders like these bring hope to young men and women in urban cities.

Joan, a single mom along with her son and five of his friends, knocked on my office door. *"Mr. Benjamin, can you please sponsor us for Pop Warner Football this year?"* Joan wasn't aware of my philosophy *(Don't ask for money, ask for an opportunity to earn money)*. She was whispering to her son and these young men what they should say to me. I immediately said, *"No, What I will do for you is:*

1. *I will give you our hose, soap, wash rags and access to use our water.*

2. *I will give you burgers and hot dogs.*

3. *I will give you a BBQ grill and poster boards to make signs to have a car wash and sell burgers and hot dogs in front of the Center."*

The look on their faces was *priceless*… They looked at each other and then looked at me, as if to say, *"This means we have to work!"* After metaphorically picking them off the floor, we set the date for their fundraising car-wash.

The community was very supportive of their project. Not to mention, hundreds of volunteers from a national youth conference were at the Center that week. Some of these volunteers, who were all white, suburban young men and women pitched in to help hold signs, sell burgers and wash cars. They were able to raise $660 at the end of this two-day event.

After paying for the Pop Warner Registration and supplies, $120 was leftover. My $100 investment into the lives of these young men yielded $560 Greater than the $560 (ROI) on my investment, these six young men and their single moms had fun and most of all, they learned *"the glory of work."*

They all came to my office later inquiring if they can have the $120 left over. I asked, *"Who worked for this money?"* They replied, *"We did."* I said, *"You are right, It's your money!"* I applauded and affirmed them for the great job they all did. After dividing the funds between them, I prayed and blessed them. The principles these young men and their single parents learned during this event will *impact their thought process and mindset long into the future.*

Deb: Paul, what a great life lesson. We can all take away some key principles from this event. We, as a society are so quick to give a "hand-out" not realizing we are missing a greater life-enriching lesson.

Don't Feed the Bears

Paul: One of the former mayors of Sanford, Florida, Brady Lessard, spoke at one of our fundraising events. He shared a story, *"Don't Feed the Bears."* A father and son, while visiting Yellow Stone National Park noticed a sign that said, *"Don't Feed the Bears."* The son asked his father, *"Dad, why can't we feed the bears?"* His dad replied, *"Son, if we feed the bears they will become dependent on us, humans, and stop fending (hunting -working) for themselves in the wild. When we stop feeding them, they will turn on us and eat us!"*

Deb: Paul, this is the same principle you have been talking about when it comes to the *"war on poverty."* It was designed to feed people *(at the expense of tax-payers/ government)* without requiring them to work for it. Now, most of these people have lost the desire and work ethic to fend for themselves. Every election cycle, when they are threatened with the removal of this *"feeding tube"* there is a huge outrage. In some communities it could result in crime and looting. Some people have successfully weaned themselves off this system and found careers or started successful businesses.

Paul: Today, we are seeing the impact of this failed system on families. 94% of people that lose their jobs are due to bad attitudes and poor work ethic. Jan, a single mom we helped to find a job making $1,500.00 per month, became frustrated because she had been receiving $1,900 per month on *tax-payer* funded *welfare assistance.*

She was not willing to pay the price to develop her skills to be promoted to the next level of income to stay off the system. After three months of work, she returned to the "system," after all, her mom was also on welfare. Just like, *"Don't feed the bears,"* Jan became accustomed and comfortable living on the *free money provided by working families.* Benjamin Carson, Secretary of Housing and Urban Development, is working to make key changes to this system.

Deb: Paul, this is pathetic. We have removed the glory of work and the desire to be industrious.

Leftwing Leaders Advocate the Murder of Babies

Deb: I was greatly disturbed when I received the news that Governor Cuomo and the New York Assembly voted to murder (abort) babies. They decided that the mother can murder the baby just before delivery. This decision to slaughter a generation of children received a standing ovation from the leftwing members of the assembly.

We the Government, Love you to Death!

Paul: This *spirit of murder* was further amplified by the Governor of Virginia, Ralph Northam. In an interview he said, the child can be murdered after he or she is born. The Governor said that the doctor and medical staff will keep the baby comfortable and decide with the mom when they would finally murder or slaughter the child.

I have a hard time understanding why anyone in their right mind (especially those that call themselves Christians) can vote and associate with a leftist political group that murders babies and call it "abortion."

If the left doesn't "value life" in the most vulnerable state, "At child birth." Why would anyone believe when these same leftist people say, "We value you and care about you!"

Just like the enemy, Satan, every time he opens his mouth, it is a lie (fake news) and millions of people will always vote and support his agenda, even when confronted with the truth.

Some women with a crushed (-5) GC who murdered (aborted) their babies are in psychiatric hospitals. Some of the men who were part of this process also suffer from the guilt and pain from their actions.

Fake Abuse with Agenda - Justice Brett Kavanaugh

Deb: This is why it makes me angry when I see women who may have been abused at some point in their lives come out and accuse innocent men like in the case of Justice *Brett Kavanaugh.*

Paul: These false claims *(fake news)* made by leftwing women against him were debunked and exposed as *lies.* Women who were actually abused and are longing for some form of vicarious public justice and vindication, were hoping that Justice *Kavanaugh would be found* guilty as accused. These **false accusations** inflicted additional pain in the hearts of girls and women that were *"really"* physically and sexually abused.

This is why the **Me-too movement** *(women and girls who were sexually abused)* was so loud and vicious. The excruciating pain it stirred up in the lives of women with (-5) Glory Codes across America is now echoing around the world.

Abort Swing Vote

This inquisition was a strategic blow of leftwing political operatives to *"abort"* the nomination of Justice Brett Kavanaugh to the bench. They feared his conservative *"swing vote"* on the Supreme Court would reverse the **murder law** *(Roe v. Wade)* that validates the *slaughter* of children (babies). The father of murder, Satan, has his people in churches, government and all sectors of society.

Parents and Pastors Commit Suicide

Deb: I was reading about another pastor who committed suicide. The pastor from Inland Hills Church in Chino, California died by suicide leaving his wife without a husband, his children without a dad and the church members without a pastor. The impact of the "FFS" is felt daily in the lives of everyone. My prayers go out to all the families that are impacted by yet another tragedy.

Paul: Many pastors are under pressure from their role and demands of the church. Compounded with their already impacted Glory Codes, some pastors struggle with thoughts of suicide. Every 6 minutes a pastor vacates a church in America.

One pastor I was ministering to had a problem with his head elder on his board. I asked him about his dad. He mentioned, since he was young boy, his dad would often abuse him and his mom. I told the pastor that the *personality of his lead elder* was a reminder of the character of his dad. When this elder challenged and questioned his actions, it caused him to shrink back in his preaching and pastoral authority in the church. After this revelation, this pastor's life and preaching ministry dramatically changed.

Rejected Spiritual Fathers

As natural fathers were designed to influence their families, Apostles were ordained to be spiritual fathers to pastors and their church family. Their role and function, as *servant leaders,* was rejected by pastors and churches. This rejection was a result of *spiritual abuse and control by so-called* false apostles.

These false apostles positioned themselves to manipulate and control pastors. This derailed their relationship with the office and function of the Apostle resulting in spiritual fatherlessness. This correlated to a greater number of fatherless homes.

Pastors don't realize, there is always a *"fake"* to everything that is *"real."* In fear of being influenced and controlled, pastors rejected the entire role and function of the Apostle in their lives. The same symptoms that fatherless youth manifest, also is present in fatherless pastors.

- Fatherless youth drop-out of school **the same way** Fatherless pastors drop-out of church.

- Fatherless youth commit suicide **the same way** Fatherless pastors commit suicide.

- Fatherless youth post their pain on social media **the same way** Fatherless pastors do in their sermons and social media.

Today, some pastors don't understand the true role and function of Apostles. This is one of the key reasons why pastors find it difficult to minister to men in their church. This role is not a priority to pastors. They cannot give what they don't have...

Deb: Paul, I didn't know about this. This would explain why over 1,700 pastors leave the church every month. Without spiritual dads, *(Apostles)* who will stand with them to walk through the maze of ministry? Can you elaborate more on this subject?

Paul: Deb, I would love to elaborate on this topic, but it would take more time to lay the foundation to bring many people up to speed. I will do that another time.

I will leave you with this one key principle to summarize the role and function of the Apostle. The Heavenly Father sent one *Chief Apostle (Chief Servant Leader)* to reach one World. This Apostle was His Son, Jesus. Authentic apostles carry the heart and DNA of The Heavenly Father. They reflect His Character and love for His Church. Therefore, Apostles are fathers *(servant leaders)* in the church.

Deb: Thanks for the extra clarification. We need more *real Apostles* to mentor today's fatherless pastors. *"No Pastor without a dad!"*

A Father's Love

Paul: Deb, you are right. Real dads love and serve their families. Real apostles love and serve pastors and churches.

David, a young man I was mentoring, witnessed his Dad putting a gun to his head and killed himself when he was 5 years old. The impact of this horrific act left David with a (-6) Glory Code. The capstone seal of love in a child's life comes from the father. So, when David witnesses his dad killing himself, it marred his GC receptor and his *ability to reframe a positive influence in his heart (CPU)*. David struggled with major drug addictions, broken relationships, divorce, re-marriage and multiple failed jobs and businesses ventures.

To renew the GC receptors and positively impact the heart, it takes a mighty impartation from The Heavenly Father. That is why as dads, we need to protect and provide a healthy image that will positively impact our children. I pray for families who have lost dads, husbands, moms, pastors and priests to suicide.

Leaders believe that by becoming a pastor or priest makes them exempt from the impact of a crushed GC. Being in the ministry *creates a mask* for them to hide behind without dealing with the *real root cause.* Working with pastors and leaders like David, there are seasons in their lives when their GC receptors are triggered. In these low moments, usually when there is a major disappointment in their lives, they may revert to former unhealthy behaviors. David is now walking in a renewed relationship with his Heavenly Dad.

Bill Cosby - Americas' Dad - The impact on Fatherhood

Deb: The impact of the FFS on dads and moms makes it difficult for children to have healthy role models. When I first received the news that Bill Cosby was sentenced to jail for his sexual abuse of women, I couldn't, or should I say, I didn't want to believe it. He was my *"TV dad."* I vicariously inserted myself into his *"TV family."* I can only imagine the far-reaching impact this sad incident has on the men, dads, fatherless children and women in our nation. My prayers and thoughts are with the women who were abused and the individuals whose "TV dad" was the only "dad" they knew. This is just a vivid reminder that none of us are exempt from the impact of the FFS.

"A TV dad is better than no dad?"

Paul: Deb, I was sad, also, when I heard the news. For millions of boys and girls like you, *"A TV dad was better than no dad."* Children that looked to him as a *"dad figure"* were also crushed by this news. Suicide is up 50% among men. Bill Cosby provided a healthy, balanced image of what a *"good dad"* was supposed to be. The fragile emotions of dads today, overwhelmed by the conflicting pressure of society, landed a huge blow to their hearts. I pray for Bill and all those that were impacted by his actions.

Deb: We need to bring hope and healing to this generation of wounded children and families.

Paul R. Benjamin, Sr.

Chapter 20

Gangs: The new Replacement Family

Paul: Justin, a young man growing up in a home without his dad, turned to various gangs for acceptance and approval. After many years of abusing drugs, gunfights and participating in all kinds of illicit activities, he longed for a real sense of family. He began a long journey across America in search of his dad.

His search led him to Central Florida. Where he found himself homeless and living in a local men's shelter in Sanford. He learned about our ministry from a local church. I received a call from the shelter to see if we would take him in. I asked to meet with Justin to see if he was, ready and willing, to commit to the plan and process needed to go from *values to victory*.

Justin arrived as scheduled. As I opened the door of the men's home, this 6-foot 4-inch dark blond man filled the doorway. He had a huge smile on his face, as if to say *"Here I am!"* He said *"Hi, Pastor Benjamin. I am Justin!"* My heart was touched, like a father who lost a son, that finally returned home. Almost with tears in my eyes, I said, *"Welcome home son!"* It was almost the same emotion I felt when a *gray-haired 65-year-old* black man came up to me after I spoke at a church about *the value of fathers* and their impact on the world. He said *"Pastor Benjamin, would you mentor me? I never had a Dad!"* The cry to be loved and accepted by a father goes deep in healing GC. From that moment on, Justin became part of the ministry home.

Deb: This one touched my heart. This 65-year old man could have been my dad. How did it end with Justin?

Paul: Deb, I was touched also when this older gentleman shared the cry of his heart. We talk often about fatherless *"youth."* This invokes a certain level of compassion, but we rarely consider, the fatherless youth of yesterday who are now our *gray-haired seniors of today*. They, too, struggle with the unmet need of knowing the seal of love from a dad.

Justin graduated from our ministry home one year later. He met a wonderful woman and I performed their wedding ceremony under the canopy of the Florida beach. The Lord blessed them with two sons. He also found his dad and was reunited with him. Just like the 65-year old man, his dad didn't have a good dad. I ministered to him for a season. Deb, we have many *"elderly people"* that are still fatherless. We can spiritually adopt them into our families.

Deb: That was heartwarming to know that Justin was reunited with his dad. I never thought of the elderly as fatherless before. This now adds another nugget to my game plan. The beach wedding sounded like fun. Maybe Joel and I can get together with you and Dawn for a beach day?

Paul: Dawn's eyes just lit-up when you mentioned "beach day." I guess that is yes! You ladies can work on your tan while Joel and I chill under the umbrella. Let's schedule that for next weekend.

Deb: This sounds great! I am looking forward to it. Dawn and I will work out the details. Now, let's return to my assignment. I have been sending John updates on my progress. He is now learning as much as I am.

Former Drug Dealer, now A Positive Mentor

Paul: I am glad you are sending John updates. After-all, he is paying for you to investigate this project.

I was in my office when a team member called me, *"There is a man named George in the conference room waiting to speak with you."* He was a former drug dealer in the city. Now, he wanted to make a positive difference in the lives of young men and women. I shared the good news about being reconciled with The Heavenly Father.

After I led him in a prayer of repentance, he was back in a relationship with The Heavenly Father through His Son Jesus. Knowing the importance of acceptance and involvement, I didn't waste time. The next day I invited George to assist in the summer youth mentoring program. I introduced him to Mr. Ward, a highly skilled leader, who was facilitating the Bible study sessions for the summer. I knew that working alongside Mr. Ward would build a dual mentoring relationship.

George began to make an immediate impact in the lives of young men. They looked up to him. Many of them knew of his former reputation in the city; and the weight and leverage he still had in the region. If any of the young men were out of line, George only had to make eye contact with them and the situation dissipated. Today he is working on writing a book about his life and how it's never too late to make a positive impact.

Deb: What a wonderful turnaround. It's great to see what God can do with a yielded person. We need to see more lives influenced like this.

Power Lunch Challenge

Paul: It's awesome to see when The Heavenly Father through His goodness draws someone to Himself. I would like to issue a "Power Lunch Challenge" to your readers. This is the Challenge:

- Pray for the Lord to place someone on your heart that doesn't know Him

- To avoid impropriety, it must be someone of the same gender *(I don't encourage married men to have lunch meetings with women alone. That's why Dawn is with me in this interview)*. This principle can help save many marriages.

- Invite that person to lunch, cultivate a friendship of trust *(Be truly interested in them)*

- Pay for their Lunch. This will be your seed gift to The Lord.

- At the right time, share your testimony and how you came to know The Lord.

- Ask if there is anything they may need you to pray for. When the timing is right, ask them if they would like to have a personal relationship with your Heavenly Father through His Son Jesus?

- Lead them in a prayer of reconciliation with The Father. Invite them to attend and fellowship with you and other sons and daughters of The Father.

Deb, I would like for you to let the readers know that they can share their Power Lunch Stories by typing *"Power Lunch"* in our *"contact us"* tab on our website: *LifeCentersGlobal.com*

Deb: Paul, this is a great idea. I will also add a link to our website. I didn't know that only 3% of Christians actually share their faith and only 4% of them read and study their Bible. I now understand why it is so easy for the Enemy to deceive them. We need a wake-up call!

Isis, Rejection, Hate

Paul: Thanks, Deb. The Heavenly Father said, *"They that know Me, will do great exploits"* by impacting lives for His Glory. This is what we are doing here today. Isis, and radical Islamic groups like them, are living with crushed Glory Codes. These groups stem from the seed of Abraham. His son, Ishmael, was rejected from being the *"promised seed."* In essence, he became a *fatherless* son. Isaac was Abraham's *"son of promise"* from his covenant wife, Sarah, and through his seed came the Jewish people. The Heavenly Father is a Father of Covenant.

Ishmael's rejection crushed his GC level to (-6) teetering close to (-7). This resulted in the same pain, anger and resentment felt by Cain when he murdered his brother, Abel. This pain and anger was passed on through the generations. Today, thousands of years later, we see the ramifications of this rejection.

In the Isis Islamic culture, when a boy is born, they are trained to hate their Jewish brothers. Many receive their acceptance and approval from their dads based on who they can kill or what damage they inflict upon Jews (Israel) or America. Their crushed and disfigured GC is only sparked and driven by hate and revenge. The only power that can heal this hardened heart is the Love of The Heavenly Father working through his sons and daughters. The greatest revival today is among this tribe of people. Let's pray for them to embrace the God of Abraham, Isaac and Jacob as their Lord and Father.

Deb: Now I understand their pain and hate. I will pray for them and for the families that have been victims of their brutality.

Dads are Protectors

Paul: This just validates the power and influence of the father's acceptance and Glory seal.

As a ***protector***, dads protect their wives, daughters, and sons. NFL player, Tony Becker, jumped into action to defend his daughter's virtue. He caught and beat-up a male ***predator*** that was peeping at his daughter. This sent a clear message to his daughter. *(My dad is honoring me as a woman and defending me as his daughter.)* My dad *"has my back!"*

Deb: We need more dads like Mr. Becker that would be *protectors, not predators.*

I am an Atheist. Leave me alone…

Paul: We were hosting a community outreach event on the University of Central Florida (UCF) campus. I couldn't avoid noticing a tall young man, about 6' 3." He seemed agitated and was irritably shaking a branch on the bald cypress tree. This was about 200 yards from the event stage where one of the pastors was speaking. As I walked up to engage him in a conversation, he took his hand down and looked in my direction. I introduced myself and asked *"What's your name?"* He quickly responded in a slightly elevated tone, *"My name is Joe. I am an Atheist. Please leave me alone. You guys come on our campus preaching about your Jesus. I don't believe in God. I am an Atheist!"*

Atheists or Crushed Glory Code?

Knowing there is no person who is an *"atheist,"* only people with a crushed GC and a marred image of the Fatherhood of God, I asked him, *"Joe, tell me about your relationship with your dad?"* Joe's face immediately became flushed. After a brief pause to regain his composure, he said, *"Well, when I was six years old my dad, who always abused me and my mom, finally left our home. We haven't seen him since then. I hate him!"*

Joe paused waiting for my response. I said, *"Joe, what is your dad's name?"* He said, *"Jim!"* I told him, *"Did you know that your dad was also abused by your grandfather when he was a 6- year old boy?"* Joe's countenance changed. He said, *"Yes! He was. How did you know that?"* I said, *"Joe, imagine your dad as a boy just like you. He was looking for the love and acceptance of his dad just like you were. Your dad couldn't give you what he didn't receive himself."*

Before I could finish, Joe began to tear-up. He asked, *"What should I do now?"* I said, *"Joe, you need to forgive your dad for what he did to you and your mom and get to know your Heavenly Dad through a personal relationship with His Son Jesus."* By now Joe was sobbing. I placed my hand on his shoulder and prayed for him and led him in a prayer of repentance. He was now reconciled with His Heavenly Dad. After this encounter, Joe was a different man. I connected him with a local church near his home in east Orlando.

Deb: I interact with some people in the press corps who claim to be atheists. My perception was they were just being intellectually dishonest and *masking the real pain of their heart*. I am so glad that you were able to pierce the veil of Joe's *atheist-shield* that he used for years to guard his heart against further pain to his already crushed Glory Code.

Drug abuse, The Opioid Crisis and Alcoholism

Paul: For over a decade, Joe masked, protected and shielded his heart by using the *coping strategy* called *Atheism (The Atheist-Shield)*. Other people use various coping mechanisms as a way to *deal with, and mitigate, their crushed GC.*

Deb: I know we are almost out of time, but could you briefly address some of the *other symptoms* we spend billions of dollars on annually like:

- The Opioid Crisis, Meth, Alcoholism and all drug addictions.

- Eating Disorders, Anorexia and Bulimia.

Paul: All the money in the world cannot solve the Glory Code Crisis. The only panacea *(global solution)* is for everyone to be *reconciled to The Heavenly Father.* This will result in the ultimate healing to their Glory Code.

First, we must address *the deception in America.* Drug abuse, the opioid crisis, and alcoholism *are not diseases.* They are *choices.* In America, what we cannot solve (fix) by *regulations,* we *rationalize* and *find ways to say it is healthy and okay.* Then we *legalize* it so we can tax it and regulate the industry. In return, many leftist operatives become very wealthy.

Disease or Deterioration of the GC

Growing up in a home with her single mom, 14-year-old Julie turned to drugs to medicate the pain in her heart. Every drug she tried could not fill the void of her (-5) GC. She tried losing weight to please her mother's boyfriend. He had sexually abused her and told her that she needed to lose more weight in order for him to like her.

Julie began to spiral out of control. Her teacher noticed she began to dress very provocatively in school. With further probing, and help from the school counselor, they found out about her abuse at home.

Child Protective Services got involved. Julie's problem was not a *Disease,* but rather the *Deterioration* of her "GC." Millions of children, like Julie, who are being raised without a balanced two-parent family (mom and dad) will always have a greater crushed "GC."

The Big Lie. *"Sticks and stones may break my bones, but words will never hurt me."* Many women, when they were girls, were told that they were either too fat or too skinny by their dad, mom or another significant authority figure. Many believed the lie they had been told. This shaped their emotional identity. Even though some of these individuals who caused them pain, are dead, today, many of these women are still trying to live up to those expectations, hoping to gain their approval.

The power of spoken words and the desire for approval goes deep within a crushed GC. We, as humans, are spiritual beings. Words *can give life or cause death.* If believed and received, it begins to mold and reshape the Glory Code.

Just like you are what you eat, your spirit is shaped by the words spoken to you. Once believed they become toxic to your Glory Code. When you realize the damage, these words do to you, it is time for a spiritual cleanse, much like a colon cleanse. You need to replace the words spoken over you with the words *The Heavenly Father says about you, His Words.* By coming into a renewed relationship with Him and embracing His thoughts and plans for your life, the renewal healing process will begin.

Deb: I know that every issue in our nation is a result of the ***FFS.*** My prayer is for people to wake up to this truth. Now that I know this information, I will cover the news stories from a new perspective.

Fear, Panic, Pause and Control
Chinese Coronavirus from Communist China (Covid -19)

This news alert just came in while we were talking! The Communist, Chinese Government suppressed and hid the *outbreak* of the Chinese Coronavirus (Covid-19) from the USA and most of the world. Now, cases of this virus are in America, Israel, Italy and other countries around the world.

Paul: All *life is precious. From the womb to the tomb.* Deb and Dawn, let's pause and pray for the families impacted in China, America, Israel and around the world. The Heavenly Father can turn this pandemic around to fulfill His Divine purpose.

Leftwing Media Exploits the Pandemic

Deb: Paul, I sense there is more to this pandemic than we are hearing in the news. Can you take a few minutes to share your perspective?

Paul: I know the Left-wing political operatives and media will use this tragedy to attack President Trump. Their agenda would be to:

1. Blame him for the virus coming to America

2. Cause Panic and stir-up Fear to *Drive-up Media Ratings and to* report negative and inflated statistics to manipulate and control people.

3. Destroy the *Trump Economy* and stock market to harm the President's chances of re-election.

4. Try to manipulate people that support the righteous cause of President Trump to turn against him.

5. Pillage the American tax-payers to further fund the murder of babies (abortion) under the pretense of emergency relief stimulus funding to help families and cities. Millions will be earmarked for leftwing special interest groups. In return, a huge part of this money will be given back to leftist individuals and causes.

6. Just like what happened after the "9-11" terrorist attack in America. This pandemic would be used to eradicate more personal freedoms. Leftist communist/socialist government leaders will inflict strong manipulating laws, controls, and regulations to subjugate people under their thumb. They will even use the fear strategy of the *"mask"* to make people think it protects them and others.

7. They will introduce control and tracking legislation to Trace and Track people that are not part of the leftist inner-circle like HR6666 being produced by the Leftwing sector of the House of Representatives in preparation for Season 5. In collaboration with China all they need to do to corral and control people is to mention the word "COVID 19." This will allow them to spark the same fear and frenzy to activate the *(intrinsic covert laws that were put in place)* to implement phase II.

8. This is only the *tipping point*. I will not share all the other plans that are being put in place as we speak.

Deb: We were just talking about some of the things that would happen before *Season Five of The Heavenly Father.* This sounds like we are in the process and *preparations for this Season.*

Paul: Deb, you are right! But, in the midst of this, The Heavenly Father is using this as a Selah Moment to pause, reset, refresh and to wake-up the Church. This will break down walls and build authentic relationships. The Church will come to realize that "Their Building is Not the Church, but, People, "the called-out ones." This will activate others to show true love for each other. People in the world and the church who are very fearful will be given a chance to know The Loving, Heavenly Father is the source of Real Peace.

Another "Spark Event" to Fundamentally Transform America

Just to give you an example of how the leftwing media *(fake news)* is out to destroy President Trump. There has been more negative inflammatory news, *false projections, falsified causes of deaths* reported in *one day* during President Trump's mitigation of the Chinese Coronavirus pandemic than the *entire year* during the 2009-2010 swine flu (H1N1) season while President Obama was in office.

This flu infected over **60** million people in America. Over **300** thousand people were hospitalized in the USA. Over one *(1) billion people* were infected worldwide. Over **500** thousand people died from this flu. There was no panic or fear during the sparse fake news reporting during that time. This mass hysteria and its national and global ramifications are in preparation *(dress rehearsal) for Season 5 of the Father's appointed times.* Millions of hearts will be turned to The Heavenly Father during this pandemic.

Deb: We can clearly see the agenda of the Enemy at work. These numbers are staggering and I don't even remember hearing anything about it. I will share this with Joel this evening. We need to start getting our house in order.

World impact from the Chinese Coronavirus
VS
100% World impact from the FFS

Paul: Many people will be more receptive during this season. We need to be ready. *The greatest pandemic* in the world is not *the 3% impact of the Chinese Coronavirus,* but the *100% impact from the **Father Fracture Syndrome.*** If we seek and pursue the "vaccine/*solution"* to mitigate the impact from the FFS the same way we are pursuing "vaccine/*solution"* for *the Chinese Coronavirus, we will begin to see a turn around. All the symptoms that we spend trillions of dollars to address the fall-out from the "FFS." It is like putting a Band-Aid on a deep wound.*

Preparation for Global Shift

Leftwing leaders and the fake news media, during the *mitigation* process will *mask* and *manipulate* this pandemic for *marketing* and *monetary motives.* **Follow the *money* and you will know the *motive.*** *More than half of the people who will be reported dead as a result from this pandemic will be fraudulently labelled. Certain people will be planted among the vulnerable population to increase the number of deaths. Thus, increasing the statistical numbers for funding leading to increased fear and control. This also will increase the "death tax" revenue for the government.*

People with (-5) crushed Glory Codes will *easily be conditioned.* Fatherless families in the urban cities will be greatly impacted and controlled because they are in the "system." They will listen to, and believe, the false information propagated by the leftist operatives. Most of them have been offended or abused by people in the faith community. They will become spies for the *communist/socialist leaders in various cities* who are laying the foundation and tracking systems in preparation for Season five of The Heavenly Father. These same operatives will increase the persecution of churches. This will help to unify the real remnant church for the end time harvest. Persecution will help purify the purpose of the church.

Dads need to know how to discern *(recognize)* fake-new from the real truth. They need to consider the source of where they are receiving their news. They should always prepare their children for Season Five and how to live in these dangerous days. Israel will be the time piece in this process. We will pray for the peace of Jerusalem.

Deb: Paul, I received news that some pastors have already been thrown into jail. Free speech has been crushed and monitored by these leftist operatives.

Paul: This will increase the number of people who are dependent on the "system." They in turn will be more pliable and many will become agents for their agenda.

Panic and Perspective

To expose and reveal how *amplified* the leftwing media and operatives have artificially *magnified this pandemic* let's take a brief look of how many people die every year *without any, or very little media coverage.* This is a *short list* of how many people die **every year** in America:

- Babies murdered by Abortion -1.3 million

- People that die in Car Accidents - 36,000

- Deaths from Cancer - 500,000

- Deaths by Suicide – 48,000 (132 per/day)

- Drug overdose deaths – 70,000

- Domestic Violence – 2,000

- Heart disease deaths – 600,000

- Cigarette Smoking – 480,000

Do you "really" believe that leftwing leaders that promote and pay for the murder and slaughter of children (Babies) **really care** about your life and the life of anyone else? Do you really believe that locking-down the country or a city is about saving even **"one"** life? Think again…

Deb: These numbers are staggering. I wasn't aware that so many Americans die from so many various categories and this is only the short list! Paul, do you believe everyone in this leftist agenda are beyond the redemption of The Heavenly Father?

Paul: Deb, as you are now well aware of the impact of the "FFS" many of these people were negatively impacted and their Glory Codes crushed. As Mephibosheth, who was "dropped" and his Glory Code crushed. He was invited to, *"live in King David's Palace and receive the King's love and goodness to heal and alleviate his crushed Glory Code.* Likewise, we need to pray for The Heavenly Father to show them His goodness and love. When He does it will help mitigate and heal their crushed Glory Codes and draw them to Himself to know His heart of compassion for them. Those who are still pliable, will be open as we pray for them. *Remember,* The Father doesn't want anyone to perish, but for all to come to know Him.

Jesus came through the human lineage of King David who showed the healing goodness to *"Mephibosheth,"* who is *a symbolic representation* of people with Crushed Glory Codes. He, Jesus, wants to *symbolically place everyone with crushed Glory Codes, at His Father's Table to show His goodness, and heal their wounded hearts. Ultimately reconciling them with His Dad, The Loving, Heavenly Father, who said; "His goodness and kindness will lead others to be reconciled with Him."*

Paul R. Benjamin, Sr.

Hate Mail and Hate Media Against President Trump

Deb: I receive so many hate texts, emails and social media posts about our President and other leaders. Many of them are so-called Christians. How should I respond to them?

Paul: I receive many of the same types of hate mail. Many people have been deceived by their dads, moms, professors and pastors who were all influenced by Satan on the left. The mouth only speaks what is already in the heart. So, every time they open their mouth, you know what's in their heart.

I would usually quote this scripture that reflects the Heavenly Father's Heart. It is found in 1 Timothy 2:1-7, *"Therefore, I exhort first of all that supplications, prayers, intercessions and giving of thanks be made for all men, for kings (presidents) and all who are in authority, that we may lead a quiet and peaceable life in all godliness and reverence. For this is good and acceptable in the sight of God, our Savior, who desires **all men to be saved and to come to the knowledge of the truth.** For there is one God and one Mediator between God and men, the Man Christ Jesus, who gave Himself a ransom for all, to be testified in due time, for which I was appointed a preacher and an apostle—I am speaking the truth in Christ and not lying— a teacher of the Gentiles in faith and truth."*

Deb, this is *not a physical battle* against any specific leader. It is a spiritual battle with the *Enemy, Satan.* He is working through them as his operatives. Every leader and individual are either led and influenced by the Enemy, Satan, or The Heavenly Father. Regardless, *we are commanded to love them and pray for them.*

Deb: I get agitated when I hear what certain leftwing leaders and their fake-news media operatives say. Then I quickly remember, *"Oh! I need to pray for them."* My prayer is that one day they will come to truly know my Loving Heavenly Father.

Paul: I have to do the same thing daily. Then I remember, they were influenced and impacted by the FFS. Their lifestyles reflect how they were raised or abused by someone in their life. The impact to their crushed Glory Code goes deep. Many of them go to the extreme to:

- Create *fake science* to justify their position and propaganda.
- Manipulate information facts to control and influence people.
- Remember the one who controls the information, controls the narrative.

- Block and destroy true information from media and conservative leaders.

- Silence pastors and churches. Yes, even place them in jail.

- Promote and publish fake information from fake preachers, priests and leaders.

- Shutdown social media and websites from leaders that speak truth.

What is Truth?

"What is Truth?" The answer to the most inquired question in the world was never furnished. The question was asked incorrectly! It should have asked, *"Who is Truth?" The answer is simple. Jesus said, "He is the way, The Truth, and the Life".* When we speak the truth, we honor The Heavenly Father. He is the source of truth. When we speak lies, we honor the father of lies *(fake news)* the devil. *Who would you like to honor?*

Deb: We need a move of God to turn our nation and world around. Fear is a great motivator, Paul, you mentioned that the reporter in Sanford from a major network said that the media strategy is to stir up fear, anxiety, and anger in the hearts and lives of people, all the while manipulating the truth to accomplish their latent agenda. I know that in the last days, people's hearts will fail *(nose-dive)* because of fear, from all the epidemics that will occur in the world. And with that note, this seems a great place to end for today.

Paul R. Benjamin, Sr.

Chapter 21

Pain and Panic

Deb: Good to see you both again. Let's jump in and pick up where we left off. What can we do in the middle of this emotional pandemic and what should be the response of dads to their families?

A Fatherless Generation is Susceptible to Fear

Paul: As I mentioned before, the voice and presence of the father can either instill *(produce)* peace and comfort like The Heavenly Father on the Right or stir-up fear and panic like the father of lies and fake news on the left. Today, with so many youths and families being raised in fatherless homes, it is easy to control and manipulate them by using fake news.

The Heavenly Father has given His children *"**His Shalom**" (Peace, intrinsic wholeness, and confident assurance)*. Those who don't have a relationship with Him will walk in *"fear."* He is our peace, we should always look to Him, not to man for comfort, wisdom, and guidance.

The agenda of the leftwing media machine is being turned around used to accomplish some good. What was designed to destroy, is being turned around for a renewed destiny:

- Dads are now able to spend more time with their families.

- Dads are also now able to reset their priorities to what matters most, *"Family."* Now, dads can function in *their role at home:*

    o The first church is in the home. Dads, as the priest of their families, can now pray for and with their families. They can lead their families in worship to The Heavenly Father.

    o The first school is in the home. Dads and moms as teachers in their families, can now impart a ***Biblical world-view*** to their children on life and the events that are happening in the world. They can teach life skills and prepare their families to navigate *the maze of life.*

- Dads who walk in peace, can transmit it to their children and families. *The Heavenly Father of Peace* will soon crush the agenda of His enemy.

- Exposed what is in the hearts of people; *Faith or Fear - Panic or Peace?*

- This has caused many people to be reconciled with others, recognizing that they may not live through this *season of fear and panic.*

- Churches *(the called-out people of God)* were forced to leave their "Buildings" *(God dwells in people, not buildings)*.

- This crushed the *idol worship* of a *"church building"* and placed the focus on God and people.

- People who never had time for God, saying, *"they're too busy"* now, they are calling out to The Lord for guidance, peace, comfort, and healing. Millions will be reconciled with their Heavenly Father.

- Bible apps and online views of church services will multiply exponentially.

Deb: Paul, weren't you asking The Heavenly Father for a *"pause"* in your busy schedule so you would have time to give me this information needed to finish this assignment?

Paul: Deb, you are right! I didn't think that The Lord would cause the entire world to pause... Now, I have no excuse. My public events were canceled. All of a sudden, I can pause and communicate the information to you for this assignment.

President Calls for a National Day of Prayer

The degree of your authority gives weight to the influence of your words. To mitigate the global impact of the *Chinese Coronavirus,* President Donald Trump called for a *National Day of Prayer.*

The Heavenly Father told King Solomon, "If my People *(His sons and daughters, the Jews, and the Christians who were adopted into the Jewish family)* who are called my Name, would humble themselves, and pray and seek My face *(favor and renewed "GC")* and turn from their wicked ways, then I will hear from heaven and forgive their sin and *heal their land.*

Symbolically, this prayer to The Heavenly Father should be made *facing the East towards Israel,* the place where He placed His Name. The same eastern gate where His Son, Yeshua, entered and where we will eat at the Father's Table forever. This is why President Trump moved the American Embassy to Jerusalem and publicly acknowledged Jerusalem as the capital of Israel. God's favor *(His Face)* turned to bless America. His hands are at work through this pandemic and His renewal is at work in our nation and world.

Decree of Favor & Protection

Deb: I know the power of this proclamation cannot be undone. I just pulled the President's Proclamation off the website. This is a good reminder. The Heavenly Father loves us and is waiting to forgive and heal us and our nations.

Paul: As a dad, I pray this protection over my children, family, and friends. When the Jews were held captive as slaves in Egypt, this protection shielded them from all the plagues and diseases that came upon the people of Egypt. While the Jews dwelt in the *land of Goshen*, they were *safe from the impact of all the plagues.* The plagues and disease only impacted and killed Egyptians. When the Jews cried out to Their Heavenly Father, *The God of Abraham, Isaac, and Jacob,* He placed His *Shield of Protection (His Right Hand)* around them.

This *Decree and Proclamation* by President Trump has *symbolically placed a **Safe-Place**, a shield, like in the land of Goshen,* over America. He is asking all who are willing to come into agreement with his proclamation to enjoy the same protection.

He is *praying* to the same Heavenly Father, The *God of* our Jewish Patriarchs; *Abraham, Isaac and Jacob.* Just as Goshen was a safe place for the Jews, The Heavenly Father is **our safe place.** He wants no one to perish but is willing for all to come into His loving arms for safety and protection through His Son, Yeshua, Jesus.

In ***Season One (Passover),*** the Jews who lived in Goshen were protected from the plague (pandemic) of death when The Father passed over those who had applied the *blood of the "Lamb"* on their doors. Let's put our hope and trust in Yeshua and embrace the eternal safety in the loving arms of The Heavenly Father.

Deb: That's ironic! This Chinese Coronavirus and this Proclamation for Protection came just before the April 2020 annual remembrance of Season One, Passover. I pray that over one billion people, including millions in China, will put their hope and trust in Him and enter His **Spiritual Goshen,** so to speak, and receive Yeshua/Jesus, as their Lord and Savior.

Paul: Barukh HaShem! (Bless "The Name," The Eternal One, Bless The Heavenly Father). We are always asking "God Bless America." It's now time for "America to bless God." For, "blessed is the nation whose God is the Lord."

Proclamation on the National Day of Prayer for all Americans Affected by the Coronavirus Pandemic and for our National Response Efforts

President Trump: *"In our times of greatest need, Americans have always turned to prayer to help guide us through trials and periods of uncertainty. As we continue to face the unique challenges posed by the coronavirus pandemic, millions of Americans are unable to gather in their churches, temples, synagogues, mosque and other houses of worship. But in this time, we must not cease asking God for added wisdom, comfort and strength, and we must especially pray for those who have suffered harm or who have lost loved ones. I ask you to join me in a day of prayer for all people who have been affected by the coronavirus pandemic and to pray for God's healing hand to be placed on the people of our Nation.*

As your President, I ask you to pray for the health and well-being of your fellow Americans and to remember that no problem is too big for God to handle. We should all take to heart the holy words found in 1 Peter 5:7: "Casting all your care upon him, for he careth for you." Let us pray that all those affected by the virus will feel the presence of our Lord's protection and love during this time. With God's help, we will overcome this threat.

On Friday, I declared a national emergency and took other bold actions to help deploy the full power of the Federal Government to assist with efforts to combat the coronavirus pandemic. I now encourage all Americans to pray for those on the front lines of the response, especially our Nation's outstanding medical professionals and public health officials who are working tirelessly to protect all of us from the coronavirus and treat infected patients; all of our courageous first responders, National Guard, and dedicated individuals who are working to ensure the health and safety of our communities; and our Federal, State, and local leaders.

*We are confident that He will provide them with the wisdom they need to make difficult decisions and take decisive actions to protect Americans all across the country. As we come to our Father in prayer, we remember the words found in **Psalm 91**: "He is my refuge and my fortress: my God; in him will I trust."*

*As we unite in prayer, we are reminded that there is no burden too heavy for God to lift or for this country to bear with His help. **Luke 1:37** promises that "For with God nothing shall* *be impossible," and those words are just as true today as they have ever been. As one Nation under God, we are greater than the hardships we face, and through prayer and acts of compassion and love, we will rise to this challenge and emerge stronger and more united than ever before. May God bless each of you, and may God bless the United States of America.*

NOW, THEREFORE, I, DONALD J. TRUMP, President of the United States of America, do hereby proclaim March 15, 2020, as a National Day of Prayer for All Americans Affected by the Coronavirus Pandemic and for our National Response Efforts. I urge Americans of all faiths and religious traditions and backgrounds to offer prayers for all those affected, including people who have suffered harm or lost loved ones.

IN WITNESS WHEREOF, I have hereunto set my hand this fourteenth day of March, in the year of our Lord two thousand twenty, and of the Independence of the United States of America the two hundred and forty-fourth.

Signed: DONALD J. TRUMP"

No leftwing leader can ***"Tear-this one up."*** **Yes,** including Nancy Pelosi. The Power & Influence of God's Word will last forever…

Deb: Amen! You are right, Nancy Pelosi cannot touch this one. The Word of God will stand for all eternity. His Word will not return void or empty. It will accomplish its ordained assignment.

Public Ridicule of Mike Lindell of My Pillow, Inc.

Paul: Deb, you are right. Nancy Pelosi displayed national disrespect for the American people and President Trump, by tearing-up *The State of the Union Speech* in front of the world sending a clear message to this generation, *"It's okay to defy, disrespect and rebel against authority."* The agenda of Leftwing leaders like her will become more aggressive because we are in *preparation for Season 5.*

Mike Lindell, after sharing his compassion *(to help with the Chinese Coronavirus)* and Christian core values on TV, received national Leftwing media mockery for sharing his belief and Faith in Jesus The Christ *(Messiah)*. Jews and Christians in America, and around the world, will experience massive Leftwing media backlash. Mike Lindell can *Rest Easy*. God has his back.

In these dark and dangerous days, dads need to build and model confidence and a strong Biblical conviction, because things are about to become more confrontational in this season.

Deb: You had to get in a little pun, huh? I will *sleep* on that one…

Paul: You are keeping up with me, too. What have I created?

Principles determine your Politics and your Politics determine your Practice

Deb: You did say, *"You become like who you hang out with."* Well, guess who that person is? On a more serious note, you were getting ready to ***talk about*** the two topics that society told us ***not to talk about***, "***Politics and Religion.***" We were told never to discuss these subjects around the dinner table with family or friends. These are the topics that separate friends, alienate relationships at work, divide families, break-up marriages, even divide churches and a nation.

Paul: Deb, you are correct! It's funny, these are the two top topics that, on one hand, could unite us as one people and nation, or divide us to create riots, wars, conflicts and broken irreconcilable relationships on every level in our homes and society.

Deb: I guess you are about to tell me that these are the two key things The Heavenly Father is very much concerned about.

Paul: You are tracking with me. One of the roles of a dad is to *live and model a LifeStyle that reflects the Heart and Character of* The Heavenly Father. *Just as His Son, Jesus, did.* After knowing the Heart and Character of Jesus, dads should be able to explain *the Principles, Politics and Practice* of The Heavenly Father. I will briefly explain this lifestyle, that was mandated for all men and dads to teach to their children.

Person, Principles, Politics, & Practice that Govern People

In the entire world there are **only two Political Platforms**. The core values and **character** of a **Person determines** the **Principles** by which they **Practice Politics** (Communicating and imparting one's core principles to influence the practice of people).

The first Failed Coup Attempt

Your core Principles will determine your Practice and Political Platform. The real source of the *Father Fracture Syndrome* started before the foundation of the world. When Satan initiated the ***first failed Coup attempt*** to overthrow the governance of *The Loving Heavenly Father* and was banished to earth. As a result of his broken relationship with

The Heavenly Father he suffered from his own "FFS." This shattered his *Glory Code to a (-7) level*. This is why he became the *father (source) of murder, death, deception and destruction.*

He and his operatives, fallen angels, with the same GC level as their leader, Satan, initiated *another coup attempt* on earth with the deception of Eve, and ultimate rebellion of Adam in the first garden. His core character stems from lies, deception and death and will always manifest in his followers and operatives on the Left. That's why individuals who have reached a (-7) GC will result in either murder by suicide or the murder of others. *Now you know the rest of the story…*

Deb: Here I was thinking that the first coup attempt was when the leftwing politicians initiated a failed coup against President Trump. I guess they were only operating under the influence of their father who launched the first failed coup.

Origin of The Two Political Systems

Paul: Deb, you are very intuitive. Their *playbook* is from the father of the Left, Satan. His *playbook was first penned in heaven when he launched his leftwing Political System. His outward Practice of the coup manifested his inward core Principles.* These are his core *Principles* that govern his *Political Platform* on the Left:

- Deception, Distraction and *fake-news* used to deceive Eve.

- Lust, pillage and theft from others to accomplish a covert agenda.

- Pride is the strength and resolve to maintain the obstinate posture and practice.

- Destroying the character and courage in others before actually murdering them. Murder and slaughter children from womb, thus, removing the value for *"life"* at any age.

Deb: Paul I never heard, or even knew, that there were only two (2) Political systems in the world. This plainly explains and reveals the **Second Political Platform on the Left** headed up by the **father of the leftwing movement, Satan,** himself. His core Principles are diametrically opposed to that of The Heavenly Father's **Political Platform on the Right.** Paul, please briefly share some of the attributes of the operatives on the Left.

Paul: Deb, you, and millions of people, are not aware of the leftwing political agenda that was given birth from the foundation of the world. People, and operatives on the Left, are being led and influenced by the father of the "FFS," Satan. They will exhibit these core characteristics:

- The murder and slaughter of children by abortion.

- Promotion of lifestyles like LGBTQ+, *sexual relations outside of a monogamous marriage between an authentically born male and female.*

- Strife, Jealousy, Division and Envy among people and the nation. *(Using key events to bring division and unrest among people to advance the core agenda)*

- Hatred, Drunkenness, Drug Abuse and Murders *(murder of anyone that may stand in the way of their agenda)*

- Witchcraft *(Sorcery. The use of demonic forces to hinder the work of the righteous and to empower or enslave others on the Left)*

- Heresies, Fake News *(Manipulating, twisting of the truth to deceive, mislead and agitate others)*

- Idolatry *(Worshiping and exalting people or things higher or above God)*

- Uncleanness, Lewdness and any other vile things *(Every type of perverted relationship and lifestyles contrary to the core values of The Heavenly Father)* imagined and contrary to the core values of The Heavenly Father.

When their covert agenda fails, they will implement more and more controlling laws to implement conformity. The ***greatest Law*** on the Left is, ***"Lust."*** Yes, take from others using deception, distraction, destruction, lust, lies, theft and murder. This core character trait is strengthened in pride.

There is hope for anyone who is being misled or deceived by these core values on the Left. They can follow the example and process that everyone on the Right had to. Repent and be reconciled to The Loving, Heavenly Father. He is waiting to forgive you and welcome you into His Family, without condemnation.

Deb: This just explains the performance of the *leftist leaders* we see on TV. It's like reading a resume. This explains when leftwing leaders are in charge there will be more restrictive laws that penalize people, families, churches and wholesome businesses.

Deception, Disillusion and Destruction

Paul: You are right. People are easily deceived and distracted by their desire for financial gain at the expense of destiny. For example:

- We are charitable. *"We care for the poor"* when in fact, they enslave them, seducing them, with the promise of **Free money**, *Free housing, Free food, Free Medical* and resulting in control, disillusionment and despair. *The war on poverty is a great example.*

- *Many people who say they are on the Right,* fall prey to this deception. Just as Eve was deceived, others are tricked by the term, *"I am for the poor and those in need."* The end product is the destruction and pillage of individuals and families.

Deb: I never drew a parallel between our government system here in America before. Now this reveals why the party on the Left is so much like the father on the Left, the devil. The things they believe and do are in line with the principles and politics of Lucifer, the father of fake news.

Paul: Many dads were never taught these core principles of how the Right and Left Political Government systems function. In the world, they represent the only two governing fathers in the world; The enemy, Satan, the father of the Left and The Heavenly Father of the Right. We cannot serve both of them. We have to make a clear choice.

Deb: This explains why so many youths are swayed to the Left, and those on the Right are ostracized for their values taught by their dads and moms at home. You mentioned 75-80% of fatherless youth grew up in poverty. They became addicted and enslaved to the leftist welfare system and are more loyal and susceptible to leftwing deception.

I also remembered when you shared the 1/3 principle, that one-third of the people will never change, so we should quickly identify those who are ready and willing to be educated, equipped and empowered to make a positive impact.

Paul: Deb, you took some good notes. I would think you are a reporter. As I mentioned before, we are about to see the fulfillment of the Fifth Season of the Heavenly Father. This is why there is an escalation of aggression, crime, murder and the revealing of the true identity of people who were hiding under the cloak of the Right to deceive others with crushed Glory Codes.

The father on the Left, and his followers, know that their time is limited. They are playing all the cards in their deck. I will address some hot topics impacting our nation today and how they are addressed from the perspective of each father, and their political platform.

First, you need to understand *one key principle* in life. For everything *real and **authentic**,* the ***artificial and fake** counterpart, seeks to distract and destroy it.* Because of the "FFS," this is true in every aspect of life. Just for example:

- Some people may say they are authentic Christians but, when they are put to the test, their lifestyle proves to be artificial. Their core values didn't reflect the character of Christ.

- Some preachers may say they are authentic men or women of God, but their manner of life and practice reflect the artificial character of the enemy, the Devil.

- Just like a boy who tells a girl that he loves her. She thinks that he is authentic and yields her virtues to him. After they have had sex, she finds out that he was artificial. He only said what she needed to hear.

- We can see this principle in every aspect of life. The level of our disappointment is based on the degree of our expectation. You may think that everyone and everything is authentic, only to find out, it was a *counterfeit, pretending to be real.*

First Political Platform, The Heavenly Father on the Right

Each Government operates by the Core Character *(Platform)* of their Father *(source)*. The motive determines the core operating purpose and mission. Their Politics *(The Communication and Impartation of one's core Principles to influence the Practice of*

People) emanates from the heart and character of the father of the political faction. Unlike the father of the second political government system, Satan, whose motive of his heart is; deception, distraction, destruction, lust, lies, theft and murder, are all rooted in his core character and strengthened in pride. His character is seen in the lives of his operative on the Left.

But the Politics of The Heavenly Father on the Right comes from the core character of His heart:

- His government and politics operate from His core ***motive, Love***. Love is manifested in these Authentic core characteristics:

  o Love gives birth to *"life"* from the womb (saving children and babies)

  o Truth *(You can trust what His faithful goodness reveals and says)*

  o Joy and Peace *(Wholeness of the spirit, soul, body and mental health)*

  o Patience *(loving others through the tough times in their lives)*

  o Gentleness, Goodness and Faithfulness *(Confident assurance of the promised hope)*

  o Meekness *(Power under control, knowing that God is sovereign overall)*

  o Justice *(knowing that The Heavenly Father will give justice to everyone in due time)*

  o Temperance *(self-control, bringing all wrong thoughts in alignment with the core values of The Father)*

  o Righteousness *(the right way of living)*.

The Father on the Right knows, if everyone lived their lives by these core values of love and righteousness, *(which comes from Him)* they would not harm another person. Families and nations would live and love each other. The ***greatest Law*** on the Right is ***"Love."*** Yes, you also have to *love your enemy,* and ***love*** *you neighbor as you love yourself."*

Deb: Paul, I am embarrassed to admit, I, too, was one of the people that was deceived by the covert strategy of the Left. They used the plight of *poor, fatherless children* to *"so-call" champion the cause,* which is really to enslave and oppress this sector of people while creating a loyal class of people to their platform on the Left.

Paul: Deb, you are not alone. There are millions of good people who are being deceived by the covert agenda of the Left. It is like what I mentioned before, *rat poison is 98% good food,* it's the 2% poison that will kill you. The deceptive lie of the Enemy was only *2% "fake-news,"* but that small percentage launched their entire world in the FFS.

Today, many people, just like Eve, believe and fall for the fake news on the Left. They listen to propaganda media outlets where almost 98% of the news is fake news. They covertly *manipulate the truth to project their agenda spawned by their crushed GC stirring up division and dissension among their deceived audience, who are influenced by the same crushed Glory Code.*

Just like the news reporter who confided in me during the Trayvon Martin media coverage in Sanford FL, she mentioned, "Our viewership and advertising revenue increased by 86% when we reported the hype and controversy, inflaming the issues. This is our new strategy."

Deb, I hope, just like your eyes are now open to the authentic truth, others will have the eyes of their hearts opened to understand the agenda of the Enemy, as he works through people.

Deb: There is a huge contrast between the two political platforms. It's the difference of "Life" and "Death." After reading this, I can't believe anyone with a healthy GC would want to align with the leftwing agenda.

Paul, can you now address some of the *hot political topics* that are influencing our nation? I believe dads need to know how to guide and train their children on these issues impacting their generation.

Paul: You are correct. We need to take a stand, not only for this generation, but for future generations. Because of time, I will briefly address a few of these hot issues and the position of the Left and Right political platforms.

Chapter 22

Values Determine Your Victory

Paul: Values determine your victory. Political platforms are connected to your values. What is your Value System? Dads are supposed to set the values in their family:

- Dads, what legacy are you leaving your children? Do your values reflect the character of The Heavenly Father? If they do, you will elevate the GC of your children and family for generations.

- What you spend your money on reflects your values. Are you supporting causes that echo the values on the Right or causes on the left that destroy families? We own nothing! But, we are the managers of it.

- God, The Heavenly Father, owns everything. What you currently possess, He has entrusted to your management. One day, we all will have to give a management report to Him.

- We give our time to what we value. How are you investing your time? You become like the one whose values you believe and embrace.

- The values you are instilling in your children will follow them through life and impact society. The leaders, who are influencing our society today, reflect the *core values they received and embraced from their dads, moms, and mentors.*

The values modeled yesterday are being reflected in people's principles, politics and practices. "You are known by your words and actions."

Deb: This is a great reminder. My values can use some recalibration. I need to make sure all my values and beliefs are in alignment with The Heavenly Father. In my mind, I disagree with you about the man being the head of the woman, but in my heart, I know what the Bible says. This is one of my values I need to reconcile.

Paul: Deb, I can understand where you are coming from. After seeing how your dad treated your mom, his wife, this marked your first reference of the role of husbands and men in general. Even though Joel is an awesome husband, your GC is slowly being renewed by your new healthy relationship.

Husbands are to reflect the image and character of Christ to their wives. To the degree we put our hope and trust in Christ to mitigate, and reconcile, this conflict in our heart, will determine how much time it will take to renew our GC. Deb, I have seen a huge change in your countenance since we started this interview two weeks ago.

Deb: Thank you for saying this, Paul. I am glad you are seeing a change. I know I feel different. My first reference of a dad, and husband, was marred. As I hang out with you guys, my heart feels lighter. A new healthier image of marriage and the role of a dad and husband is being reinforced. Thanks for being patient with me. I love you both!

Dawn arose from the table and walked over to Deb, and gave her *a huge hug* and said. *"Deb, I can relate with you. Paul and I are here for you. We love you too…"*

Deb: Thanks Dawn. It's good to know I am not alone in my journey. I would love for us to have some girl time. Let's arrange to do coffee sometime.

Dawn: I would love to. Text me some dates and times when you are available.

Paul: It would be great if you ladies could connect outside of these interview sessions. But, there is only one disclaimer, when we hangout as couples, you and Joel will have to endure my puns. By the way, did you and Dawn schedule our couples beach weekend?

Deb: As a matter of fact, we decided the weather looks great this weekend. It should be 80 degrees, perfect beach weather. Joel and I are looking forward to it. We, girls, have already worked out the details. We will be going to New Smyrna Beach, followed by dinner afterwards.

Paul: Wow! I knew when it comes to beach days, Dawn would make it happen quickly. For quick beach getaway, our beach supplies are always kept in my car.

Deb: Now, Dawn and I are connected. We will be having more of these beach excursions. Paul, I am anxious to hear your perspective on these political hot topics. Let's get started.

Political Hot Topics

Hot Topic 1

The Murder and Slaughter of innocent children (babies) by Abortion

The Platform on the Right is Truth

Paul: The core value of the government on the Right is **"Life."** The very source and giver of all "life" is God, The Heavenly Father. He knows every child before they are conceived. He requires justice for the murder and slaughter of every child. Leftwing political operatives, fueled by the father of their agenda, *Satan, the father of murder,* used deception by changing the words *murder/slaughter* to *"Abortion, Pro-choice and Women's Health Issues."* They fund Planned Parenthood *with tax payer's money to murder and slaughter babies.*

Deb: You started out with a hot, hot, topic! What about those people who would argue about women who were raped and abused. They would ask, *"Why should you punish the victim by letting them carry the baby to term?"* Or in the case of having to choose between saving the mother or the baby in a life-saving surgery. You definitely came out of the gate hot! How would you respond to this?

Paul: Deb, these are all valid points and questions. Because of time, I won't be able to go too deep into each topic now. Just a reminder, there is no crushed "GC" that The Heavenly Father cannot renew and heal.

The Heavenly father can turn any tragedy of rape into triumph. The baby can be given up for adoption. He can turn this mess into a beautiful mosaic, if it is submitted to *His Healing Glory Source*. Yes, Yielded to His will, someone with a (-7) "GC" can receive a renewed (+6) Glory Code.

Saving a mother or Child

When we discuss ***saving a mother or a child in surgery***, that is a different situation. We are not talking about murder, but viability for survivorship in a medical procedure.

In this situation, if a child dies in the process of saving the mother's life, it is not murder. There is a difference between death and murder. When a child dies during a surgical procedure to save the mother, that is "death." But, when a girl or woman goes into an abortion (murder) clinic and makes a conscious choice to murder the child (baby), that is called "murder," the slaughter of a child.

Fatherless, young women and men are 500% more likely to "Approve" the murder of their children (babies). Already dealing with the pain from being abandoned or rejected by their fathers, these young women with a (-2) "GC" find it easy to reject and murder their child (baby). Abortion workers and clinics prey on single-parent, fatherless communities, enticing these young ladies to commit this gruesome act to their children.

Deb: Now I understand why so many women are adamant about murdering their babies. Many of them never felt wanted or loved by their own fathers. This makes it easy for them to say, *"Why should I care about my child, when my dad didn't care about me!"*

Paul: To alleviate the emotional pain, and the thought of murdering their child, these young ladies are trained to use emotional softening words. They may use words like, *"It's a blob of tissue," "This thing," "It," or "The fetus or embryo."*

Deb: This explains why hard working *"Tax-paying families"* are forced investors to pay for the mental health issues of these girls, women, and men after the murder of their children in these abortion clinics.

Paul: It is sad to know that America, a nation founded on the core principles of God's Word has strayed so far to the Left. We sanction the murder and slaughter of over 1.3 million children (babies) every year.

It's no wonder, there is so much bloodshed on our streets. We are saying to this generation and the world, *"We do not value life at conception, which means, we do not value Life itself or The Father of Life, God, The Heavenly Father."* In our society impacted by the FFS, many dads who are being influenced by the father on the left, have no reverence, respect or fear of God.

The platform of the Left is built on Lies (Fake News-Deception)

The Left: The very foundation of the Left is murder and death. The father of the Left came to steal, kill *(murder)* and destroy everything that is from the Right. The core character of the left is built on the foundation of Lies, Fake News from the very beginning. After all, he is called, the father of lies (fake news).

The platform of the left encourages, celebrates and promotes the murder and slaughter of children (babies), all under the deceptive cover called, *"Pro-choice, women's reproductive health, and a woman's right to choose."*

Standing Ovation for the Murder of Children

Leftist, Democrat Governor, Andrew Cuomo, of the State of New York, in 2019 celebrated with his Senate as they erupted into a thunderous standing ovation for the passage of their new law to murder and execute children (babies) up to the time of birth. This was their landmark bill of death, in keeping with the agenda of their father of murder and death Satan.

Deb: This was one of the most disturbing events I have ever witnessed in my life. Seeing these Senators applauding the slaughter of children made me appalled. Just to imagine, the *blood of those babies is on the hands of all those who voted for these same leaders.*

Murder after Birth

In his 2019 *State of the Union Address* to America, President Donald Trump, referenced the comments and the supportive posture of Virginia's Governor, Ralph Northam for post birth murder and slaughter of children (babies). Under the leadership of Governor Ralph Northam, this new law would allow the parents to murder and slaughter their child after the baby is born. He said all you have to do is to make the child comfortable until they discuss options with the doctor before deciding to murder the child. These are the same people that would send you to jail, if you crush a turtle's egg.

Deb: I was shocked when I heard what the Governor of Virginia said. I wonder at what age can a woman decide to murder/slaughter her child or children. Maybe she can decide to murder her child in kindergarten, or maybe at elementary age or even in high school? When will it end? Paul, I cannot believe the level of deception I had. I even went so far as to associate myself with the left. I guess, I did it because my father was a preacher and a big hypocrite. He always endorsed the left, saying *"They are for the people. They care for the poor. Boy, was he wrong!"*

Paul: Deb, you and many other Christians, have fallen for this deception. They forget that Jesus said, *"The poor we will always have with us."* The Heavenly Father said the best way to help the poor was to give them dignity, *value and self-worth.* We bring glory and honor to the poor by providing them with an opportunity to work. Work is worship, through which we bring glory and honor to God. He created us to work and bring Him Glory. He is still working today and so should we.

The quickest way to enslave people, is to make them dependent on you

This is what the father on the left has done to a generation of people. By using the welfare system to entice them and enslave them, He has made them loyal and dependent to the evil leftwing agenda. The Jews were lured into Egypt for food and welfare. Then, they were enslaved for 430 years before The Heavenly Father freed them from their physical slavery. While thousands remained mentally and spiritually enslaved *because of their unbelief and rebellion.*

Are you still a Slave? (To the god of the left?)

The same is true today. Millions are physically "free," but mentally and spiritually they are still slaves to the father of fake news and the leftwing agenda which tells them, *"Stay angry. Never forgive the past hurt, pain or injustice of racism, abuse or abandonment. Don't embrace the Love of The Heavenly Father. Join others who feel the same way. Let your venom overflow into all aspects of your family, your place of worship, your workplace and society."*

Deb: This further validates the role of dads to educate and guide their children and families. The decisions we make today impact future generations. A child *left* to their own evil devices will go astray.

I feel sorry for anyone who associates with and endorses the leftwing agenda. They have become a party *(partaker/partner) with their murderous platform.* They will have to answer to The Heavenly Father of the Right. Every judge, every public official who signed or supported the document (law) to murder children, the blood of these millions of children will be on their hands.

Paul: Deb, this is sad, but true. The hearts of so many people are hardened to this truth because of their crushed (-4) GC.

Fathers, who are influenced and yielded to the father on the left, will steer and influence their children and families to support the destructive leftwing *Agenda, Core Values and Beliefs.*

Dads, who know and have an authentic relationship with The Heavenly Father on the Right, will lead and positively influence their children. Together they will function and be a blessing to society. Now, imagine this generation of fatherless young men and women trying to navigate through the maze of society, without the positive influence of a dad.

Who will lead and influence them? Will it be a leftwing father-figure, who recruits them to his leftist agenda, or a father on the right, who will positively influence them to victory? Time is of the essence. Who will get there first to mentor them? Would it be a father on the left, or right?

Deb: Paul, you can count on my husband, Joel, and my boss, John. They are all in, on the right. They will lead and positively influence this generation to follow the path of The Heavenly Father.

Hot topic # 2

Promotion of the LGBTQ+ Lifestyle

Deb: This is a hot topic in our nation. When former President Obama, the *champion of the* **left**, endorsed and validated the *LGBTQ+* community, he fundamentally transformed America.

By endorsement of using the bathroom of choice, there has been an explosion of radical acts and events in our nation. The legalization of same-sex marriage by the **left** has been another affront to The Heavenly Father, the author of marriage between one man *(born male)* and one Woman *(Born female)*.

I remember a 12-year-old girl who was abused and molested in a girl's bathroom by a man claiming he was transgender. He entered the woman's bathroom and molested the girl. This was just one of the hundreds of abuse and molestation cases that happened after President Obama unleashed this abomination on America. The ripple effect is now being felt in kindergarten, elementary and the government school system. Children are now being subjected to education about accepting the depraved lifestyle as normal. They use words like, *"tolerance, homophobe",* and a plethora of other words when anyone objects or speaks out about anything contrary to their lifestyle.

Paul: As I mentioned before, The Heavenly Father loves people but, He hates the lifestyle they have chosen to live in our FFS society. He knows that their Glory Code was impacted. He knows many of them have a (-2) to a (-6) GC. He said, *"Let the person who has no sin, cast the first stone,* (words of condemnation).*"* Then He says, *"Go,"* (Get-up, repent, be reconciled to me, be healed of your wounded GC state, receive my Love, and Healing through forgiveness, acceptance, and approval. Now walk-in victory and in obedience to my Word) *"and sin no more."*

Deb, because one of the five core needs of every human is acceptance, just knowing that their lifestyle is wrong and rejected by the mainstream society, they force and influence laws that will cause society to accept them. Their (-3) to (-6) GC gives them the drive to champion the cause of the LGBTQ+ community. They are forcing their quest for acceptance into all aspects of society, from the White House to your house. They even work through covert leftwing judges that sit on the Supreme Court, like Justice Roberts. Justice Roberts along with other leftist Judges passed a landmark ruling that redefined sex discrimination against the LGTBQ+ community. This is another endorsement of this lifestyle that further erodes the value of "family." This will impact businesses and the faith community.

In summary, the platform on the Right (The Heart of the Heavenly Father) *is that He loves the person, but* the lifestyle choices are an abomination to Him. He allows everyone to repent and receive His Love and forgiveness, in order that they may walk in His blessings.

Hot topic # 3

Illegal Aliens (Unlawful &Criminal)

Deb: Illegal aliens is another hot topic. This is a major violation and invasion in America. The left says it is immoral to stop people from invading our nation.

Paul: Dads and families on the Right know, and see, through the agenda of the left about this invasion of our borders. They know that:

- Some of those invading our borders are planned and funded by the left.

- Criminals, gangs, and sex-traffickers are amongst those trying to enter.

- The left agenda needs the poor, fatherless, single-mothers and needy families who are angry and feeling victimized or marginalized.

- The more people they can seduce into dependency on the welfare system, the more power and control over the working dads, mothers, sons and daughters they will have.

- Freedom to think for one's self is the greatest *threat* to the left.

If the left celebrates the murder of babies, nothing else in life has any value to them. So, when they say that they care about anyone else, it's a lie. Remember, they serve the father of lies, he is the father of fake news. *You know who they are by their actions (lifestyle).*

We know, if you and your family are asleep in bed and burglars break through your window, that is illegal. You have the right to protect and defend your family. You can call 911 and have the law enforcement officers arrest them and take away the intruders. That is why we place doors on our homes. We do our best to protect our families, the people we love.

Dads are supposed to be the protectors of their families. We are all supposed to:

- Protect our hearts *(guard our hearts against the hurtful influence of the father on the left)*

- Protect our minds *(refuse to act on negative, radical thoughts that invade)*

- Protect our body from physical abuse

- Protect our children and families

- Protect unborn babies from being murdered and injustice against the weak.

- Protect the core values of The Heavenly Father and the legacy He has given to us.

- Protect the families in your nation, by protecting its' borders.

- Protect your belief and build strong core values based on Love from The Father on the Right.

The Heavenly Father on the Right has borders and boundaries. No one can enter His kingdom without following His Plan and Principles.

Hot topic # 4

Climate Change, Global Warming, Green New Deal

Deb: Paul, we only have 12 years before the world will end!! If I had $10 for every person on the left that said the world would end, or the north pole would melt and flood the world, I could have paid off my mortgage by now. Most of the calls we receive at our office reflect that many individuals are fed-up and do not believe this Big Lie.

Paul: It is a huge, fake-news agenda and attempt to plunder hard-working moms, dads, and youths through the use of more regulations and taxes on companies, which is passed on to families. Most of these families recognize the hidden agenda, knowing the truth.

This is a hoax (deception, fake news) perpetrated on the American people to levy *(collect, pillage, legally take)* more taxes from working families through increased and unnecessary regulations on families and businesses.

Each regulation imposed on a company affects families financially. The billions of dollars taken *(leveraged through fees and taxes)* from hard-working families goes to benefit special business and political leaders *(some through stock options in the company)* and very little goes to mitigate the alleged problem.

When President Obama took office, he implemented about **3,000 new regulations** which was almost a **$900 Billion** impact to children and families in America. The **increased cost,** caused by penalizing companies, is passed on *(Charged to families to recover the increased expenses of the regulations)* to hard-working families in the form of increased:

- o   Product expense in supermarkets and stores
- o   Gas prices
- o   Cost for purchasing homes, property taxes, etc.
- o   Airfares and travel rates
- o   Sticker price to purchase cars and vehicles
- o   Fees for water, sewer and garbage services and much more…

I would summarize this with a few words. Most people did not know when President Trump took office, in his first year, he was able to **remove over 1,600 of these destructive**

regulations. This was why the economy began to flourish. By removing these burdensome chains, he brought freedom for families to flourish again.

Youths and individuals who don't know what the core values and the Word of The Heavenly Father says will easily fall victim to this agenda of the left. The core values of the right should reflect the core values of God's Word:

- We cannot change the times, temperatures and seasons (Winter, Spring, Summer & Fall)

- We are stewards of the Earth

- We cannot stop divine weather patterns

- We know that God promised to Noah that He would not flood the world again, but will renovate the earth *(melt the entire earth with fervent heat before bringing down the new heaven upon the new earth)* with great heat. This is to clean up the mess, pollution, and contamination that humans have inflicted upon the earth. This will address the global warming propaganda. God will warm the entire world and melt it at the end of His appointed season. If people walk in His law of Love, we will do what is good for each other.

Deb: Wow! I forgot it says in God's Word that He would melt the entire world. Well, I guess this will take care of all the global warming and climate change proponents. Paul, you also mentioned that we are about the enter the Fifth Season of The Heavenly Father. This season is where things in the world will become radically revealed and the enemy (Satan, the Devil) will unleash all of his servants. You mentioned that even in the Church, the authentic followers of the Heavenly Father *(His true sons and daughters)* would become solidified in their core conviction and begin to take a strong stand for their faith when they are challenged. The people who choose to be on the Left will begin to reveal their true colors and even begin to physically lash-out against those on the Right.

Paul: I am glad you remembered. You only have to turn on the news to see this playing out across our nation. Deb, there is a temporary open window of favor and blessings for those who are alert and aware of this season. It is time to maximize this moment to positively impact as many as we can in this generation before it is too late.

Paul R. Benjamin, Sr.

Chapter 23

Hot Topic # 5

Minimum Wage Scam

Deb: Every time I turn on the news there is some politician on the left promising to raise the minimum wage to $15 per hour. I remember when I started my first job, I worked in a printing shop filing and cleaning the office. I was paid $4.50/hr. Then, my wage was based on my knowledge, skill and value to the company. A fire sparked in me, I wanted to earn more. So, I took the initiative. I decided to learn how to operate the printing press, and with the help of my co-worker, I also learned how to input the data in the computer.

After six months of learning and improving my knowledge and skills, my boss called me into his office and said, "Deb, you have shown great initiative and work ethic. You have grown in your skills and knowledge within our company. You have become very valuable to me and the company. We will increase your hourly pay by $2.00, which would graduate you to $6.50 per/hr."

I can still remember how I felt back then. I was so excited that I couldn't wait to catch the bus to go home to tell my parents. I asked my boss if I could use his office phone to call my parents to share the exciting news.

Paul, please briefly explain the ramifications with leftist leaders trying to force and mandate employers to pay $15.00/hr. This minimum wage rate will now become the birthright to new and existing employees.

Paul: It is great to hear how you were rewarded for your work performance. Today, we have removed that fire of desire, creativity and initiative from many of our young men and women in the marketplace. That drive to learn more, and find alternative streams of income, just like Colonel H. Sanders, the founder of KFC who at age 40 branched out from just selling gas. Now, millions of people are enjoying Kentucky Fried Chicken around the world. Or, men like S. Truett Cathy who tested many ways to perfect a chicken sandwich. Today, we can all enjoy a wonderful chicken sandwich at a *Chick-fil-A*. All the cows are celebrating that they are not on the menu.

Deb: Funny, Paul! I think the cows should have a memorial for the chickens. I was reading about Chick-fil-A. They provide college scholarships for students who would like to improve their education, move on to a higher wage and even become a business owner. It is amazing. When we allow freedom in the marketplace, individuals and companies will prosper and promote employees from within.

Paul, I usually tell people my story when others complain to me about the minimum wage. I tell them that they have the freedom to improve their knowledge and skills and if there is no promotion within their company, find a company that will pay them more. I also tell them they have the freedom to start their own business.

Paul: Most people forget. Business owners were youths who had a dream to have their own business one day. They paid the price. They woke-up early in the morning and learned the skills they needed to know about starting and operating a business. Most of them went to trade school or college to obtain the needed knowledge.

Many saved their money from washing cars, doing lawns or various side jobs while in school. This sacrifice enabled them to go after their dream with the hope of one day owning their own business. The goal was to make a better life for their children and families.

Some may even get financial help and partnership investment from their parents, in the form of a loan or even a trust fund, but the work and creative management is up to them. These are the same principles we teach single moms and youths in Life Centers. They are learning how to **A**ctivate their **P**assion into **P**urpose, (APP).

Forced Pay Raise without Work Performance

When political leaders on the left appeal to their audience, it's a gimmick to capitalize on the victim mentality. It speaks to individuals who believe they have been robbed of the opportunity to prosper, despite being afforded the greatest economic freedoms accessible in America. The ability to work, learn, advance and to earn unlimited income is based on their efforts and hard work.

By threatening to force business owners to reward employees *(who may not even have the skills or performance value)* with a mandate to pay $15 per hour, it is tantamount to criminal. This audience is unaware of the huge ripple effect. They are not aware, what they receive in one pocket, will quickly go out of the next. This is a shortlist of the impact, if this is forced into law:

- Many people will lose their jobs immediately. 2020 Socialist, Presidential Candidate Bernie Sanders, is one of the leading proponents for forcing *(Mandating through the force of Government)* families, who own and operate businesses, to pay $15.00 per hour as a minimum wage. His political ploy backfired on him when his employees were being paid less than $15 per hour. He then realized, to pay them the $15 they requested, he would have to either fire some or reduce their work hours. Thus, reducing their income to what it was before. Realizing, if such a law was passed, it will increase unemployment for youths who are now seeking to enter the workforce and rob them the opportunity to learn a new skill.

- When the pay scale begins too high, employers cannot afford to hire new employees at that rate. It limits the number of youths that can be hired. They will miss out on the chance to increase their knowledge and performance, just like Deb did at her first job. Employers will have to cut overhead expenses to maintain their same take-home income in order to feed their children and families. Many companies are now turning to an automated kiosk in preparation. They are reducing the number of employees that will be needed to operate their business profitably.

- This will increase the cost of goods and services to consumers. For example:

  o The drivers that deliver the goods would be paid $15/hr.

  o The employer of the driver *(The youths that are now adults, who worked hard to own a business)* passes on this fee. He increases his charge to the company purchasing the items that are being delivered.

  o The results in increased prices at the grocery store, restaurant or wherever items are delivered. *(Some of these companies will also have to fire employees to remain profitable to keep their stock owners profitable or to be able to take home their same paycheck to feed their children and families)*.

o   We will also see an increase in rent rates and employee terminations. (Apartment companies will have to pay their employees more money. This increased expense will be passed on to each tenant in the form of higher rent).

o   Gas prices will soar, as the principle applies to all aspects of society. Every industry that has given people a chance to get started in the workforce will have to pass on the increased cost to consumers *(working mothers, fathers and youths)*

o   Unemployment will go up; millions of people will lose their jobs.

o   Taxes and insurance rates will escalate. The government will take more taxes out of paychecks. The company that may have given a youth the chance to prove themselves in a job, may say no because of the high cost of hiring and training.

Wages that had been set lower to give employees a chance to start and grow in their skills and knowledge, now had to be raised based upon the proposed salary fee. This will limit the number of candidates hired.

In America, there is the freedom to learn and improve your skills and knowledge. This gives you the ability to advance in your career as you move from one job to another. If you want to go further, you can even start your own business, just like your boss did. These failed manipulative policies and strategies will never work in the "real" world.

One of the core reasons we teach business principles to youth, single mothers and families *(those who would like to improve their life situation)* in our Entrepreneurship Development program is to let them know that, everyone is an entrepreneur. Every job is providing them with the skills, knowledge, and training for their ultimate assignment in life, their (APP). All we are doing is Activating their Passion into Purpose.

Capitalistic or Entrepreneurial

America is not a *capitalistic* nation. We are a nation founded on core values that allows freedom for individuals to pursue their *God-given* dreams; the freedom of *entrepreneurship* being one of them. We are like no other country in the world. You do not have to wait for a politician on the left to force your boss to give you a pay raise to $15/hr. Why not improve your skills and make $30, or even $75 per hour? People perish because they lack knowledge. Don't be one of them. Increase your knowledge and move to the next level in life. You can do it. You can do all things through Christ. He will always lead you to victory. *"Your values determine your victory."*

Hot Topic # 6

Religion and Politics: Two Things that Rule the world…

Deb: Paul, thanks for adding such a well-defined perspective to another one of the deceptive strategies of the left. One of the big questions I keep getting almost daily is about the shadow government/deep state *(Covert operatives who are entrenched and hold key positions in the government. They are only loyal to the leftist agenda and mission of the father of death, Satan, to subvert the positive mission of the right and the nation).* I hear about the high-level secret government documents or phone calls leaked to the news media. Corrupt ex-officials publish books about all of their covert operations while they served the agenda of the left. Paul, when will this stuff end? Is there any hope of change? My email inbox is full of these and many other questions I cannot answer.

Spiritual Perspective overlooked by the Church, Media & Society

Paul: Deb, when you look at or listen to the news, you are only hearing what is happening from a natural, 2-D perspective *(Who said what about whom. Who tweeted about a controversial topic. etc.)* That is why the media only answers in this realm. But, we are 3-D *(Three Dimensional beings. We are spirit, we have a soul, and we are housed in a temporary body, which we try to keep looking young forever.)* We live in a three-dimensional world. This deception and evil agenda will get worse, until Season Seven of The Heavenly Father, when He would put an end to all of this.

As it was in Heaven, so it is on Earth

In heaven, the father of fake news, the Devil, organized the first coup attempt. He, and his *deep state/shadow government operatives,* executed a failed coup to overthrow the Heavenly Father. His desire was to be worshipped and to become the supreme ruler of the entire universe. As we all know, his plans failed. When he was expelled, he and his covert operatives came to earth. They are now implementing their strategy by working in and through his human agents in key roles in society. *(Dads, mothers and youths who have yielded their lives and are now slaves to his will. They are used to execute his agenda of rebellion, death, and deception upon the human race.)* He works through individuals in homes, schools, churches, television and radio stations, newspaper outlets, companies, coffee-shops, social media, co-workers and government offices *(From the White House to your house)*.

Many dads, moms, and youths on the right profess to be Christians. They only look at political issues through their natural eyes and senses. They are inspired by the charisma and charm of a leader and totally disregard character flaws; immoral, core values; failed ideology and the platform they represent for the father of the left.

These same people will complain about a leader who lacks charm, eloquence, charisma or social manners. Yet, if the leader keeps his promises and upholds the moral values and character of the right, this leader is ostracized.

They do not realize when they align with a person or the platform of the Left, the blood of millions of babies and children is also on their hands. One day they will have to give an account to The Father of The Right, God. Himself. I pray the eye of their hearts would begin to see things through a spiritual perspective. Christians do not realize there is a battle for the hearts of people that started from the foundation of the world, between the father of the left, Satan, who works through his operatives on the left, and the Heavenly Father on the Right.

Holistic Perspective: Spiritual, Natural, Social

Deb, I will give some quick examples of how I look at the things in the world through holistic lenses. This is the missing perspective that is not covered in the news. In politics there are (5) core principles to keep in mind:

1. **Person**: Does the person represent the call and purpose of The Heavenly Father on the Right? Do they defend the life of babies from conception? Do they honor family values, justice and freedom from exorbitant, burdensome taxation on families? Do they promote freedom to work with honor and dignity providing for themselves and their family?

Freedom from the System

What about freedom from being enslaved to the system of generational hand-outs, only with the threat of losing it if you do not submit and vote for leaders that control the system? Are they in favor of your *freedom to save and invest your money* or *start your own business,* so that one day you can become wealthy and provide jobs for others to contribute to society? Do they champion your freedom to protect and defend yourself and your family from the evil intrusion of corrupt individuals?

2. **Personality:** Does the person's words match their actions? What is the character of the person? Do they keep their word? The only true thing we all own is our word. Everything else is temporarily managed. Our words will live on long after we are gone.

3. **Purpose**: The leader's purpose will determine their policies and platform. The purpose is determined by who they are serving. If they are serving God, The Heavenly Father on the Right, it will reflect in their policies. *(Just like Jesus, He came to serve the Father's will by implementing Life, Love, Joy, Peace and by showing us the right way to live)*. If they are serving the Devil, it, too, will reflect in their policies. *(Murder of Children, fake news to deceive families, lust, poverty, increased taxes to destroying families)*.

4. **Policies:** Reflect the **Purpose**, **Platform**, **Personality,** and character of the person. Like Jesus, His policies were simple; love God and love others, as you love yourself. On the other hand, the Devil, his purpose, is reflected in his policies; steal and corrupt the truth by speaking lies, *(fake news)*, killing children *(babies)* and destroying the destinies of families.

5. **Practice:** Consistency of character is reflected in the practice of an individual. Your principles will become your public practice. Any imperfect person, who chooses to submit his or her life to a Perfect God, *(The Heavenly Father)* will change their principles and practice to reflect the character of God, resulting in a positive, profound impact upon others and nations. So, by the practice *(fruits, actions, policies)* of an individual, you will know who they are serving; the father on the left or The Father on the Right.

Paul R. Benjamin, Sr.

Chapter 24

Politics in our Society is Impacted by the FFS

Paul: There is only one perfect, political leader in the world. His name is Yeshua, Jesus, Son of the Most-High God, Father of the Right. Until He establishes His physical Kingdom and rules over the whole Earth, we have to choose broken, fallen men and women who represent the platform and principles of either the father on the **left,** the Devil, or the Father on the **Right,** The God of Abraham, Isaac, and Jacob.

Deb: I am glad you mentioned which God we are praying to. Many people say we all believe in the same god. As you mentioned, we pray to the one, and only, true God of our Jewish patriarchs. I know many of our Jewish families are deceived and vote for leftist leaders because they were enslaved in Egypt and are very sympathetic towards poor and underprivileged people. We need to enlighten them to the real truth of the agenda on the left.

Paul can you speak at my Synagogue before the Barack Obama Election?

Paul: Deb, this is huge in the Jewish community. They were always encouraged to care for the needs of other. Now, they have fallen for the deceptive plot of the Enemy.

In the summer of 2008, knowing that 99% of the congregants in his synagogue would vote for the presidential candidate on the left, Barack Hussein Obama, Rabbi Cohen invited me to speak at his synagogue. I shared the spiritual and natural impact, if candidate Obama were to be elected to the most powerful office in the world:

- As the first Muslim President in America, he would turn against Israel. There would be an increase in Anti-Semitic actions in America. There would be increased Muslim influence in all aspects of government. Sharia Law *(Islamic Law)* would begin to influence our society and pave a path for many other Muslims to infiltrate all aspects of our government. It would implement an Anti-Judeo-Christian agenda and for the first time in our history, America would turn against Israel and the Jews.

- This candidate would pillage the treasury of America to fund special interest groups and Muslim causes to subordinate and destroy America, from the inside out. As the most powerful, military force in the world, America would be attacked, not by another military army, but from within.

The Deception is Real

Deb: How did this one slip by me? I am in the media, and I didn't know Obama was Muslim.

Paul: This one slipped by many Christians. The *fake-news* media *covered-up* his true allegiance and faith.

Sorry to say, my speech was not well received by the Jewish people in this synagogue. Many of them came up to me after I spoke and said they "fact-checked," they liked him and will vote for him. I received letters from others who didn't get a chance to speak to me in person, expressing the same views. I know many well-meaning Christians, and pastors, were excited and voted for the left agenda.

Pocketbook: Pity or Principles

Many well-meaning individuals, and even key Christian leaders, aligned with the agenda of the Left. Just like in every election, people vote and align with radical agendas based on three categories:

- **Pocketbook.** *(It's all about the Benjamins; the $100 bill with a picture of Benjamin Franklin on it, money, $$$.)* People will vote for a candidate who will lie to them and promise them free stuff; like medical and dental. If you like your doctor, you can keep your doctor. You may receive increased welfare checks, Medicare or Medicaid, free college, slavery reparations, free student loan forgiveness program, free housing program, etc. Free, Free, Free. *(All this free stuff means more taxes on the backs of hard-working families)*. We will tax big evil corporations. Remember, the same principle with the $15/hr. wage minimum increase. When you increase taxes on corporations, they pass on the increased expenses to you, the consumer…which means, higher prices on goods and services.

- **Pity.** Many people will vote out of *"pity for, or identifying with, a people group"* to show that they are not racist or to give someone a chance; whether they be black, brown, female, etc. After all, they have suffered and were victims for decades. These emotional people mean well in their hearts. If only they knew the holistic view.

  There is nothing capricious in life. *(Nothing is by accident. There is a spiritual agenda and actual purpose and reason behind everything.)* There is an agenda on the left. *(It is to steal, kill, spread fake news and destroy you, your family and society from the inside out.)*

- **Principles.** I am grateful that we have many people who see things in our nation and world from this holistic view. Others reject truth because they willingly do not want to face the pain of reality. With increased knowledge, comes increased sorrow and responsibility.

  Those who don't want to face the truth, prefer to live life in a bubble until it is too late. This is why we were taught to stay away from the topic. It reveals the only two agendas that are at work every second of every day, from the foundation of the world. One day, they will wake up and say, how did all of this happen so suddenly? When it was slowly occurring right in front of them every day.

Paul R. Benjamin, Sr.

Chapter 25

Assumption:
Being "Black," Automatically Means You Are a Leftist

In the summer of 2008, I rushed into Wal-Mart. It was a warm 82 degrees on a Friday afternoon, around 2:15.3 PM. Just like clockwork, I was accosted by someone who knew me. It was an older black gentleman in his mid-sixties. He knew me as a minister in the city. He said, *"For the first time in America's history, "we" (blacks) will be voting for one of our "own," referring to the first black Presidential candidate, Barack Obama."* His natural assumption was, everyone who is black, naturally votes for the *"left"* or for the *"black person."* After-all, we have to support *"our own!"*

After I introduced myself, I found out his name was Roy. I said, *"As a man of God, do you think the principles and character of God, as revealed in His Word, would support and endorse a person, party, or political platform on the Left? In good faith and conscience, should I endorse the left which promotes:*

1. Removal of God from their platform.

2. Embracing of Baal worship *"The murder of children (babies)"*

3. Celebrating the LGBTQ+ lifestyle

4. Hatred of Israel and the Jews

5. Rebellion against God's Word by promoting the demise of monogamous families that God established to reflect His heart and character *(One man and one woman in marriage)*.

6. Gender confusion *(Anyone can decide to choose their own sex or gender based on how they feel; male, female or "other".)*

At this point, the cashier began looking intently at both of us, as if to say, *"I want to hear the rest of the story?"* After paying for our items, we made our way towards the exit. Roy looked startled, his face became pale and he was speechless for about 30 seconds. After regaining his composure, he said, *"I was never told this or understood this before."*

Today, there are many people like Roy who attend church every week and serve the cause of the Enemy in their daily lives. He was only conditioned to support and endorse the agenda of the left. Sad to say, millions of people like him who *profess* to be Christians, after knowing the agenda of the father of the left, Satan, will still run and support this leftwing agenda.

Dads, you need to know how to teach and model the character of The Heavenly Father on the Right. The destiny of your family and nation depends on your leadership and influence.

Political, Biblical Worldview

Deb: These true principles and facts are so easily overlooked by the church. Millions of churches and Jewish people supported former President Obama. Under his Presidency, America was fundamentally transformed. I know you are almost out of time, but I want to get as much information as I can to take back to John.

Can you give a brief list from a biblical perspective regarding the impact that former President Obama inflicted on our families, country and the world?

Paul: Okay, Deb. This will be quick. The full list of consequences from the Obama presidency would take too long to explain. His presidency awakened and activated the right, while exposing the real character on the left.

I will Curse those who curse the Jews (Israel)

Under his presidency, he turned America against Israel ushering in the judgement of God against the USA. As I mentioned before, the degree of your influence amplifies the impact of your words and actions.

If I were to list all the negative things, along with the spiritual and natural effects, it would take me a week. This is the shortlist:

Just by being *aligned with the principles, party and platform on the left* sends a message of accepance to young men and women.

Former President Obama turned his back on Israel and their Prime Minister, Benjamin Netanyahu, the leader of the *most powerful nation in the world*. The only nation in the world that The God of Heaven, The Father on the Right, has sworn himself to be their defender and protector. Thus, making them the greatest protected nation on earth. No enemy or agenda from the left can stand against Him or His chosen people.

Now that the Jews are back in the land God gave to them, no one will ever be able to remove them from their inheritance; the place where the New Heaven will come down upon one day. Any nation or person who turns their back on Israel, God will turn His blessing from that person and nation. *Former President Obama* also took $4 million from working families (tax-payers) in an effort to defeat Prime Minister Benjamin Netanyahu in his re-election.

America Cannot be Great again Until we return to God Again

The moment *former President Obama* turned his back against Israel the Spirit of God began to activate His champion, who was prepared before the foundation of the world to stand in the gap for Israel and the USA. America is blessed because America was founded, and established, on the Jewish foundation, which had given birth to Christianity. That champion was Donald Trump. He is not a politician representing the agenda of the left, but an ambassador executing the agenda of God, The Father of righteousness, on the right.

He will not follow the agenda of man. He follows only his God-given assignment. He will yield to God's agenda. He knows that, *"The only way America can be great again, is that we must turn to God again."* He, in essence, knows that we must repent for dishonoring Israel. He is a man of his word. He is the first President in Americas' history to acknowledge Jerusalem *(The city of the Great King)* as the Capital of Israel, as God ordained it to be.

When *former President Obama* turned his back on Israel and the Jews, he launched an open defiance against the Jews. Synagogues began to be attacked and burned like never before in American history. This emboldened the enemies of Israel to attack from all sides.

Funded Israel's # 1 Enemy

Former President Obama gave Iran, Israel's number one enemy, $150 Billion in released assets and $1.8 Billion in Cash, to fund their agenda of destroying Israel. Iran's #1 goal is to destroy Israel. We know this agenda from the left will always fail. The God and Father of Israel is King and Ruler of the Universe. No agenda can stand before Him and His chosen people.

Rejection of America's Pastor, Dr. Billy Graham

Former President Obama implemented laws that limited the freedom of religion. He even rejected America's Pastor, Dr. Billy Graham, who has been a source of wisdom and counsel to many previous Presidents.

Endorsed Homosexual Marriage & The LGBTQ+ Lifestyle

Former President Obama endorsed and *promoted homosexual marriage and the LGBTQ+* lifestyle. He promoted and sanctioned the use of any bathroom (male or female) based on how the individual "felt" about their gender. This scandalous proposal increased the number of rapes and abuses of children in public bathrooms. Men, who wanted to rape and molest girls or women, would put on a dress and enter a woman's bathroom only to rape them. Now, parents are asking their children to choose what they want to be; boy or girl. We, as a people and nation will pay a huge price for this. If we thought the mental health crisis was bad, look for what is to come.

Increased Tax burden on Families

Former President Obama promoted dependence on the government **welfare system** by adding 13 million people. This created an employment crisis in America. Employers could not compete with *"FREE."* Many people stayed home rather than go to work. They were making more money staying home, living off the taxes of hard-working families. We will always have more jobs available than people who are willing, or equipped, to fill these jobs.

Global promotion of the Murder of Babies

Former President Obama promoted the **murder and slaughter of children** (babies) even up to the latest possible moment prior to birth. This process was also promoted to other countries, and funded by billions of dollars from taxpaying families in America. Today, because there is no value for human life from its' inception, murder and crime against youths and adults are rampant around the country and the world. Knowing that their fathers abandoned them and leaders who sponsor and murder children, gangs and fatherless youth find it easier to murder and kill each other, law-enforcement officers and anyone that gets in their way. Just look at Chicago, President Obama's home town. It celebrates some of the highest murder and crime rates in America.

Disrespected American Heritage

Former President Obama's world-wide *"condemnation"* tour of America sparked additional disrespect for our nation, both at home and around the world. This denigration of the most sought-after nation, where people flock to its' borders legally and illegally, paved the way for radicalized people to commit more violence in America and around the world.

Attacked our Patriotism

Patriotism is now at an all-time low. *(At least, that is the perception the media on the left is espousing.)* Some groups are paid to burn the American Flag in public, in an attempt to add fuel to many fatherless youths and gangs who are already discouraged and disillusioned about their situation. Now we are witnessing more hate crimes against individuals, law-enforcement officers, clergy and the Jewish community. This national Anti-American sentiment has activated the authentic, patriotic spirit in America for the flag that represents its' greatness.

Rashida Tlaib and Ilhan Omar Continue the Obama Legacy

This Anti-American spirit has emboldened and activated many Muslim, Anti-Semitic American people to run for public office to entrench themselves in key leadership roles in America. This Trojan Horse effect *(To revolutionize America from **the Inside-Out** by introducing opposing radical ideology)* is already making great strides.

Key leaders are now in congress, courts and over 30 strategic, powerful leadership roles in America. Some of the most visible leaders that are continuing The Obama legacy are Rashida Tlaib and Ilhan Omar. These two radical Muslim women, who were voted into power by some American people, are very vocal about their Anti-Semitic American bigotry and their association with radical Islamic groups. ***Let us pray*** for the healing of *the hearts of all of these leaders. The Heavenly Father, desires that no one would perish, but that all will come to repentance and experience His Love.*

Alexandria Ocasio Cortez, a Sephardic Jew?

Alexandria Ocasio Cortez, *(AOC)* a Sephardic Jew, daughter of Abraham. She, not knowing her true Jewish heritage, is making extremely radical Anti-Semitic American statements. Her radical ideology and policies are bad for America. This is another example of dads not letting their children know who they are, their legacy and their purpose. In 1492 the Sephardic Jews were forced to convert to Catholicism or be persecuted. They were part of the diaspora that came to America.

To hide their identity, many of them changed their names. Her statement, linking America's border crisis to that of the Jewish Holocaust stirred up generational pain for many Jews around the world. I would like AOC to know that she and all of her friends and family are greatly loved. I pray that her heart would be healed and she would know her Jewish Messiah who loves her very much and would like her to be a champion for the right cause. She can let many other Latino, Sephardic Jews know who they are and to awaken them to walk in their true identity, as His chosen people.

Creating a Dependent State

Highest Un-Employment rates among Blacks and Latinos due to many burdensome regulations and high taxes. Why work? 11 million people took the offer and signed up for welfare. Companies were afraid to hire new employees. ***The cost of Obama Care*** also forced millions of families and companies to pay more for health care. This reduced the workforce and caused millions of people to lose their jobs. Home ownership went to a 50-year low. The economy grew at its slowest pace in decades. Consumer confidence was at an all-time low.

Deb: Thank you, Paul. I know this is only the short list. As a nation, we will experience the ramifications of his presidency for generations. Let's wrap up for today. Joel and I are looking forward to our beach day with you and Dawn tomorrow. See you then.

Paul: We are looking forward to it. I already have my tan. I will let you ladies work on yours. Please say hi to Joel and the children for me. Have a blessed evening.

Chapter 26

President Trump Restored Hope

Deb: I am still basking in the glow from our weekend at the beach. Dawn and I enjoyed our girl time together while working our tan. Paul, you have an awesome wife! Not to mention, Joel enjoyed his guy time with you. He was able to ask you some of the troubling questions he wanted me to ask during our interview. I told him to wait and ask you in person when we got together. We must do this again soon…

Paul: Deb, we enjoyed our time with you and Joel. He also confirmed his commitment to be part of the national mentoring team.

Deb: Dawn and I will be arranging more of these weekend getaways. We are now sisters.

Paul, let's pick-up where we left off. You were about to discuss how President Trump is a blessing to our nation.

Paul: I am glad you ladies will do all the planning and implementation for our mini-getaways.

When President Trump took office, he ***removed the burdensome regulations*** that enslaved the American economy. This was like bringing "freedom" to slaves who were held in (Economic chains) for eight years. He also reduced the income tax rate and ***removed the high-tax penalty of the Obama Care*** mandate, and its penalty on hard-working families *(People living in radical States with higher tax rates didn't get to enjoy the full benefits)*. This produced an economic resurgence in the American economy like never before. Businesses began to prosper and give their employees raises and bonuses.

Under President Trump the "**un-employment**" rate for blacks and latinos became the *lowest in American history*. This is the difference between the agenda on the Left; to steal, kill and destroy and the agenda on the Right; to bless and bring freedom from

Governmental systems. Families who were on the "system" can now be released from tax-payer funded programs into prosperity, thus, enjoying life.

8 Years of Obama Pillaging the American Tax-payers

Former President Obama in just 8 years, managed to double the National debt, outspending all presidents before him combined. He added over 9 trillion dollars in debt, just as I had told the Jewish people he would do. This also includes the 1.5 billion dollars for funding the *Muslim Brotherhood* and other community organizations in charge of paying protesters for radical activism in cities. The trade deficit of over $700 billion didn't help our economy. When you add all of these items, (along with the open borders that allowed millions of illegal immigrants to join the American welfare, medical and prison system) it exponentially increased our national debt.

The creation of a pandemic from one Spark Event

Former President Obama Fundamentally Transformed America when he hijacked the Trayvon Martin and George Zimmerman tragedy in Sanford, FL. He said, "If I had a son, he would look like Trayvon and nobody understands the plight of Black males."

These and many other agitating remarks, along with the national rebuke and constant criticism of law enforcement, spawned these local and national consequences:

- *Law Enforcement officers are being murdered, abused, and publicly ridiculed by* youths who are pouring water on them in New York. Today it's water, tomorrow it could be contaminated liquids or …

- *Black youths have become emboldened to commit acts of violence against whites, and all kinds of crime.* Mayors and Governors, who are on the left, have become strengthened in their resolve against the core values of America. They have given criminal illegal aliens a free pass and refuge in their cities, resulting in multiple youth rapes and the killing of Americans. They promote anarchy in their cities by rebelling against the national rule of law. These same rebellious leaders are perplexed by the increase of crime and violence by rebellious, fatherless youths in their city and state.

- *This gave birth to the Black Lives Matter movement and Put Your Hands Up, Don't Shoot Movement.*

- ***The rise of anti-America sentiment*** among many black pastors, political leaders, athletes like, Colin Kaepernick, and students in college across the nation.

- ***Division in Families, the Marketplace and the Church.*** Now more than ever, the division in families and the Church has become so clear. The **two topics** that we were told not to discuss, (Religion and Politics) are now, the greatest core values that have divided the world. It is like a volcano that has finally exploded after decades of being suppressed.

Which Political Team are you on?

These two topics are inexorably linked (They are one and the same) your politics are dictated by your religion *(Faith-Beliefs)*. Everything in the world hinges on *your true relationship with The Heavenly Father, on the Right.* He said, *"If you love Me, keep My commandments."* Yet, millions of people who profess to be Christians will align with the agenda of the Left.

Now, the world will know which churches and families are on the Right, and those who are on the left. There is no more hiding. The authentic will have to take a stand of courage or compromise their faith and join the leftwing operatives. There will be a price to pay. Joshua said, *"Choose you this day. Who will you serve?"* The God of Israel, The Heavenly Father on the Right or the Enemy, the god, and leader of the Left agenda. Dads, moms, and the youth of today will have to make their decision!

Dads, you have to set the example in your family.

Men, I recommend that you follow Joshua's example. He chose the winning team. He chose to follow the God of Israel, The Father on the Right.

Deception and Distraction Strategy

The Russian Collusion Hoax *(deception strategy)* was the biggest crime, and coup, attempt perpetrated upon a sitting American President. Just like the father of *fake-news*, the Devil. He tried to launch the first failed coup, was kicked out of his office in Heaven, and now his operatives are seeking to do the same thing here in America. He used former President Obama, and his administration, to launch his failed agenda in an effort to destroy the legacy of America and its key role with Israel. Despite all of their attempts to distract and derail the *God-given* mandate of President Donald Trump, The Heavenly

Father strengthened his resolve to accomplish more, in a shorter period of time, than any president in America's history.

Benghazi, The Uriah Effect

Deb, I will end on this last major topic, the tragedy at Benghazi. The slaughter and execution of American Ambassador, J. Christopher Stevens, by Islamic militants angered millions of Americans, and our armed forces. Emboldened by the weak posturing of America by *Former President Obama,* radical Islamic groups were given a green light to attack American troops and our facilities. After attacking the American Consulate in Libya, they executed the US Ambassador and his support team. A massive cover-up campaign was launched. Fake-news videos, in collaboration with the leftwing fake news media tried to distort the truth. This, and many other events, where the American armed forces were told to stand-down, at the cost of American lives. The Father and source of Truth *(The Father on the Right)* will expose the leftist agenda (from the Clintons to the Covert Operatives behind this agenda). He will bring justice in His due time.

To add fuel to the fire, Former President Obama allowed and endorsed open homosexual and lesbian relations in the military, while restricting Christian Chaplins from the full practice of their faith. On the other hand, he allowed free and open Islamic prayer. Being encouraged by their champion in the White House, by their newly endorsed freedoms, Islamic soldiers began murdering other soldiers by opening gun fire on various military installations.

America and our military strength were laughed at around the world. This is why President Trump invested his time and effort to rebuild the honor and morale of the brave men and women who serve in all the branches of our military.

On the anniversary of America's Independence, July 4, 2019, in order to honor and salute our brave men and women who serve in all branches of our armed forces, President Donald J. Trump, held an *"America Strong Military Flyover."* This event brought tears and renewed hope to the families that had lost loved ones, while restoring courage and confidence in the hearts of our great men and women who are serving in our military.

What You Bless, Builds in Value

President Trump knew that, **What You Bless, Builds in Value** (Whether in people, relationships, marriages, children, companies and yes, in our country). **What You Disrespect, Decreases in Value.** In the eyes of the world, the previous positive perception of America was decreased due to the Disrespect shown for America, (Because of our Jewish and Christian heritage) by former President Obama and his administration.

Disrespecting the American flag decreases the value and image of our Country, which, in turn, decreases the value of homes, stock portfolios, the value of education. This reduces the value of self and the value of our children. It's no wonder, we find it so easy to murder babies.

The only thing that increases is mental health issues. This results in school and community shootings; like El Paso, Texas, the shooting at Wal-Mart and the one that occurred in Dayton Ohio. Youths and individuals who are already on the edge with a (-6) "GC" level from their crushed Glory Codes, only need a small spark to push them to a (-7) "GC" level, which is equal to suicide or shooting.

If the place where we live has no value, then that means we, as individuals have no value. A country is not just a geographic location, it is made up of its people. It is the equivalent of saying, the children of Adolph Hitler went to school and held their heads up high in pride, knowing that their dad was despised as the most notorious mass murder of over 6 million Jews. Just like today in America, so many people are changing their last names so they don't have to associate with the shame and dishonor of their fathers' name. Influenced by corrupt leaders who disrespect America, individuals begin to emotionally disassociate themselves from the ideals that once reflected our greatness.

Will President Trump be Re-elected in 2020?

Deb: With all the failed attempts to destroy President Trump and the influence of the fake new empire distorting everything he says and does; do you think that he would be re-elected in 2020?

Paul: *There is a strong resurgence* under the leadership of President Trump. God has given America a brief reprieve from the evil agenda of the father of the left. Satan is always working through his agents on the left in the warfare for the hearts of mankind. I believe that God will bless America with one more season (term) under this great President.

Paul R. Benjamin, Sr.

Chapter 27

The Contrast of Two Leaders (Right & Left)

Deb: What a contrast in leadership and influence upon our country. These two diametrically opposed men, one serving the dark agenda on the left and the other serving the agenda of God on the Right. One *disrespecting and seeking to destroy America,* the other seeking to *Make America Great Again. As you said, "America cannot be great again until we return to God again."*

Paul: God has given America another chance. He appointed an imperfect person *(Just like all of us)* who has the hutzpah *(Courage and conviction)* to fight for the heart and soul of America. *When an "imperfect person" meets a "perfect God," together, they can change the world.*

If America rejects God's gift in President Donald Trump, yes, even with his unorthodox style, tweets, and strategies, do not think for one moment, we would escape His judgement. Do you think God wasn't aware of his past sins and shortcomings before He chose him from his mothers' womb?

The USA has been given a short window of opportunity from the onslaught of the dark left. This short window is to get the church ready for Season 5 of The Heavenly Father. This opportunity is so the church can reach His lost children before it is too late. If we don't, future generations will pay a high price.

Many people think that President Trump is here to serve at the pleasure of a *particular party or platform.* No! He is on assignment from God, Himself. He will be loyal to His purpose and agenda. In blessing Israel, America as a bi-product, will be blessed.

Deb. Paul, there are millions of men, women, youths, who hate President Trump. His past lifestyle with women has struck a nerve in their already crushed Glory Codes. How would you address this hurt and feelings in the lives of women on the right and left? This has amplified the radical left in Hollywood, the court system, media and many churches.

Why Some Women are Angry with President Trump

Paul: I will address this from all three aspects, the spiritual, soulish and natural realm. As I mentioned before, we are living in a FFS society. None of us are perfect. When we have a society where 1 in 3 women and 1 in 4 boys, who are now men, were physically and sexually abused. This leaves multiple millions of hurt, wounded and angry people. These individuals are now in key influential positions in government, our court system, schools, churches, Hollywood and many are CEOs of large corporations.

Their GC level would be about a (+2) and many of them would even be at a (-3) GC. Deb, that means many of them have not properly processed through their crushed GC as a result of their abuse. Remember, 75-80% of the abuse against these individuals was committed by a male, and the male was a step-father. In fewer cases, the abuse came from a biological father. In other cases, it may have been at the hands of a priest, pastor, mother, aunt, uncle or neighbor. Physically, many of them may carry the scars, bruises or burn marks on their bodies today. Their soul *(mind, will and emotions)* is crushed. Their GC could be at a dangerous level. Some of them have seen family members reach a (-7) GC and commit suicide. They may be bordering on that level. Spiritually, many blame God, The Heavenly Father *Who Loves them.*

Pain Always Seek a Target

They are angry at Him, saying, "Why didn't you stop this abuse and pain." Some may say, "If you loved me, why didn't you stop it from happening in the first place?" "I hate you. You say that you are all-powerful. Why don't you stop my pain and make it go away?" "I will become an Atheist. I don't believe you exist anyway. You weren't there for me or my family." This type of thinking is only the tipping point of how many of them feel towards God. Most of them reject traditional religion and turn to other forms of spirituality while looking for hope and healing.

Others join causes trying to alleviate the pain. Millions have turned to opioids and other illicit substances in an effort anesthetize their pain never realizing they will only be truly healed in a restored relationship with God, The Father. For many, just mentioning the word father stirs-up bad memories and rips the band-aid off their unhealed wounds.

They do not grasp the fact that they do not have to carry it anymore. They only need to receive the healing that only comes from Jesus.

Deb: This outcry has become nasty and radical. The profanity from some of these celebrities, and others in our nation, is destroying their own screen image, and ultimately impacting the souls of today's youth.

Global Threat to your Moral Integrity

Paul: Under President Trump many things and people that were hidden and subdued, have begun to manifest. Now, picture a man who is a father. He had a colorful past with women and said colorful words about women. He now in the most powerful position in the world. Deb, can you imagine the depth of pain being experienced by these women whose GC is (-3)? They will strike out with *unbridled venom.* Based on the degree of their influence in society, will be to the degree of their impact upon the hearts of other wounded bitter, angry and abused women and men. At ***Justice Brett Kavanaugh's*** confirmation hearing, the nation heard the outcry of many women who are still dealing with their past or current abuse.

Women who were abused, have not yet been healed and hear of these false accusations are *retraumatized* when these women are used as pawns by the left to destroy strategic leaders. *These false claims of abuse are attempts to derail good moral leaders on the **Right.*** These accusations *belittle, demean and minimize* the heinous act of physical or sexual abuse.

The Father of Truth, on the Right, will always expose lies and bring forth the truth. It may not happen immediately, but the Truth will always win in the end. The agenda of the left failed and was exposed for what it was *fake-news,* Justice Kavanaugh now has a seat on the highest court in America.

Keeping the Pain & Anger Alive (Politicized Pain)

Every time a woman brings false accusations against a man, it triggers the emotional pain in their crushed Glory Codes. I pray that these women will reach a healing relationship with the Heavenly Father who loves them and is waiting to help them.

Deb: Paul, that was very insightful. This explains why the left always uses women to lash out. I noticed when one of the leaders from the left is caught in a sexual or physical abuse scandal against a woman, it is the woman who is then marginalized, ostracized and ridiculed for coming forward with claims of abuse.

Paul, what is the process for someone to find healing?

Chapter 28

The Healing Process in our FFS Society

Paul: Deb, my heart is touched when I hear of the abuse of girls, and boys who are now grown men and women. The healing process is based on their current relationship with The Heavenly Father. For those who have been reconciled with God through a relationship with His Son, Jesus, and have made Him Lord of their lives, all they need to do is:

Acknowledge the Pain that was Inflicted

Acknowledge the abuse that was inflicted upon them. This is important because many times after the abuse, individuals will suppress the pain from the incident. Many times, this is done to protect the perpetrator who is usually someone they know, and even live with. If the abuse is repeated over and over the individual may even become numb and begin to emotionally disassociate themselves from the abuse.

Process the Pain

Mourn the loss and the pain that was inflicted upon you. Some people cry, scream or punch a punching bag. There is nothing wrong with showing and experiencing strong emotional pain, anger, and grief. Remember Janice, the young lady I mentioned earlier, who had two children by her Dad? I was able to provide a point of identification with her pain. She was able to cry and scream to release the deep hurt in her soul.

Forgive and Renew Your Thoughts

Next, I led her to verbally forgive and release her dad. This is the same process you should follow when forgiving the perpetrator that abused you (speak out clearly, not silently). For people who cannot speak or are on a dying bed, another person can speak it out for them and ask them to blink, or nod their head as a sign of acknowledgement. Remember, when Jesus took all the pain and sin of humanity upon himself on the cross, He said, *"Father forgave them, (the people that nailed Him to the cross) for they do not know what they are doing."* The real test of our love for God is in our ability to forgive. That is why He said, *"Love keeps no record of wrongs committed against the one loved."*

Jesus walked in love. He forgives all who come to Him in repentance of their sins. He has called everyone to do the same. When King David murdered Uriah, after having an adulterous relationship with his wife, He said, *"God it's against you alone I have sinned."* This also refers to anyone who has been abused. Their perpetrator has sinned against God! The Lord will ultimately give you justice. Jesus askes that we forgive those who have caused us our greatest pain, (those who have sinned against Him) by abusing, molesting, or even raping you. Caution, if you are still living with the abuser, it may not be wise to be in the same environment. Forgiveness doesn't mean permission to do it again.

Embrace your Healing from The Heavenly Father

Here is the sample prayer I asked Janice to pray.

"Heavenly Father, thank you for your love and grace towards me. I acknowledge the pain and abuse committed against me by _____. I am furious, bitter and angry at _____ for what _____ did to me, but, according to your Word, you commanded me to forgive those who sin against me. In obedience to you, I choose to forgive and release _____ for all the abuse and pain that _____ caused me. I speak blessings over _____. Heal _____'s heart. Let _____ come to know you and be healed so _____ won't hurt anyone else. You said that your goodness leads us to repentance. Father, show _____ your goodness. Let your great love swallow up all of _____'s pain as you would take away all of my pain. Thank you for the victory to walk in my healing from this moment forward. I will comfort and help others with the same comfort you have given me by faith today, in Jesus Name. Amen.

Just a reminder, Jesus said all prayer is directed to His Dad. Prayers that get access to His (Jesus') Dad are to be prayed in His Name. Many people pray to Jesus because there is a pain associated to the image of father.

Share Your New-found Freedom & Victory

I encouraged Janice to share the *freedom and release* she experienced in her life with other ladies, suggested she seek support from someone in her church, or find a good Godly counselor, like my wife, directed her to find a good Bible to study, asked her memorize and highlight key scriptures and reminded her to read out loud so she could hear herself, because faith comes by hearing the Word of God.

Set Your Expectations

I always caution people to manage their expectations. I recommended to Janice to download a good audible Bible app on her smartphone. I said, listen to it when you wake-up, drive, go for a walk, and before you go to bed; saturate your life with the Word of God.

In the early stages of victory, only share past hurts with people you trust. Some people will use the "prayer line" as a form of gossip. When you are comfortable with your story being shared with others, then you have received your healing from your past. Some people may try to capitalize and take advantage of your past vulnerabilities. For example, if you struggled with co-dependency, you may not have developed new healthy behaviors yet. Someone may pretend to fill that gap and potentially repeat the abuse. Keep you inner circle small with people you can trust.

Keep confessing & Walking in Your Victory & Freedom

When the thoughts or memories of past abuse comes to mind, as it will from time to time, you may still bitter or angry. You may not have received the full manifestation of peace yet. Just continue thanking your Heavenly Father for your victory, healing, and peace. Keep speaking blessings over the person or persons who inflicted the wound. After doing this for a period of time, the frequency of the memory will become fewer and further apart.

When you realize there is no more pain or anger, you have received your full victory. For some people it is instant, and for others, it happens over time. Many churches have programs or processes for helping individuals through abuse and trauma.

Some areas of abuse may go deeper and require deliverance at a spiritual level. This part I will not discuss now. This is an area that requires more in-depth, face-face help and guidance. Holding on to past hurts and not forgiving others may allow the Enemy may be at work in your life. Many church congregations help to facilitate this process. They surround you with loving, caring sisters or brothers as you walk through the process of healing to gain complete victory.

Don't be Afraid to Seek Godly Help

Some seek out professional, Christian, Biblical Counseling. This helps to navigate through new life-changing behaviors, breaking off old patterns and creating new ones.

This could take a person to the next level. The goal is to get to a (+6) GC level where your mission will be to help someone else walk through the same process.

Deb: Paul, that was a beautiful prayer and explanation of the process. I have learned this and applied it to my own life as I have prayed and forgiven my Dad. What about others who don't have a relationship with The Heavenly Father, but would like to experience the same healing, peace, and victory in their life? I know you mentioned in the relationship cycle number four, repentance, is that where they need to start?

Prayer to Reunite with The Heavenly Father

Paul: Deb, for anyone to receive the peace of God, they need to know Him. He is the personification of peace. He is The God of Shalom *(complete wholeness in mind body and spirit, living and walking in peace)*. All they have to do is to invite Him to be the Lord of their life. Remember, He gave His Son, so you can be reunited with Him. He is waiting to welcome you into His loving arms.

Here is a simple prayer: "Heavenly Father, I acknowledge I have sinned against you. I believe you sent your Son Jesus to pay the price for my sins by dying on the cross so I can be reconciled to you. I also believe that you raised Him from the dead for my justification *(Just as if you never sinned, placing you in the right relationship with Him)*. Please come into my heart and be The Lord of my life, in Jesus' Name. Amen."

Your New Birth Certificate

Congratulations! Welcome to the family. Your birth certificate says "God is your Daddy." As His child, you now share in the inheritance with Jesus. You are now joint-heirs with Him. You are seated with Jesus at His right hand. You are blessed with all spiritual blessings in Him.

Now, that *you are reconciled with your Heavenly Father*, you are in His Family again. He, also, loves the person or people who abused and hurt you. It is your turn to follow what your Heavenly Father is leading you to do for you to embrace the fullness of His grace and peace in your life. Follow the guidelines that were given earlier and walk in your new season of victory and peace. You are no longer a victim, but a victor *(champion and a winner)*. Walk in victory and hold your head up. Your Dad is a Champion. So are you. Go and help someone else become a champion like you.

Chapter 29

Promise Keepers Orlando
"I need to be Mentored"

Deb: Paul, you once mentioned in 2000 during a Promise Keepers (PK) event In Orlando you had a booth for the men to sign-up to be mentors to fatherless youth. Remind me, did you say that instead of the men signing up to be mentors, 9 out of 10 of them wanted to be mentored? I was alarmed that such a high number of men were seeking fatherly mentoring and guidance.

I know you made mention that most men were raised with either no dad, a bad dad or step-dad, a good dad or an emotionally and sometimes physically absent dad. As you referenced before, as the men go, so go the families and the world...

Taking Thousands of Fatherless Youth to Promise Keepers

Paul: The greatest pandemic is the fatherless crisis in our nation and the world. I will be teaming up with men's ministries, like Promise Keepers to engage, equip and train men to stand in the gap for this generation. Beginning in 2020, I will be mobilizing thousands of fatherless young men to attend the Promise Keepers and Better Man Events.

Deb: Paul, that is awesome! I will talk with my boss to sponsor some of these young men. It will be great to see men being trained to mentor the next generation of young men.

I know that it is getting late, but, could you please give some quick nuggets that men and dads can use in raising and leading their family. I will share these with Joel. He is a great dad, but we can all learn from each other.

Paul: Deb, if I continue adding more information we can end-up with an encyclopedia. But, you are right, men and dads need some core principles that can be applied in their lives with their children and families. I will give you an A-Z Topical Guide on Manhood.

Fatherhood and Manhood Nuggets (A-Z)

A

- *Acceptance* is the key principle in every relationship and family. Dads need to first need to accept their children from the womb to the tomb, not based on what they do, but based on who they are.

- *Approval* is the foundation in the life, and soul, of a child or any individual. It activates and draws them into their purpose. Approval unlocks hidden potential.

- *Assignment* is key. It brings clarity and a sense of destiny. We mold and shape destiny by the clarity of the assignment.

- *Authority* activates trust and faith. It is the fuel to implement your assignment in life. You will know you are covered and someone has your back. By having the badge of authority, you can walk in the blessing of your dad for maximum impact.

- *Affirmation* adds staying power and endurance for the assignment. What we affirm, we get more of the same. Whoever we affirm will grow in appreciation.

- *Attention.* What we give attention to grows and prospers. What we neglect grows away from you and out of control.

- *Access.* The degree of access is the degree of your relationship. The greater the Access, the greater the relationship and influence. If children do not have access to their dads, they lose access to be influenced by you. That is why, we have full access to the Heavenly Father because he is the source of our life, love, hope, and approval. Access = love.

B

- *Blessing* seals identity into destiny. Every child needs and yearns the blessing of their Dad. The Blessing solidifies the Glory Code in a child's life. Grown adults, today, are still waiting for their dad's blessing.

- *Belief* builds confidence, cultivates relationships, draws out the best from within and fortifies staying power.

- *Belonging* is life! One of the greatest desires in the human soul is to belong and be part of a family. The word family comes from the word father. That is why acceptance and belonging equals family. Dads set the tone and the stage for belonging in the family.

- *Boundaries* bring freedom and clarity. Adam and Eve were given the entire world, except one, boundary. Without boundaries, you become bound, not knowing healthy limits.

C

- *Compassion* is caught, not taught. Model compassion to your wife, children, and others. Compassion is also knowing when to say no. Children will do what they see you do.

- *Covering* Dads are the covering *(spiritual and physical)* in the home. What they get involved with enters the home. Dads provide good covering by being a role model of the character of Christ to his wife and family.

- *Clarity* builds community. Set clear goals and expectations and applaud defined outcomes.

- *Character.* Your words must match your actions. Don't say, "Do what I say, not what I do." That is hypocrisy. Character is not taught, it is caught.

- *Covenant* is the foundation of Character. We exist because of the covenant and character of God. Honor your covenant with God and Man. The covenant is only as good as your character.

- *Conviction* is the strength of your core values. When your core values are challenged, your convictions will defend and protect them. If you do not defend it, maybe, it isn't one of your convictions. Is truth one of your core convictions? When it is challenged by fake news, your convictions will defend it. Is life, and the protection of children and babies, one of your core convictions?

- **Commitment** reflects the follow-through of character. Our first commitment is to God. If you are married, your next commitment is to your wife, your children, your work/job, your church, and your friends.

- **Correction** is a manifestation of love. Who you love, you will correct. Ask any parent who had to correct their two-year-old child when the child tried to touch the hot stove or tried to cross the busy street without looking. It is the way of life…

- **Counsel** from Christ-centered Christians will lead to character building conduct. Seek good, Godly counsel. There is wisdom in it. To the degree you yield to the counsel of God's Word, that is the same degree to which your children will yield to yours.

- **Conscience** is fed by the conduct of your character. Develop a Godly character and your conscience will text you when you are going off track. If you keep ignoring your conscience, then it will post your behavior on Facebook and Instagram.

D

- **Discipline** helps to set your **D**irection which will determine your **D**estiny. Correction sets your orientation, but discipline is the rod that keeps you on the path. Discipline your children while they are young or the government *(Law-Enforcement)* will detain them and do that for you. *Society will then have to pay the bill.*

- **Dreams and Desires** should be cultivated, not crushed or dismissed. You do not stifle the stride of a stallion. You stear it in the right direction. Joseph's brothers tried to kill his dreams, but he became the second most powerful man in the world during his time. Don't kill their dreams. Kindle a fire of expectation and hope. You may be coaching the next president.

- **Determination** to hold on to Core Values. Walk with courage. Your Dad is God of the universe. With Him at your side, you will have all the determination you need to face the challenges of life. Your children are looking to you for the same courage. Tell them from whom you received yours.

- **Danger** awareness is really common sense on steroids. Read the book of Proverbs for yourself, and with your children, and then carefully consider the path of your feet. So many laws are changing about the use of bathrooms. Caution your daughters about men dressed like women seeking to use their bathroom. Boys use the *word love* to get their way with them, etc.

E

- **Expectations** are the roadmap to avoid the maze of disappointments while building clear outcomes. Set reasonable expectations for yourself and your children. This will reduce stress and bring peace in your life and home.

- **Encouragement** is the spark that ignites the fuel of creativity. What you encourage, will maximize its potential.

- **Ego** is not to be crushed. It should be cultivated to advance the positive impact of the Kingdom of God on earth. It is the *sanctified zeal of God* working within to pursue and accomplish great things for Him. Do not fall for the lie, that Ego is (Edging God Out). There is ego on the *left* to fulfill the agenda of the father of fake news, hate, and death. Use your ego to advance the cause of The Father of life, love, peace, righteousness, and joy on the *Right*. Which Father will get the Glory?

- **Employment & Entrepreneurship** start at home. Do you give your children a hand out that we call an allowance or do we give them responsible work duties and reward them with cash?

Teach them the 10, 10, 10 principle. The first 10 goes to God, The Heavenly Father, as a Tithe (a sacred memorial offering, in honor and celebration of Him. We honor His Strong, Right Hand, Jesus, who paid the ultimate price to reunite us with Him). Even though He has no personal use for money, He owns everything on Earth, and in the universe. He has entrusted you to manage all He has given you; life, health, strength and the ability to earn through your employment or entrepreneurial endeavors. You honor Him by returning the first 10% (sacred memorial offering) from your income in celebration of all He has done for you. This brings Him Glory! The tithe is then used by churches, and Apostles, (regardless if you can get a tax-write-off or not) to bless the fatherless, widows (single moms) and positive causes reflecting the heart and character of The Heavenly Father. In return,

He will bless you, your family and business in ways you would never think possible…

Your children will also learn how to honor God with their finances from your example. The second 10% should go long-term emergency savings and the third 10% should be for fun and recreational activities, including self-improvement books, training, etc.

The father who Prays and Plays with his family has the maximum potential of keeping his family together.

- ***Environmental*** beauty is to bring glory to God. All worship and praise goes only to Him. We do not worship His creation, we worship Him. We do our part to take care of our environment, but one day God will renovate the entire earth and make it new. Teach your children not to get caught up with fraudulent, fake-news stories from national leaders about climate change *(only to steal more money from working families through increased taxes by increasing regulations, to benefit the agenda on the left)*.

- ***Enjoyment.*** Dads are responsible for having fun and bringing games in their families. Work and play need to be balanced. Break off old patterns that say, you cannot have fun and work. Live your life to its full.

F

- ***Faith*** in God is the **foundation** of the family. Fathers and mothers are responsible to model and live out their faith publicly. The number one reason why youths leave the church is that they heard their parents talk about their faith, but they haven't seen them live it out at home and in society.

- ***Family.*** Where dad spends his time declares what he values. Fathers, spend time with your family. It will show them you value them.

- ***Future, Favor, Fitness.*** Dads are responsible to let their children know that God made them to have a productive future by walking in His favor and blessing to do His will. As physical fitness is beneficial to the physical body, so spiritual fitness is to our spiritual body. Men, spend time reading and studying God's Word with your family.

G

- *Glory* code. It determines your destiny. Dads, model and live a life reflective of the Glory Source from your Heavenly Father. As a result, you will raise children with healthy Glory Codes to be positive influencers in society.

- *Guide* your family by walking along the path that leads towards the Heavenly Father.

- *Govern* as a servant leader. Jesus said that he came to serve others. Dads, model by first serving your wife. Men, do you open the door for your wife? Do you help your wife wash the dishes? Do you clean-up after yourself? Do you help with chores around the house? Do you serve in community projects with your children and family? How you serve your wife and family will create their perception of the Heavenly Father, as modeled by Christ.

- *Guard* the hearts of your children and family by protecting and monitoring what you allow into your home. What music, movies, and morals are allowed to be portrayed in your home? This will determine how their hearts are being influenced. What we put in, will influence what comes out.

H

- *Honesty and Honor* are two key characteristics that dads model and bring to their family. Protect the honor by keeping a good name.

- *Humility and Humor* are foundational to receiving and modeling God's favor and blessings. God withholds his favor from those who walk in pride, but He shows His favor to those who walk in humility. Humor is key to keeping a happy heart because laughter is good medicine. Laughter releases healthy endorphins. Don't forget the value of "dad puns."

I

- *Integrity* is the maximized character of Christ. Who we are, privately, will ultimately manifest publicly. The Heavenly Father is molding us daily into the Character and Integrity of Christ

- *Identity* is established by Dads. Many dads do not even know who they are and what their role is in their family. Your words begin to form and shape the identity of your child or children even from the womb. Identity is not only by blood, but by spirit. Your words are spirit. Use the Word of God to speak life over your children and shape their identity into the character of Christ. When fathers choose to reject or accept the gender of their child, it will directly influence their emotional perception of self. Thus, causing identity confusion.

- *Influence* is a result of a good relationships. Dads, build a good relationship with your children. The greater your relationship, the greater your influence in their lives. The relationships you build with your friends can yield dividends of influence and favor for your children in the future. King David showed favor to Mephibosheth because of the good relationship he had built with Johnathan, his Dad. Influence can bring you before kings.

J

- *Joy* for the journey starts with a mindset. Knowing you are a child of God, you have a joyful expected destiny and eternal fellowship with your Heavenly Father and His family.

K

- *Knowledge* of the "why" makes you the employer. Knowledge of the "how" is the employee. Don't be dismissive of your children's questions. Teach them the why because they will be the leaders tomorrow. Dads, teach them how to address the source of problems. It will help them mitigate the symptoms later.

L

- *Love* is the source of life. God is Love. We were made in His image. We were made to model His love to our families and the world. Love conquers, and covers all sin and wrongdoing, it is the fulfillment of the law. Walk in love. There is no such thing as *"I can't love that person"* Love is a choice. The Heavenly Father commanded us to love each other. Dads, your role is to take the lead. Love your wife, your family, and others. You represent the Heavenly Father here on earth. As Jesus walked in love, we, too, need to do the same. One of the greatest gifts you can give your children is to love their mother. Their "GC" depends on it.

- *Legacy and Leverage* is the marriage that unlocks the doors of favor for your family in the future. Dad, your good name is worth more than gold. So, leave the legacy of a good name. It will provide leverage to endless possibilities for future generations.

- *Leadership* is conferred upon Dads to provide clarity and direction to the children and family. Even the weakest person is looked-up to for leadership by someone who is even weaker than they are. *Remember, someone is always watching.*

M

- *Marriage* is the greatest covenant that reflects the loving safety that children yearn for, and thrive within, its boundaries.

- *Money* is a tool to provide for your family, not to master your life.

- *Memories.* Turn key moments into lasting memories.

N

- *No.* The greater your yes, (purpose and value) the easier it is to say No! Build a great yes by spending time with your wife and children. Show-up for weekly date nights, family nights and vacations. With a great Yes, it will become easy to say NO! No, to things that are not equal in value.

O

- *Obedience* to the Heavenly Father unlocks favor and blessings in your life and your family.

P

- *Prayer* builds your relationship with The Heavenly Father and releases His *Prominence, Position, Provision Protection* in your life and your family.

Q

- ***Quiet time*** will orient your relationship with The Heavenly Father which helps you to avail yourself for ***Quantity Time*** with your wife and family.

R

- ***Relationship*** with healthy, wise friends builds ***Resilience*** to ***Recovery*** during tough times in your life and family.

S

- ***Savior.*** There is only one true savior. His name is Jesus. Dads, your one main mandate is to lead your families into a lifesaving relationship with The Heavenly Father through a relationship with His Son, Yeshua. He is the ***Source*** that brings ***Soundness and Security*** to you and your family.

- ***Sex.*** A gift of God to declare His Glory in the context of marriage between a husband *(Male at birth)* and his wife *(a female at birth)*. Dads, your children will have a healthy knowledge of sex within the marriage covenant as you explain this gift is nor for everyone, but to be saved for the person that will honor them in the protection of marriage.

T

- ***Truth*** builds ***Trust.*** This is the foundation of a long-lasting relationship. Build your marriage and family on this foundation.

U

- ***Unity*** in the family. Unite as one. As one cluster of grapes *(many grapes, one cluster)* when squeezed, produces a wonderful tasting grape juice. After time, it produces a great tasting wine of great value. In 1992 one bottle of wine was sold for $500,000. The longer you stay together as one, *(squeeze together to produce wine)* the greater value you will have in the world. The taste will be sweet.

V

- ***Values*** will determine your ***Victory.*** Your ***Vision*** will perpetuate your values to many generations. Dads, we are called to lead our families with the values that come from the character of Christ which will lead us to victory and will fulfill

The Heavenly Father's vision to let the world know and experience His Glory Source. Men, it is time to declare His Glory by living and influencing others to follow you as you lead.

W

- *Wisdom* is the principal thing in life. Get it and walk in it. Speak *words* that will shape and heal the hearts and lives of your families to become more like Jesus.

X

- *"X" out* the negative and embrace life, joy, and peace from the Heavenly Father.

Y

- *Yesterday* was a teacher. Tomorrow you have the potential to practice what you have learned from your teacher.

Z

- *Zeal.* Zest for life (and the purpose of The Heavenly Father) is to positively influence the world for His Glory.

- *Zero.* Balance the books. Forgive and release the things that keep you from being in a harmonious relationship with The Heavenly Father.

Paul R. Benjamin, Sr.

Chapter 30

Word Theft: Counterfeit or Real

Deb: Thanks for that A-Z guide. These are some helpful tips for dads. I have a random though that I'd like to bring up. I have friends at work who say they are Christians, but their actions, and world view, reflect the character of the father of the left.

Paul: The freedoms and values of authentic conservatives are based on their core belief in The Heavenly Father producing a balanced, healthy society. Armed with this heart and character, they can, in turn, positively impact their families, communities and Nation. The Heavenly Father's *Government* operates on the core values of: Love, Joy, Justice, Righteousness, and Peace. Conservatives comes from the very character of Christ. A true conservative is someone whose lifestyle *(politics)* reflect the character of Christ.

Anyone can align with the right, based on personal preference, but an *authentic conservative* will always support God's *"right"* because of the conviction in their heart. Who you are in private *(character)* will manifest publicly *(lifestyle)*.

Voting On the Right should reflect key characteristics of The Heavenly Father: Saving lives of babies, children and police officers because "all lives matter;" moral integrity in marriage (one man to one woman); and lowering taxes to enable families the freedom to spend more time with each other.

Voting On the Left will reflect the key characteristics of the father of the *left, Lucifer, the devil*. Core values of the left: Lying *(fake news, twisting and manipulating the truth)*, murdering (freedom to murder babies; in and outside a mother's womb and freedom to sell these baby parts to individuals and companies), promoting and endorsing immoral lifestyles, pillaging families by raising taxes and placing unnecessary restrictions and regulations on businesses.

Deb: With this information, people will now have a clear understanding of the only two working systems in the world. You mentioned in the beginning, once people know this information, they will be held accountable for what they do with it. Paul, this is a little off topic. With the recent death of Jerry Epstein, I am hearing how many women and families were impact by pornography. Could you please address this?

Pornography Impacts Families and the World

Paul: Pornography destroys families. Not only does it impact dads, but their wives and children. Former President Bill Clinton's dad had a profound effect upon him and our nation. When he was a boy, former President Clinton was exposed to the *power and influence of pornography.* He came across his dad's pornographic magazines, and as they say, the rest is history. Today, 60-70% of men, and pastors, struggle with pornography.

Pornography gives a false, elusive gratification to the GC, making it hard to remove or renew. It's like abusing a drug, a temporary fix. It provides a *"high,"* but it never satisfies the "GC." Men, and women, don't realize when they have authentic intimacy with The Heavenly Father, the less they will desire to quench their crushed (-5) GC with unhealthy, addictive behaviors.

Sex in the White House

Former President Bill Clinton's oral sex scandal became public and caused a ripple effect across the nation. The impact from that event is still entrenched in the fabric of our society.

Deb: I was furious after I learned what former President Clinton did. Not long after, I began to hear of young children experimenting with sex in school. We need to restore hope in our children and families again.

Paul: We sure do, Deb. Many children, within the school systems, believe the lie. They think that because it is not *sexual intercourse*, it is not classified as *"sex."* I am deeply saddened by this turn in our society.

Blood Drive canceled. 95% of students tested positive

Another shocking moment, with far-reaching implications, occurred when a local school held a blood drive. It had to be cancelled due to the fact that 95% of the students tested positive for a sexually transmitted diseases (STD). Some were proud of this fact, stating, *"At least we are not having 'real sex' and are still virgins."* The moral implications from the choices the students made will be felt for generations to come. As I mentioned earlier, to the degree of your influence, is the degree of the impact. In our FFS impacted society, children seeking to fill and satisfy their crushed GC and will use anything, or anyone, in an effort to fill the void in their lives.

One of the roles of dads is to protect their daughter's virginity until she marries. It is an honor for a father to present his pure daughter to her husband on their wedding day. Jewish dads would give their daughter's husband a white sheet for their wedding bed. When they consummate the marriage on their honeymoon night, the blood from her hymen would be on the white sheet. This blood-stained sheet would be neatly folded and returned to the bride's dad. This was a sign of her virginity. Her dad would be honored, knowing that he had fulfilled his mandated responsibility to raise and protect his daughter until marriage. This would bring him glory in the community.

Girls, sexually abused by their Dads, have Shattered Glory Codes

When a girl has been sexually abused by her dad, *(the man mandated to protect and preserve her virginity until marriage)* it shatters her Glory Code at the deepest level. This violation will alter the beliefs she holds; toward self, as well as, any current or future relationships. Her intrinsic self-worth is erased and replaced with anger, bitterness, self-hatred, worthlessness and resentment towards The Heavenly Father (who was not there to stop the act). She now feels dirty all the time!! *(It's like taking a shower over and over, yet, never feeling 'clean')*

When these women choose to get married, they may experience a vast array of interpersonal struggles. (It would require a full day seminar to cover this topic completely.) When I counsel husbands, I discuss the importance of knowing the relationship between their wives and their fathers. This will let you know what to expect, and how to minister to her. The marriage bed can become a very cold place.

The Pain of Truth is Difficult to Accept

One day I hosted a team of mature women; ranging in age from 58- 79 years old. They were from a local church in the community. They were looking for ways to volunteer at the Center.

10-year old gives Birth to Twins

While giving them the tour of our facility, I mentioned the story of a 10-year-old girl from the community who had been sexually abused and given birth to twins. One of the ladies flatly refused to believe what I said, and even accused me of lying. She said there was no way such a thing could happen! Needless to say, I never saw her again.

We, too, respond much like this woman when presented with the atrocities of life. In an effort to insulate and protect our hearts, we block them out, pretending they never occur. Our mind will attempt to preserve and safeguard our GC.

Estrogen-laced meats, filled with growth hormones, cause female reproductive organs to quickly develop. Nowadays, all you have to do is turn on the news to hear about multiple 10-year-olds giving birth. The men perpetrating these atrocious against these young girls are under the assumption their abdominal acts will never be uncovered. They assume if they stop before the young girl has her period, the abuse will stay hidden.

Deb: I can identify with the pain these older women feel. Listening to their stories, I understand why they disassociate in an effort to guard their hearts from the painful reality.

Dressing Provocatively

Paul: I, too, can empathize. Girls, who have been sexually abused, lose a sense of self-worth. They attempt to regain perceived value by dressing provocatively in order to attract attention, almost unconsciously seeking to quench their crushed "GC." They may move through multiple relationships and alternative lifestyles seeking to fill this void. The impact to their "GC" goes deep…

Spiritually Renewed Glory Code

On average, 24 people per minute are abused in America. Millions of them have lost their virginity, the precious intrinsic gift The Heavenly Father gave them as part of their Glory Code. It was intended to be a gift to their husbands to seal their *covenant* relationship on their wedding night. The Heavenly Father sealed His relationship in Season One with the blood of His Son.

My heart goes out to every woman, girl and boy who lost their precious innocence. The Heavenly Father wants to bring hope and healing to your heart and life. He wants to mend your shattered "GC" and bring renewed spiritual virtue to you.

He is saying, *"I am waiting for you to give me all your pain and broken pieces. In exchange, I will give you a renewed Glory Code. I will heal your heart. You no longer have to live with the pain, shame and anger of your past. I will give you my peace and restored Glory Code that is only satisfied in Me. Every pain and hurt you felt, I felt, also. I placed it on myself. In Season One, I nailed it to the cross.*

One day, in my appointed Season, I will come for all my children. In my presence, there will be no more pain or tears. I Love you with an everlasting love." Your loving, Heavenly Dad.

Father-Rophe (Rapha), The Heavenly Father who *heals, restores, and brings renewal, by turning bitter things into blessings.*

Deb: The thought that there is hope awaiting all who have been abused gives me some grace to endure all the pain I witness in the world. Just when I think it's getting a little better, something worse happens. Can you give some insight into the tragic murder that happened in Volusia?

Paul: Let's address this tragic murder tomorrow. I happen to know the victim that was involved.

Deb: I know this one may be heard for you. We will continue tomorrow. See you then.

Paul R. Benjamin, Sr.

Chapter 31

Children Abusing
and
Killing their Parents

Paul: Welcome back Deb. I know you must be ready to jump right back in to our interview.

Deb: Hi guys. I brought both of you some hot coffee. Let's pick-up where we left off.

Paul: Thanks for the coffee Deb…

My heart is constantly bombarded with disturbing news. Every news article only further validates my mission to bring life and healing to families and the nations.

A 15-year-old young man, Charlie, murdered his mother, Cheryl. Charlie, and his two friends, buried his mom's body in a church yard in Volusia County, Florida. This tragic event caught the attention of the national media. Cheryl, a single mother, had volunteered for the Center a decade before. Years later, she got married and brought her new husband into her *"mother-son relationship."* Our thoughts and prayers are with her son and family.

Charlie had been seeking his biological dad's acceptance and approval. In 2018, Charlie brought home a "D" on his high school report card. Cheryl threatened to show his report card to his biological dad. This news sent Charlie over the edge. While she slept, Charlie strangled her to death. He will be tried as an adult with the possibility of life in prison.

Wisdom for Single Moms

Cheryl didn't know threatening her son, Charlie, would be the catalyst to push his (-6) "GC," to (-7) "GC," the critical level that results in either murder or suicide. In this case it was murder.

Unaware, that showing her son's failing report card to the man who gives him his capstone approval, was like saying, *"I will take away the oxygen of your soul."* Compounded by anger and resentment from his parent's break-up, Charlie's crushed "GC," had been at a dangerous point building up to this final moment.

Subconsciously, or consciously, children blame their custodial moms for the separation from their dads. Regardless which parent was at fault, or who caused the separation or divorce, children still seek the intrinsic seal of love from their dads. Most parents are not aware of this *capstone seal* that a dad brings to their child's Glory Code.

Another key principle, most single moms don't recognize, comes to light when they remarry another man. They need the blessing, approval, and acceptance of their children, especially their sons. Single dads planning to remarry, also need the same thing, especially from their daughters. (Another all-day seminar would be required to address all the ramifications associated with single parents and blended families.)

Deb: Paul, this was another devastating tragedy. Single moms need to learn these principles. If Cheryl had known the principle regarding her son's crushed "GC," it could have been a game changer.

Workaholic and Performance-Based Relationships

Paul: These principles when integrated can change the fabric of society.

Ray, a former volunteer at the Center, never received approval from his Dad. He worked his day job before coming to volunteer. This 5' 2," 42-year-old blond man could outwork any young man I knew. It came to my attention how many hours he worked (volunteered) at the Center each week.

I invited Ray to lunch. He acknowledged his dad never affirmed any work he did at home. Even after his first job, he didn't receive his dad's approval.

At this point, Ray's dad had been dead for five years. His unconscious quest for his dads' approval drove his work performance. Today, there are so many men and women who are still *"performing"* for approval and acceptance from their dads or moms.

As I spoke with Ray, he began tearing up as I prayed the Father's blessing over him. As I mentored Ray, he became equipped with this new revelation and began to implement greater balance between his work and home life.

Sexual Abuse by Pastors, Priests and other Religious Leaders

Many single moms came to the Center seeking assistance with rent payments or utility fees. When asked if they had reached out to their local church or pastor, quite a few of them would respond by saying, *"My pastor wanted sexual favors in return for helping me with my rent."*

During my years of working within the community, I mentored several pastors. One in particular comes to mind. He informed me when he took over a new church, the women who had been abused by the previous pastor invited him to meet their daughters; all "fathered" by the prior pastor. They offered up their daughters to the new pastor to carry on the same legacy.

My heart goes out to those who have been abused. These spiritual leaders should have been reflecting the true Heart and character of The Heavenly Father, instead they were abusing the authority for their own personal gain. Many women and men have rejected the Love of The Heavenly Dad because their image of Him is so marred by dads, priests, and pastors.

Core Values or Corrosion through Coercion

The dad sets the final seal on the core values in the family. Children usually reflect the core values they have seen modeled in their homes. Children who were raised in two-parent homes with a mom and dad on the right are more likely to hold on to stronger core values. Children raised in homes where there is no dad are more likely to be easily influenced, intimidated, and pressured to follow other unsavory youth in school and the community.

Because so many youths are being raised without dads, their GC is crushed and they are looking for acceptance and approval from their peers and other authority figures to substitute as a father or mother figure. Not having solid core values based on knowledge and relationship with The Heavenly Father, they most times will not have the courage to stand up under the *pressure of coercion.*

Strong Core Values become Stronger Under Pressure

Today we are witnessing leaders who do not have solid core values. Under the slightest pressure, they cave-in. Dads and moms who influence and instill strong core values in their children, when these children are challenged on their core values, instead of caving in to pressure – they instead grow stronger under pressure. Just like a diamond, it is forged under pressure. Dads need to help prepare their children to become diamonds. Today, more than ever before we need more men to become Diamond dads.

Chapter 32

The "What is to come" Phase

Deb: I have seen many leaders print retractions after receiving criticism from the media. They were courageous and made statements that needed to be said. However, later backed down from their stance when leftwing media inflamed the story, claiming they were racist. Paul, we really need men of courage today to take a stand, regardless of the cost.

Paul: Deb, many of these men were raised by single moms. This doesn't mean that all men, who were raised by single moms, lack courage, but this principle is true most of the time. Men get, and embrace, courage from watching their dads act courageously.

The Greater the Expectation, the Greater the Disappointment

Call 911!! I would like to report a crime of identity theft (The misrepresentation of the true heart of The Heavenly Father in the churches of America and around the world).

Please forgive us. We, the children of The Heavenly Father, have misrepresented His True Heart and Character in our FFS impacted world. You might have heard the phrase, the greater the expectation, the greater the disappointment. Well, the same is true for, the greater the hurt, the deeper the wound (to the Glory Code).

When someone attends a church, or a place of worship, they go with an expectation of hope and healing. They are seeking answers to quench the burning desire in their heart. They want to understand why their Glory Code is shattered. However, before deciding to give church a try, they may have tried everything else including drugs, food, work or sex. Some may have attempted suicide. Finally, after exhausting all efforts, they give in and decide to give it a try.

Many become shocked and disillusioned when they walk into a church and are greeted by people who look down on them. They might even hear things like, your hair is too long, your tattoos are offensive or your clothes are not acceptable. Many are chastised for not discipling their children and told they need to learn how to become better parents.

Some churches are much more offensive saying comments such as, "You are a wicked sinner. If you don't repent, you are going to hell!"

If you, or anyone of your family members, have visited one of these churches, please forgive them. They have grossly misrepresented the true heart of The Heavenly Father. It is His goodness that attracts us to Him, not the harsh baseball bat approach. There are many good churches out there, reflecting the true heart of our Heavenly Father. He loves you where you are, but He loves you too much to leave you where you are. He is waiting to give you His Acceptance, Approval, Authority, Assignment and Affirmation. He wants you to walk in your new Identity as He renews your Glory Code. Your season is now!

Deb: You just described some of the things that went on in my father's church. If we, his children, felt condemned at home, imagine how the church members felt when he kept criticizing how they dressed and what they did. Now, I have a renewed image of The Heavenly Father and I would like to invest my life making this known to the world.

Life Center Missional Impact

Paul: Deb, you are an example of what God can do to bring healing to individuals who surrender their lives to Him. The church is made up of broken, fallen people. They are seeking healing for themselves. Once received, they then share their hope and victory with others.

As I mentioned to the pastors who came to my office many years ago. The answer is not in more government programs. The mandate to minister, and influence, the community belongs to the church. The church is called to be salt and light; beginning in their own community, city and the world.

We are the Answer

This story is a perfect example of why we need to be the answer to our community...

Two blocks from my former office, a 12-year-old girl returned home from school. The short, 300-yard walk seemed like a mile in the heat of the day. As she turned the key to the front door of her subsidized apartment, she sensed that someone was in the house. Her mom's boyfriend entered the room and began stroking her hair. He progressed until he raped her. He said if she told her mother, or anyone else, he would kill her and her family.

Two miles away, in an effort to prove his manhood, her 15-year-old brother was stealing a car from a gated community. This was part of his initiation to join a gang. His actions didn't disturb him in the least. After all, his dad was currently serving 15 years in prison for armed robbery.

The same girl's 14-year-old sister was pregnant with her first child. Not unlike her own mother who gave birth to her at the same age. Crying and shaking in fear after the horrific rape, she heard a knock at the door. It was her 7-year-old sister arriving from school.

After the mother of these children, Jay, finished smoking marijuana at her friend's house, she went home. Just as she was about the enter the apartment, the social worker from the child the protective service showed up at the door. She had previously been warned that she is in danger of losing her children to foster care. She began to panic and decided to reach out for help!

She went to the neighborhood churches and all eight of them were closed. The sign said, open on Sundays 9:00 AM and 11:00 AM for services. She began to cry. Eight churches and they were all closed! She thought to herself, "They are not there when I need them." *(Not unlike most churches in America, her neighborhood churches were only open 3 to 7 Hours per week)* What a waste! Jay returned home hopeless, discouraged and fearful that she may lose her children to the foster system.

Deb: Wow, this story validates the need for change!

Paul: One of the local pastors reached out to me. He asked about the Life Center Strategy for communities. He invited me to share the vision with him and his board members. They fell in love with the vision, were trained and hosted a Life Center Vision Event, in hope of raising funds to funds to launch a Life Center in their area. The event had a great attendance. Business leaders, public officials and other partnering churches got behind the vision. Together they were able to raise approximately *"$120,000"* that was needed to operate the Center for the first year.

They asked 120 people to invest $1,000 for the first year. The second year, the original 120 people would ask one of their friends to do the same. And so on, up to five years. At the end of the five years the Life Center should be *self-sustaining* from its own business and development activities.

Bringing Hope to the Community

Let's refer back to the story of Jay. She was home crying one day when she heard a knock on her door. It was a volunteer from the Life Center outreach team. They mentioned the Center is open Monday – Friday providing programs and services for the entire family. These included:

- Obtaining a high school diploma/GED
- Finding and maintaining a job/career
- Offering individual and family counseling
- Mentoring for men, women and youth
- Learning a trade
- Signing up for a high demand, career-based college degree
- Learning effective business principles in the Entrepreneurship Training Program.
- Media, Digital Marketing, Website Design, Video Production, Arts
- Real-Estate, Property Management, Investing
- Business and Accounting Management
- Culinary Arts, Restaurant Ownership/Management, Hospitality Industry
- Construction, Plumbing, Electrical, Steel, HVAC, Trades Industry
- Lawn Care and Landscaping Business
- Medical and Dental industry
- Franchise Ownership
- Banking, Insurance, Financial Investments
- Automotive, Air and Land Transportation Industry and much more…
- Investing in a home (real estate). Fix and Flip Income Properties
- Teaching them how to reinvest in their community, and leave a legacy.
- Navigating through social ills within their families and resolve conflicts

- Addressing human trafficking concerns

- Embracing the strategy of **(8)** Diversified Entrepreneurial *Streams of Income*

After graduation from the Entrepreneurship Training Program, business leaders *provided small micro loans to invest* in families who had been trained in the following business arenas:

Jay was so overwhelmed with their offer to help that she hugged all the volunteers. She said, *"When can I come to the Center?"* They said, *"We are hosting a huge community event at the church to introduce the Life Center to the region."*

Looking back, it's amazing to see how far Jay and her family have come. She is working as an assistant manager for a local business in the community. Her children are doing great in school. Her family is attending the local church and reaching out to help other families.

Deb: Wow! We need these impact centers in communities across our nation and around the world. The impact that one person can make in the life of another is priceless. I will do my part in my city.

Mark Meadows hears the Mission

Paul: While having breakfast at one of my favorite places, *Chick-fil-A,* Mark Meadows came in with his police security team. I introduced myself and shared our mission to mitigate the impact from the FFS in cities across America and around the world. After our 8.5-minute exchange, Mr. Meadows handed me his personal business card with his phone number on it. He said, *"Paul, this is a great mission. Let me know how I can help?"*

Deb: If I were you, I would call him to further discuss this strategy with him.

The Power of One

Paul: I may reach out to him, but the solution to our problems need to be initiated and implemented by the "church," not government. The government may help give influence and key relational contacts, but the faith community needs to take the lead. Many of us are conditioned to look outside of ourselves for the solution that resides within us. I know it is easier to deflect our problems thinking if I ignore it long enough, it will go away; or I will let someone else take care of it. This mindset is part of the problem and has led us to where we are today as a society.

It only takes one person who decides to say, *"I will make a positive difference in my generation."* With this mindset, we can see our homes, communities, and the world transformed. There is someone out there with a crushed Glory Code waiting for a word of encouragement from you, someone in whom you can invest your life and make a difference. For even the weakest person, there is someone weaker, looking to them as a role-model.

The Murder of George Floyd

Deb's I-phone eleven began ringing. It was an urgent call from her office.

Deb: Paul and Dawn please excuse me. I have to take this call. It's from John. It must be urgent! I will return shortly.

Paul: Sure Deb. I hope all is well? Let's all pause and meet again in 29.7 minutes.

Deb: Dawn and Paul I am sorry for the interruption. John called to let me know of a national breaking story. It's exploding around America and the world.

Paul: Deb, this must be big! Please share with us what this big incident and event is?

Deb: Sure Paul, as a matter of fact, John sent me the video link. Let's look at it together. I must caution you and Dawn, this is a very sad nine-minute video. It may even bring tears to your eyes when you watch this white police officer murder this black man, George Floyd. Paul, John would like for you to give your comments about *this global spark event.* He would like to how we, as a people and nation, can address this pandemic. He will like to publish your response in special news edition.

"I can't Breathe!"

Paul: Deb, it was disturbing to watch the tragic murder of *George Floyd.* I was moved to tears watching him gently appeal for oxygen. *"Officer, I can't breathe..."* These were the last words that George cried as he appealed to the white, Minnesota Police Officer, Derek Chauvin, who held his knee on his neck for about eight minutes.

Let's Pause and pray for George Floyd's family, officer Chauvin's family, the healing of America and the world. We need a wave of The Heavenly Father's Love to flow into every heart to turn around what the Enemy meant for evil and use it for good. We also need to pray that God will give President Trump the wisdom and favor to navigate our country through this difficult season.

Deb: Thanks for praying. The pain of seeing this murder has touched many people around the world. It's like reliving the Trayvon Martin tragedy all over again. Paul please share your perspective. How can we address this international back-lash?

Paul: The crushed Glory Codes of the 9 out 10 black youth who are growing up without their dads, in urban America, witnessing this tragic incident, metaphorically represents their own cry, *"I can't breathe." Remember,* The Glory Code is the oxygen of the soul.

Deb: This was a good reminder. So, in essence, everyone with a crushed Glory Code attached their own pain to the pain stirred-up by this tragic incident. This was the same pain that was manifested during the Trayvon Martin shooting.

Ethnic Bigotry (Racism)

Paul: The Trayvon Martin tragedy gave birth to Black Lives Matter (BLM). As I mentioned before, we don't have a racism problem in America, we have a "sin" problem!

Before I address the ramifications of this tragedy, I would like to say, *"Thank you,"* to all the good, loyal, and faithful *police officers,* who serve and put their lives at risk for us every day across our nation and around the world.

In every sector of society, we have good, and bad, Right and Left. There are *good pastors* and *bad pastors.* We have *good priests* and *bad priests.* There are *good plumbers* and *bad plumbers.* Nationally, we are witnessing *good police officers,* and *bad police officers.* We cannot ridicule and condemn all police officers because of the 2 to 10% bad "cops" whose actions are incongruous to the core principles of policing.

There is only one race, the human race. We are many *ethnic groups* of one blood and stem from the lineage of Adam, our earthly father. The excellence of The Heavenly Father made us male and female in various colors, sizes, and heights to reveal His Glory. The Enemy on the left, has used our *"external differences"* to divide and destroy, causing us to forget we were made in the image of God.

Deb: As of now, we don't know why police officer Derek Chauvin did what he did.

Paul: There could be many reasons why this officer committed this murder. It could be because of his ethnic bigotry, bad training, or *"Post Traumatic Stress Disorder."*

Deb: God knows his heart and motive.

Paul: Every day since the launch of Black Lives Matter movement, police officers and their families woke up to the BLM chant, *"What do we want?" "Dead cops!" "And when do we want it?"* Now! *"Pigs in a blanket, fry them up like bacon!"* "Black males" that time began murdering police officers after the Trayvon Martin shooting which gave birth to Black Lives Matter.

Just imagine, the wives of these police officers knowing when they kiss their husbands goodbye, it may be the last time they see them. When their children hug their fathers, it may be the last embrace they receive from their dad. This is the reality police officers face daily. Many of them became *fearful, and hyper* when arresting a black man. Many white officers over compensate, out of fear, when arresting black men.

Deb: I never thought of the stress and pressure these officers and their families are under on a daily basis. How is the generational pain, abuse, and injustice that blacks endured playing out in this national outcry?

Pain, Protest and Pillage

Paul: Just as some police officers may suffer, many blacks are dealing with negative stories of past abuse, mixed with current-day injustices and marginalization. This fact, mingled with their crushed Glory Codes makes black men and women *primed, poised and positioned for explosive behaviors*:

- **Pain:** Some blacks may march in a *peaceful protest* and seek healing and reconciliation with whites that reach out and embrace them. These actions pose a threat to pastors and pundits on the left who do not want reconciliation, as they prosper financially by keeping blacks bitter and angry. Forgiveness brings true "freedom" and healing and stops the pain and pillage.

- **Pain to Purpose:** Teams of Christians began hosting community outreach and revival services at the site where George Floyd died in Minneapolis. People who are looking for hope are being reconciled with The Heavenly Father. Many of them are being baptized. Others are reaching out to their friends to share the good news of Jesus.

"Except a seed falls to the ground and die, it abides alone." George Floyd's death was that seed which God can use to help turn around what the Enemy meant for evil and use if for good. This is a great response from the faith community.

- **Pillage:** Many black pastors and national sports figures, like *Collin Kaepernick, are in* support of rioting and looting. Kaepernick wore a picture of a "pig" on his socks, echoing the BLM mantra, the call for the *"murder of police officers.*

- **Black looters kill other blacks**, including *black* police officers. They are encouraged by leftist leaders to destroy black-owned businesses in their own communities. Not knowing, they are destroying their own ***"opportunity zones"*** that will help them to prosper in the future. The destruction of businesses will keep them hooked and loyal to the *"system."*

Many looters and rioters didn't even know "the name" of the black person who was "killed." Their only motive was fueled by a *"lust for money."* It drove their actions to pillage whites, and others. Many were paid leftwing protesters funded leaders and organizations to create ongoing division and unrest in our nation.

Hijack and Pillage White America

Deb: Paul, you mentioned, Black Lives Matter was initially birthed as an outcry after the shooting death of Trayvon Martin near your home. How can whites, including business owners and the faith community, *respond and not react* to this *deceptive and divisive movement?*

Paul: This feels surreal, Deb! I don't have much time to go into greater detail. I am reminded of the conversations I have had with white pastors and business leaders since 2001. I encouraged and challenged them to join me in reaching the urban black communities before they reached us with crime and violence in ours. Now, the urban "black" community, powered by BLM, is influencing the world, and seems to be dictating the narrative of the day.

God Sent His Son to Reveal Himself as "Father"

What we neglect today, will get our attention tomorrow. God is the Father to the fatherless. I believe He is making a loud sound. The blood of the fatherless is crying out for justice. The Heavenly Father's justice leads to true peace, not like what you see and hear from the leftwing media. Many young men and women from the urban, black community are fatherless and they are making the loudest appeal. Their quest for justice hijacked by the father of fake news, Satan, who is operating through the BLM movement.

Deb: I know you don't have much time left, but could you briefly share what should be the response of the President, churches and business leaders?

Paul: I would like to address this but, Dawn and I are going out of town. I will have to answer these questions when we return.

President Trump's Response

Deb: Welcome back folks. It's good to see you. Paul, you promised that we could pick-up where we left off.

Paul: I have outlined some key responses that President Trump, churches and business leaders can implement to help mitigate this social pandemic.

Remember I mentioned before, we don't have a crime problem, we have a "sin" problem. Radical rioters vandalized St. John's Church *building* in Washington, DC. This was grossly disrespectful. Anger and rejection of God, and "His Word," symbolizes the platform of the left.

President Trump walked from the White House to the "House of God." *(God dwells in people, not buildings.)* President Trump picked-up the "Bible" that was firmly ensconced on his Presidential Desk. This Bible, passed on to him by his mom, had been used in the *Welsh Revival.* This act symbolized his dependence upon God for wisdom. He asked God to bring the same *"Revival and Renewal to America."*

As President Trump walked to the church building, he was taking a stand for "Justice and Mercy," reclaiming the lost ground leftist operatives had stolen. When he held up the "Bible," he made a public declaration that The Heavenly Father is the *"only hope"* for the healing of the crushed Glory Codes in the lives of people in our nation and the world.

Dads, we need to be men of courage to hold-up the Word of God, "The Bible," as the standard for our lives and our families. Symbolically, we need to stand with the

President and hold-up the same standard. Just like Aaron and Hur who held up the hands of Moses, we need to stand together in order to have victory over the Enemy on the left.

Deb: To see our President holding up the "Word of God" was a powerful image. This brought hope to me. We need God to bring us through the chaos in our nation.

The Church's Response

Paul: While we were talking another black man, Rayshard Brooks, a 27-year old, was shot by an Atlanta, Georgia police officer in a Wendy's parking lot. In retaliation, the mob burnt the Wendy's to the ground, leaving the black employees without a place to work. We will pray for all families involved in this, yet, another avoidable shooting.

Pastors are already calling me for strategic ways to address this crisis in our nation. I caution them, not to fall for the BLM, deceptive agenda. This is not a quick fix. I encourage them not to react, but respond with a careful, long-term lifestyle change and ministry initiative.

For many decades, white churches have neglected the plight of urban, black America. They represent the undesirable, non-performing assets or people, who are a burden to their ministry team and finances. Not to mention, some white churches still practice and walk in the sin of ethnic bigotry (racism).

Recently, a black pastor who sounded "white" on the phone was invited to apply for a preaching position at a white church. Without doing their due diligence, to learn more about him, they were shocked when this "black" pastor showed up for the interview. He was rejected due to the color of his skin and not the content of his character.

External events do not necessarily produce internal Change

Pulpit Exchange. For many years black and white pastors have exchanged pulpits. This is a great gesture, but all too often, this transaction does not yield favorable results. Authentic unity and reconciliation can only happen at the Cross of Jesus.

When a white pastor finds an authentic black pastor, one who is not playing the restitution- racist guilt game, there can be great brotherhood between them, and their communities can be impacted.

God requires John 17 unity among his children (That we would be *one* just like He, Jesus is *one* with His Father, God). After all, we have one Father, one Lord, one faith and one baptism. As the Apostle Paul said, *"Why do some of you say, I am of Paul or I am of Apollos or of Cephas?"* In like manner, I would ask, *"Why do we claim, I am Baptist, or Presbyterian, or Lutheran?"* Is Christ divided? It was Jesus who died and paid the price for us to walk in His Love, expecting us to reach the world on His behalf. As He was, so are we in this world.

Missionaries Launch Urban Impact Centers

When the white church abandoned the urban community their character and influence left a huge vacuum in urban America. Crime increased due to the lack of fathers. The opportunity for interracial mentoring was lost. We overcome evil by doing good. 90% of mission funds are sent around the world. Less than 10% of a church's missional budget is invested at home, and even less is spent to improve the conditions in our urban communities. Sorry to say, but some white pastors would rather see the urban black areas obliterated as referenced in Pastor David Platt's book, "Radical."

The Heavenly Father said, "If we see others being drawn away and killed *(Like what we see daily in black America)* and we hide ourselves (by not making a difference) we will have to give an account to Him. I am **coaching pastors and leaders to "Respond" effectively.** With the proper training they can work together to establish a L.I.F.E impact centers across the nation. Initially, these relationships need to be facilitated to protect the white leaders who would be targets for "Blacklash" (pillage and guilt manipulation). This is another all-day seminar.

Urban Family System Reform

Deb: Paul, this is what I noticed in the church we attend. We spend huge amounts of money funding all kinds of mission work around the world, but the community around our church building is falling apart. Most church members drive in from other communities and are not really concerned about the plight around the church building. All they have to do is drive back to their nice gated communities. This explains why there is such neglect in urban cities.

Paul: Deb, you are tracking with me. One of the key indicators of the church's neglect is it's of true missional work to the fatherless. Blacks represent about 13 to 15% of our population, yet they make-up 80-85% of our jail population.

All too often, many sons meet their dads for the first time in jail or prison. Why is that? With over 90% of black youths being raised in urban America without their dads, the bi-product is more crime, drugs, violence and rage. With this said, now you know why we have more police incidences and calls from this sector of our nation.

George Floyd lived in a tax-payer funded government project called Third Ward Community Projects before moving to Minnesota. Just like many fatherless young men, he was involved in multiple crimes and was in and out of the prison system. Based on some reports, he had reconciled his life with The Heavenly Father and for about five years he was involved with community outreach before relocating to Minnesota.

As I mentioned before, if we are going to see any real, long lasting impact in the black urban communities, we need to restructure the welfare system that emasculates the black dads and their role in the family. If the church is going to respond to this crisis and not react by becoming part of another *"Free, free, hand-out program."* These, and many other key reforms and re-framing strategies that I teach, need to be implemented in the church, and community.

Like so many failed government, tax-payer funded programs, large churches and large businesses with huge budgets, will be part of the same failed system. After all, they have enough money to throw at the problem. The media coverage helps their image, but lifestyle and generational change is a *"four letter word…"* work! Yes, it means getting out of our comfort zones and been equipped to make a true difference.

Cower or Courage

Coach Mike Gundy of Oklahoma State University (OSU) acquiesced when his leftwing players objected to him wearing a T-shirt with the One America News (OAN) logo. One America News is a conservative news network. Later, I spoke to a loyal Oklahoma University fan, dyed in the wool (OU), "Boomer Sooner" fan who always had great respect for Coach Mike Gundy… the operative word being "had." Coach Gundy took off his shirt today, what will we take off tomorrow…?

Today, we need dads and men of courage and conviction who would take a stand for their faith and Biblical values, regardless the cost.

The Covert Agenda of BLM

Deb: Could you please leave me with some quick key points and indicators that I can add to what you have already given me?

Paul: Share, I will share some short bullet points. Here are just a few:

- ***Profiling is not ethnic bigotry (Racism),*** it is a common-sense response coupled with experience and knowledge. I might have mentioned before that I was robbed at gun-point multiple times by black men in hoodies. When a black man came into my store, my experience (Robbed by "black men wearing hoodies") triggered my response to press or keep my finger on top of the "police alarm button." Was my response based on my ethnic bigotry (racism) or knowledge (common sense) that I was robbed by black men.

  Leftwing operatives use the word "profiling" as a means to guilt and manipulate whites, law enforcement and other to believe that they are "racist" when they react with caution or concern. Many times, it is because the *"TV and Hollywood image of black and brown men"* portray them as muggers or gangsters. These two ethnic groups represent the largest sector that are fatherless.

- ***Deception and control.*** Deep Fake News leftist agents produce reality videos to stir-up and activate individuals with crushed (-6) Glory Codes to act-out in cities across America and even around the world. The national unrest is used to manipulate key leaders from being in office, like President Trump.

- ***Idolatry of "unforgiveness."*** To leverage money from whites and businesses, and to gain more power and control, blacks and the BLM keep stirring up "spark events" by inflaming selective key incidents between blacks and whites. Unforgiveness keeps the fire of rage and resentment alive. *Pastors are caught up with their cultural identity and not with their identity in Christ. Many black pastors are seeking financial restitution before they even address their own "ethnic bigotry" and unforgiveness.*

- ***All Lives and Blue Lives Matter.*** Merely mentioning *"all live matter or blue lives matter"* is rejected and labeled as "racist." This is so BLM can keep the focus and funding flowing only to their movement. These funds go to key leftist leaders to fund their agenda to destroy families and the core values of America. In 2020, their goal is to abort the Trump Presidency. *Laws may regulate your lifestyle, but only God can renew your nature. We cannot legislate the sin of "ethnic bigotry" from the heart of mankind. It will always find a way to manifest.*

- ***Companies are caving to the coercion.*** In fear of the national "Black-lash" *companies are changing their products and marketing partnerships. Companies bowed a knee to Black Lives Matter, whose agenda is to silence anyone who speaks out against them like conservative TV host, Tucker Carlson that airs on the Fox News network. Some of the companies that pulled their ads are: Angie's List, Jackson Hewitt, Disney, T-Mobile and Papa John's Pizza. Who will be the next victim of their hate agenda?*

- ***Do Black Lives matter to BLM?*** *Many well-intentioned whites fall prey to the deceptive agenda of the BLM machine. People believe they really care about black lives. These misinformed individuals do not know that BLM only uses "high profile inflammatory incidents of perceived racist acts between whites and blacks" to create unrest and financially pillage America. If they really cared for "black lives" why is there no national outcry when:*

- ***18 blacks were murdered in Chicago the same week that George Floyd was murdered.*** Hundreds of *"black on black"* deaths occur each year on the streets of Chicago without any outcry or concern from *Black Lives Matter.*

- ***More black children (babies) are murdered by abortion in New York*** than those that are born alive. All of this is happening without any outrage from BLM.

- ***White doctors murder (abort) "black" children*** (babies) under the mask of "women's health" without any response from BLM. Regardless of age, a son murdered and slaughtered at 4 months in utero or George Floyd at age 46, is still murder.

- ***Black men kill black police officers*** all the time without any response from Black Lives Matter. Blue lives matter and all lives matter.

- ***Employers are terminating employees if they remain "silent"*** on the job (by refusing to post Black Lives Matter propaganda on their social feeds).

- ***Seattle Washington held hostage*** *resulting in violence and death. There is no response from BLM.*

Deb: It seems that every media personality has an opinion on how to solve this social pandemic. ***Rush Limbaugh called a black talk show*** seeking to find common ground for bringing peace and unity in our torn nation. The men on the show were dismissive of his suggestions to help solve our confits.

Chick-Fil-A's CEO, Dan Cathy, reacts from white guilt. His answer to the problem is for white people to polish the shoes of blacks to demonstrate and show repentance for the sin of racism. Paul, this is the kind of reactions you were talking about.

You mentioned before that blacks were sold to whites by **black slave owners**. Blacks have also forgotten it was the whites that fought alongside them to free them from slavery. America has produced more black billionaires and millionaires in the world than any other country.

Paul: The greatest injustice today is the leftist agenda to keep poor blacks on "the system." Many people don't realize that leftist blacks are not seeking unity or reconciliation. The head of one of the black clergy alliances spoke with me. She said, *"Paul, we like what you are doing, but we are not with you. You are seeking peace and reconciliation. We don't want that."*

As I mentioned before, forgiveness is a choice and a conscious act of your will. If I had to wait for every white person or police officer that treated me unfairly to come and wash my feet before I could forgive them, I would still be angry and bitter today. When you are in an authentic relationship with the Heavenly Father, you quickly realize, mankind is not our Enemy, Satan is. He works through people. So every problem we face today is a sin problem. We do not have a "racism" issue, we have a sin issue…

At the cost of losing their lives, the three Jewish boys didn't "bow" (take a knee) to the leftist demonic statue in Babylon. They were men of faith and courage. Today Black lives Matter and the leftwing operatives are asking us to "bow" (take a knee) to their Anti-Christ agenda, that is covertly hidden in the statue of "racism and BLM." We need to exhibit the same faith and fortitude to take a stand for the cause of Christ and lift our banner of life and liberty for this generations to see and follow.

Nations Bow to the Agenda of BLM

Justin Trudeau *(Prime Minister of Canada)* bowed (took a knee) during anti-racism protest in Ottawa. People around the world are falling for the deception of this movement. Some well-meaning people are caught-up in the shadow of this agenda. Many are using this movement the mitigate their own pain form their crushed Glory Codes. As I mentioned before, this is only the tipping of the "FFS."

To whom we "bow" (take a knee) we submit and serve their agenda. Today, if we all "bow" before The Heavenly Father, we can stand as "one unified people. "This is why the Apostle Paul said, "I bow my knee to The Father of my Lord and savior Jesus."

Men, we will stand tall before of our children, families and nation when we "bow" (take a knee) before our Lord, Jesus, The Christ.

Deb: A leader of BLM from New York said if they are not given what they want, they will "burn down" the system. Bob Johnson, the former owner of BET, said we need 14 trillion for slavery reparations. Leftwing operatives, including many black pastors, have been seeking financial reparations for decades. This is one of the kay motives behind their *"unforgiveness, racism movement"* Their quest is to make the white man "pay" restitution.

Paul: Deb, no amount of money, (reparations) shoe polishing, or painting of Black Lives Matter on a wall will quell this problem. It will take true forgiveness and walking in the love of God to see the healing in the hearts of men and women in our nation and world.

Quincy Mason, the 27-year old son of George Floyd said, during a press conference on June 3, 2020 *"No man or women should be without their Father."* Today, as I sound the alarm of the fatherless in our nation and world, join me in being a positive influence in your city and community. *Pray for the people on the left that they will truly get "right" with The Heavenly Father.*

The Father's Tunic Was Torn

Jesus paid the ultimate price upon the cross in Season One of the Heavenly Father. The moment when He died, the thick veil/curtain *(about 4-6 inches thick)* in the Jewish Temple was *torn from top to bottom.* This veil separated the holiest and sacred place in the entire temple. Only the High Priest could enter once per year with the atoning blood of the sacrifice to place on the mercy seat. This veil (curtain) was also known as the Father's Tunic *(Robe).*

The tearing of the Father's Tunic has a triple meaning:

1. It represented the tears and mourning of The Father for the death of His Son.

2. It represented the acceptance of the pure and perfect, atoning blood of His Son. This satisfied his perfect requirement for the disobedience of all mankind.

3. It represented the joy He felt knowing His children who were separated from Him could now have full and fearless access to Him forever.

Nothing can ever separate His children from His Love. He has not only covered all of our sins, but washed them away, separating them as far as the east is from the west. He will never use them against us. It is forgiven.

Now, The Heavenly Father is asking you to do the same for those who crushed your Glory Code. It may have been your dad, mom, uncle, pastor, priest, brother, etc., but, He wants you to follow His example of forgiveness. You will be a model for others in how to do the same.

Turning of Hearts

The Heavenly Father is longing to bring healing to wounded hearts and nations. He is calling fathers to turn their hearts *(forgive and be reconciled according to the relational cycle of life)* towards their children, and for children to turn their hearts towards their fathers *(mothers)*. He wants us to get our hearts right with Him before it is too late. Today is the day. Tomorrow is not promised to any one of us.

There are three areas he is calling us to turn our hearts:

The First turn is towards Him, The Loving Heavenly Father. He has already turned towards us. He paid the ultimate price in Season one while we were still in our rebellion. It is only after we turned to Him and were reconciled with Him that we could have the power, and His Love, to do the next two.

The Second turning is towards our earthly dads. He is calling us to forgive, bless, and release them for all the wrong they have committed against us. He wants us to tear the veil that is over our wounded, and hardened, hearts. The Father wants you to: *Acknowledge* your Hurt or the Abuse committed against you. *Mourn* the loss it caused your Glory Code. Finally, He wants you to *Forgive and Release* your dad or the person that caused you the pain. Speak blessing over the person and rejoice that you were able to obey the voice of your Heavenly Father.

For your obedience, you will be refreshed by Him. Just like Jesus was obedient to Him. Celebrate the joy, peace and freedom which comes only through forgiveness.

The Third, and final turning, is towards Israel, His chosen nation and people. The Jews are our Spiritual fathers. They brought us His written Word (Torah) and the living Torah *(Yeshua, Jesus)*. If we honor the Jewish people and nation we will be blessed, and the Favor and blessing of The Heavenly Father will rest upon us, our families and nation.

Paul R. Benjamin, Sr.

Chapter 33

Bringing L.I.F.E to the World…
Principles put into Practice

In determining where they should build the next jail facility; investors and government officials, look for communities where children are being raised without their dads in the home. The same principle is true for Pawn Shops, Rental Centers and businesses that feed on poor and fatherless youth and their families.

That is why one of the key principles in launching Life Centers (LC) is to work with healthy, Life-giving *(authentic)* churches that reflect the true heart and character of The Heavenly Father. One of the courses we teach is *"Lifestyle Mentoring"* to train their mentoring team to bring – LIFE to their city.

3 Levels of Life Centers (LC1, LC2 & LC3)

Life Centers *(Impact Centers)* are not just facilitated from a physical location, it's a *"Lifestyle"*. The acronym stands for:

•**L** = Love. Life. Legacy.

•**I** = Integrity. Influence. Intimacy.

•**F** = Faith. Family. Future.

•**E** = Entrepreneurship. Empowerment. Evangelism.

Every word in this acronym has a purpose and action plan. Details are taught in the Life Center training and coaching when a church or ministry request in launching one from their facility.

We impart knowledge, but reproduce *character though our Lifestyle.* At the core, the Lifestyle of the team members at each Life Center, without any apologies, should model the Character of The Heavenly Father. This transformational influence will positively impact the lives of men, women, and youth in communities around the world.

Deb: If a church called you and would like to *launch a Life Center,* do they have to use the name *"Life Center"* or could they use a name of their own choice?

Paul: The term *"Life Center"* is not the name of a facility or program, it is an Acronym for the core values and principles that should be implemented in any Life-Giving Christ Centered church or ministry in a city.

Every Life-Giving Church Can have an Impact (LC1)

LC1 – Life Center 1, is based on churches hosting *The Father's Family Table* once per week at their facility. For every church that would like to join the global healing process in the hearts of this generation, *we provide training in each level* and process of The Life Center. Each church must be trained. They will avoid many pitfalls by learning key principles and some do's and don'ts. Principles learned and experienced over 30 plus years. LC1 calls for *male* Husband and *female* Wives and their children to host single moms and their children at the table. The principles taught through this process will impact everyone involved.

I Gave up on Men

"I will not date another man or get married, I gave up on men!" Hurt and abused by men, Dana, a single mom lived by these words. The father of her son Josh had died. Feeling hopeless, she began clicking through TV channels in search for a "male" mentor for her son. While channel surfing, she came across one of my TV interviews about fatherless youth and the impact of Godly dads.

Influence of the Father's Family Table

Dana contacted our ministry and requested help in finding a mentor for her son. I invited her and her son Josh to be part of our *"Father's Family Table".* Just like The Heavenly Father in Season Seven, we will all be at *His Father's Family Table* (FFT). At the FFT, there is fun, games, life interactions, joy, peace, family discussion, vision casting, and dream building. All culminating in the ultimate healing of our GC.

I want to get married

Dana, two months after she and her son, Josh, participated at our *Father's Family Table,* said, *"I want to get married! Seeing Paul in his role as a man, husband, father, and* mentor, painted a picture in my heart of what authentic manhood, marriage, and fatherhood looks like. I want this for myself and my son."

Manhood, Fatherhood, Marriage, and Family are not taught in a classroom. It is caught, through a modeled relationship with authentic men *(male at birth)* and women *(female at birth)*. *Today, Josh has his own son and family.* Male *Grand-Fathers* and Female *Grand-Mothers* are very important.

About **30%** of children in single-parent families are being raised by their grandmothers. In some instances, grandfathers are involved. We train grandparents *to be part of the FFT.* Children raised without dads, often, don't have grandfathers who can *stand in the gap as a positive father role model.*

LC2 Based on the operational budget of the church and the united effort to raise the necessary operational funding for a full-blown LC3, we recommend a church grow from LC1 to LC2 (unless the budget is raised for an LC3). In the LC2, the church would choose to go through a corporate structure strategy by forming a separate Non-Governmental Organization (NGO) or Non-Profit Organization (NPO). This will create a legal firewall, separating the activities of the church from that of the Life Center *(The church will choose whatever name they would like to call their Life Center).*

LC2 Would be facilitated one day per week, usually on Wednesdays, because it is on a day when most schools release children early and it is also a day when most churches have their mid-week service. There would be activities and the FFT. Other key programs can be implemented from the recommended list, based on the age group of the attendees and the staff available on site.

LC3 Will be a full functioning center based on the funding and staff at the center. The church will choose from the program list based on the audience, staff and community partnerships in place. In all three Life Center levels, the FFT is the one key structure and relational bond that impacts the entire process. Full details would be in the LC training.

We also teach some of these key *principles of FFT to be implemented in public schools* during the lunch period or a special weekly session. The process helps to bring healing to many youths with a crushed Glory Code (GC). You may read a book to a child, but the child will *read your **Lifestyle** (your life).*

Emasculation of Men

With so many millions of men and women in media and society who were victims of crushed Glory Codes by their dads, the anger, hate, and resentment towards the very image of dads goes deep. The Emasculation of Men (EM) was given birth to destroy the value and impact of the capstone, sealing-love that the dad brings in the lives of their children. Just like in school, when the children who see other children with dads, they become jealous and enraged, intrinsically wanting the same; but because of the rage and anger of not having it, resulting from their crushed GC, they take out children who do have a balanced relationship with their dads.

"Don't follow me, I am Lost"

These words were leaping into the air from a bumper-sticker forced into the cluttered chaos of what was about 30 other stickers vying for attention on the back of a 1980 Ford Pinto. It was nestled between two stickers, one saying, *"Save the mother earth"* and the other saying *"World peace now!"*

Who are you following?

I said to myself, this is a true representation of this generation. So many people are lost, and the quest for true inner peace has eluded them. Today men do not have a clear authentic model of Manhood or Fatherhood. Let me leave you with some parting wisdom, as a Man, Husband, Dad, Mentor, and Coach, there is hope. The Apostle Paul from the tribe of Benjamin Said, *"follow me as I follow Christ (The Messiah)." Christ came to model what authentic Manhood and Fatherhood is. He did and said all that He saw His Father do and say. He revealed the character of His Dad. Therefore, the true measure of a man is Christ.*

The question is, *who are you following?* I shared many quick principles; your destiny will be determined by who you are following. If you desire to know Peace, then you need to know the source and Father of Peace. If you desire to know and experience love, joy, happiness, and a family who has a Loving Father, then you need to know Jesus The Christ, He will bring you to The Heavenly Father. Jesus said, *"Follow Me"*, this is my recommendation...

Connect with The Loving Heavenly Father Today

If you are ready in your relationship cycle of Repentance, I would love to lead you in a conversational interaction *(Prayer)* with The Loving Heavenly Father. After reading about His Love for you, He is waiting to be reunited with you and to welcome you into His loving arms.

Pray this prayer: "*Heavenly Father, I acknowledge that I have sinned against you. I did things not pleasing to you. Please forgive me and cleanse from all of my sins. Thank you for sending Jesus to die in my place so I can be reunited with you. Because Jesus rose from the dead, I too will now arise from the death of my sins, to walk in victory and righteousness as your child. Thank you for giving me the power by your Holy Spirit to forgive others as you have forgiven me. I pray this by faith and I believe it in my heart, in Your Son's Name, Jesus, Amen.*"

Deb: Paul, that was a nice and simple prayer. I prayed the prayer for myself too. I felt a new peace all over me. What should anyone who prays this prayer do next, now that they are reunited with their Heavenly Father?

Paul: Awesome Deb! Welcome to the family of God! Everyone who prays this prayer to The Heavenly Father is now a child of God. As a new baby is welcomed into the family and given milk, so, everyone who just joined the family should now *drink the milk of The Word of God (Read and Study The Word of God – The Bible, 1 Peter 2:2)* and connect with families from a healthy Life-Giving Church *(Remember, Church is **not a building**, The True Church is the Loving Family of Christ-loving people who should reflect the Heart and characteristics of The Heavenly Father)* where you can serve, encourage others and be a positive influence to your community and this generation.

Men, because most pastors never had a good father relationship with their Dads, most churches only have a passive ministry to men. If you are already in a church that doesn't have an active ministry to men, please contact our office for some ways to help your church start a vibrant ministry to men.

Deb: I am overwhelmed! I remembered at the beginning of our conversation, you mentioned and cautioned all the readers, that once they are equipped with this knowledge, they would become accountable to get off the sidelines and do something. I would like to be the first one to respond to this challenge:

(1) Now that I am armed with this knowledge, I can positively engage with the vision and make a difference. First with the person in the mirror (myself) then in my family and society. I would like to talk with my husband Joel, but I am confident we would like to be one of the first families to invest $1,000 as a seed gift for a Life Center in our city. We will also volunteer to be a

mentor family at one of these Life Centers. I cannot sit on this information and do nothing to make a positive impact.

(2) I would like to set-up an appointment for you to speak with my pastor about starting a Life Center at our church. I can rally a team of volunteers from my church and job to pray and volunteer also. I will ask my boss John to invest $10,000, he will be very supportive of this initiative.

(3) He can even mobilize some of his wealthy friends and associates to sponsor multiple Life Centers across the nation and world, he is very influential and connected. He may want to totally fund a Life Center in his home state, Pennsylvania.

(4) We will become ambassadors for this cause, Paul, I know we need some Life Centers in Chicago. There, the crime and murder rates are higher than most of our wars. California, with all the human waste, homelessness and crime. West Baltimore, where conditions are worse than most third world countries. New York City, where there are so many crimes and *blatant disrespect* for Law-Enforcement officers and all of the high crime cities and states across America and around the world.

Paul, I know many people will be offended by this truth. Others will realize they can turn things around, and *make a positive impact.*

This information has awakened the powerful potential in my *Glory Code.* I will positively engage others through my news articles, blogs, social media, and relationships. Paul, thanks for taking so much of your time to share this information with me. Dawn, thanks for spending time with me also.

Paul and Dawn, I have to tell both of you, after learning these principles and the impact of the "FFS" I now know the "why." I have forgiven my dad for all he did. I feel such a peace, like never before. It's like the sword in my hands was finally laid at the feet of The Heavenly Father.

I can't wait to share my heart with Joel and my family.

Paul: Dawn and I were blessed to spend this time with you. Thanks for being a positive influence in our nation. If this information positively impacts even one person, it was worth our time. As Dawn suggested, I kept my comments as brief and to the point as possible. *More to come* in seminars, and interviews on your **website**: *Global impact Magazine.com*

The Heavenly Father's Thoughts & Blessings

Deb: Paul and Dawn, I know I have taken up so much of your time gathering all of this valuable life-changing information. What would you like to say to my readers before we part ways?

Intimacy with Your Heavenly Father

Dawn: I believe, the greatest joy and fulfillment in your life will come when you learn to develop an authentic father and child relationship with your Heavenly Father. Like the Apostle, Paul said, *"That I may know Him,"* Jesus, in His final report to His Father, just before He returned to heaven to be with His Dad said, "this is eternal life, that they, your children, may know *(have a deep abiding intimate relationship with)* you… This is why, my favorite scripture is Psalms 46:10 *"Be still and **know** that I am God: – your Heavenly Dad…"* because, in knowing Him, I confidently know who I am, which solidifies my glory code. As I pray *(communicate and hear His heart, and act upon His will)* I get to know His heart and sense His divine purpose in situations on earth.

Deb: Love it!! Dawn, this will now become my new favorite scripture. From this posture of knowing who you are in your Dad's presence, empowers you to live and walk in victory.

Paul: Deb, I cannot top Dawns' posture and statement. Everything first and foremost proceeds from the Bosom *(heart)* of the Heavenly Father, there is no better place to be. It is from this place of intimacy we get wisdom and guidance to:

- Live our lives on purpose and activate our passion
- Find a partner to travel through life's challenges
- Make difficult decisions and so much more…

In conclusion, I will like to reveal the Heart of The Heavenly Father. God's will is that no one would be eternally separated *(perish or die without being reconciled with Him)* from His Loving arms and presence. I pray for the healing of everyone who is currently existing with crushed glory codes, as a result of the FFS; may they all come to know The Heavenly Father.

The Heavenly Father's Glory Code Blessing

Knowing that the world would be impacted by the deadly ramifications of the FFS. The Heavenly Father places His *Glory Code* blessing and Father's Seal on His chosen people, the Jews, and all of those who are adopted into the Jewish family by placing their hope, and trust *(those who are reconciled with Him in the cycle of life)* in Him through a relationship with His Son, Yeshua, Jesus. Knowing what your Heavenly Father thinks of you and having His acceptance and approval, solidifies your "GC" and activates your *purpose in life.*

The Seal of The Father

"Your Heavenly Dad bless you, *(He sets his Seal, of approval to protect your glory code)* and keep you; His face shine *(His expression of Love and smile of acceptance)* upon you and is gracious to you *(Wrap His arms of Love around you and comfort you in times of trouble)*. The Father will lift His countenance upon you and give you His Shalom *(Peace, wholeness and renewed Glory Code)* "

This is the heart of The Heavenly Father. He is not like any other dad on earth. He will never leave you or abuse you. To prove His everlasting Love for us He placed His name upon His Son Jesus, *"Ever Lasting Father." He will be your Dad forever!* Those who are willing, can; if they embrace His plan and purpose for their life, can walk in a healthy *renewed Glory Code*. I invite you to join me and millions of other brothers and sisters who are walking with our Heavenly

Dad…

The Lord's Prayer

Deb: This is an awesome blessing and true reflection of The Heavenly Father's heart towards us.

Paul: Many preachers and people call the *"Child of God's Prayer,"* The Lords' Prayer. As children of The Heavenly Father, this is how we should Pray:

"Our Father in heaven, Hallowed be Your name. Your kingdom come. Your will be done on earth as it is in heaven. Give us this day our daily bread. And forgive us our debts, as we forgive our debtors. Lead us into temptation, but deliver us from the evil one. For Yours is the kingdom and the power and the glory forever. Amen."

Deb: From a girl I was taught this was the Lord's prayer. Tell me what is the Lord's prayer?

Paul: Deb, you and millions of people were told the same thing. The Lord Jesus (Yeshua) about twelve hours before He paid the ultimate price on the cross, prayed to His Dad, The Heavenly Father. This, is the prayer of His heart. He is still waiting for its fulfillment. There are times in our lives when we pray for someone. There are other times when we can be *"the answer"* to their prayers. **This is that time!** We can all be an answer to *The Lord's Prayer*. What if?

What if the reason God The Father hasn't answered your prayers yet was because He is waiting for you to be an answer to His Son's Prayer?

Paul: Deb, you and millions of people were told the same thing. The Lord Jesus (Yeshua) about twelve hours before He paid the ultimate price on the cross prayed to His Dad, The Heavenly Father. This, is the prayer of His heart. He is still waiting for its fulfillment. There are times in our lives when we pray for someone. There are other times when we can be *"the answer"* to their prayers. **This is that time!** We can all be an answer to *The Lord's Prayer*. What if?

What if the reason God The Father hasn't answered your prayers yet was because He is waiting for you to be an answer to His Son's Prayer?

Jesus spoke these words, lifted up His eyes to heaven, and said: *"Father, the hour has come. Glorify Your Son, that Your Son also may glorify You, as You have given Him authority over all flesh, that He should give eternal life to as many as You have given Him.* ***This is eternal life, that they may know You, the only true God, and Jesus Christ whom You have sent.*** *I have glorified You on the earth. I have finished the work which You have given Me to do. Now, O Father, glorify Me together with Yourself, with the glory which I had with You before the world was.*

*"**I have manifested Your name** to the men whom You have given Me out of the world. They were Yours, You gave them to Me, and they have kept Your word. Now they have known that **all things which You have given Me are from You.** For I have given to them the words which You have given Me; and they have received them, and have known surely that I came forth from You; and they have believed that You sent Me.*

"I pray for them. I do not pray for the world but for those whom You have given Me, for they are Yours. And all Mine are Yours, and Yours are Mine, and I am glorified in them. Now I am no longer in the world, but these are in the world, and I come to You. Holy Father,

keep through Your name those whom You have given Me, that they may be one as We are. While I was with them in the world, I kept them in Your name.

"Those whom You gave Me I have kept; and none of them is lost except the son of perdition, that the Scripture might be fulfilled. But now I come to You, and these things I speak in the world, that they may have My joy fulfilled in themselves. I have given them Your word; and the world has hated them because they are not of the world, just as I am not of the world. I do not pray that You should take them out of the world, but that You should keep them from the evil one. They are not of the world, just as I am not of the world. Sanctify them by Your truth. Your word is truth. As You sent Me into the world, I also have sent them into the world. And for their sakes I sanctify Myself, that they also may be sanctified by the truth.

"I do not pray for these alone, but also for those who will believe in Me through their word; that they all may be one, as You, Father, are in Me, and I in You; that they also may be one in Us, that the world may believe that You sent Me. And the glory which You gave Me I have given them, that they may be one just as We are one: I in them, and You in Me; that they may be made perfect in one, and that the world may know that You have sent Me, and have loved them as You have loved Me.

"Father, I desire that they also whom You gave Me may be with Me where I am, that they may behold My glory which You have given Me; for You loved Me before the foundation of the world. "O righteous Father! The world has not known You, but I have known You; and these have known that You sent Me. And I have declared to them Your name, and will declare it, that the love with which You loved Me may be in them, and I in them."

Deb: Paul, that brought tears to my eyes. Knowing that Jesus said this prayer to His Dad only hours before He was about to die on the cross. He revealed the heart of His Dad and now, He is asking us to do the same. His wants His children "the Church" to be unified as "one." We are so divided. Everyone is doing their own thing and building their kingdoms. I read this prayer before in John 17 and didn't realize it's significance.

Paul: Pastors and churches do not realize the power and impact of this prayer. Jesus mentioned to His Dad to give us His Glory (GC) that He had while He was here on earth. He asked The Heavenly Father to heal our crushed Glory Codes, so we can accomplish His mission that He assigned us to accomplish. As He was, so are we in this world today… Let's be about our Heavenly Dad's Business!

Who would you like to Acknowledge

Deb: This was a great closing mandate for the Church. This concludes our interview. I would like to acknowledge you and anyone else that you would like for me to mention when I publish this article.

Paul: Deb, it's was great working with you on this assignment.

I would like to first thank my Heavenly Father and my parents, Fred and Shirley Benjamin for raising me in a Godly home and modeling the character of The Heavenly Father. They set my feet on the true path of life and introduced me to the one true source of all life. They were great role-models to me growing up in the Benjamin Household. (The Tribe of Benjamin)

Deb: So, Paul! What you are trying to say is, ***It's all about the Benjamins***? No pun intended!

Paul: That's cool Deb! Even at the end, you are trying to get your last *pun* in. I guess I have corrupted you through this whole process. You know the Proverb, you become like the people you hang out with.

Dawn: Deb, now I see, he has won you over with his puns. Now you are going to take it home to Joel and the children. I will pray for you! We need to have some girl time to help you get over all of these.

Paul: Thanks, ladies! I would like to wrap things up here!

I would also like to thank and acknowledge my wife Dawn, she was the driving force behind me to give you this information. In the midst of her busy schedule, she kept reminding me to *move it along* and finish this assignment. Sometimes she did give me *the look…* I would also like to honor our children: Paul Jr, Nick, Leah, Erika, Simone, Sammy and our son and daughters in love, Kevin, Amy and Samantha. I would also like to honor my good friend and partner in the ministry, Dr. Bill Davis and all of my former board members who served alongside me and always encouraged me to share these principles with the world.

Deb: On behalf and John and our team, we can't thank you enough for investing your time over these last weeks to complete this important assignment. We are looking forward to your contribution and insight on future news events. I will miss our time together. Dawn, you and I will still plan our girl time and family events. I love both of you.

Paul: It was my pleasure to share this information with you and your audience. This is not a goodbuy, but see you later or until our next interview.

I want to end by speaking blessing over all the men, women and youth who were impacted by the Father's heart through my ministry to them. They are now sons and daughters in the faith. May the legacy continue until the appointed season of the Father. My goal is to see the earth filled with the knowledge of The Glory Source (GS) that comes from The Loving Heavenly Father, God Almighty, as the waters cover the sea.

End Notes – Resources

Any biblical reference (or paraphrase) in this book is sourced from the New King James Bible. For ease and reading flow, the author did not add direct scripture references to each chapter or whenever an allusion was made from a Biblical Truth from The Heavenly Father. In using the paraphrased method, the author was able to paraphrase complete words or thoughts into modern-day language and understanding. Subsequent books, study guides, and even blogs will go deeper into key areas of interest and topics that would be of interest to those seeking deeper understanding.

Paul: As previously mentioned, I only briefly touched on this vast subject. I went only into the shallow water in the ocean of insight and information available on the Father Fracture Syndrome, the Glory Source (GS) and the Glory Code (GC). Follow my blogs and subsequent seminars for more information.

Connect with us @ LifeCentersGlobal.com

Give the best gift this Christmas, Give the Gift of "You." Sign-up to be trained and become a *Lifestyle Mentor and Family* to a fatherless child or children. Your life and theirs will never be the same…

Know your Glory Code – Know your Impact

Would you like to ***Know your Glory Code*** and how it impacts your personal life, mental health and other sectors in your world? Go to: *GlobalImpactMagazine**.com***

Connect with Deb, learn more about these and other life impacting symptoms from the FFS at: *GlobalImpactMagazine**.com***

Questions or concerns about:

- Personal Life (Am I a real man or woman?)
- What's my Glory Code Level?
- How can I be a better dad or mom?
- How can I deal with troubled teenagers?
- Tips for being a better single mom?

Paul R. Benjamin, Sr.

- How can I start a Life Center in my community?
- Why do I keep dating men like my dad?
- Why can't I find a good man that would marry me?
- Why don't I feel fulfilled in my relationships?
- Why am I attracted to older men?
- How can I find a mentor for my child?
- How to deal with the anger of my child?
- My son is beating me, how can I address this problem?
- My wife is cold in our marriage, how can I renew my marriage?
- My husband is verbally, or physically abusive, how can I find help?
- Your Job and Business (Job Performance, Business Start-ups, Partnerships)
- Ministry (Your Ministry Impact, Pastoring, Youth Ministry etc.)
- Behavioral Issues and conflicts with youth and parents
- Fear and Anxiety – (how to cope in times of fears and trouble in the world)
- How to break the cycle of control and abuse, while learning to walk in victory

Paul R. Benjamin Sr. is available for interviews or speaking engagements. For more information contact:

Paul R. Benjamin Sr.
C/O Advantage Books
P.O. Box 160847
Altamonte Springs, FL 32716
info@advbooks.com

To purchase additional copies of these books, visit our bookstore at:
www.advbookstore.com

Advantage BOOKS

Longwood, Florida, USA
"we bring dreams to life"™
www.advbookstore.com